CALIFORNIA

Its Government and Politics

FIFTH EDITION

Michael J. Ross

San Diego State University
Palomar College

Wadsworth Publishing Company

An International Thomson Publishing Company

Belmont • Albany • Bonn • Boston • Cincinnati • Detroit • London • Madrid • Melbourne
Mexico City • New York • Paris • San Francisco • Singapore • Tokyo • Toronto • Washington

Political Science Editor: Tammy Goldfeld
Editorial Assistants: Kelly Zavislak, Heide Chavez
Copy Editor: S. M. Summerlight
Design: Donna Davis
Photo Research: Laurel Anderson / Photosynthesis
Illustration, Production, & Composition: Summerlight Creative
Print Buyer: Diana Spence
Cover: Cassandra Chu
Printer: Malloy Lithographing, Inc.

Printed in the United States of America
1 2 3 4 5 6 7 8 9 10 — 02 01 00 99 98 97 96

For more information, contact Wadsworth Publishing Company:

Wadsworth Publishing Company
10 Davis Drive
Belmont, California 94002, USA

International Thomson Publishing Europe
Berkshire House 168-173
High Holborn
London, WC1V 7AA, England

Thomas Nelson Australia
102 Dodds Street
South Melbourne 3205
Victoria, Australia

Nelson Canada
1120 Birchmount Road
Scarborough, Ontario
Canada M1K 5C4

International Thomson Editores
Campos Eliseos 385, Piso 7
Col. Polanco
11560 México D.F. México

International Thomson Publishing GmbH
Königswinterer Strasse 418
53227 Bonn, Germany

International Thomson Publishing Asia
221 Henderson Road
#05-10 Henderson Building
Singapore 0315

International Thomson Publishing Japan
Hirakawacho Kyowa Building, 3F
2-2-1 Hirakawacho
Chiyoda-ku, Tokyo 102, Japan

Library of Congress Cataloging-in-Publication Data
Ross, Michael J.
     California, its government and politics / Michael J. Ross. — 5th ed.
       p. cm.
     Includes bibliographical references and index.
     ISBN (invalid) 05340231128 (pbk.)
     1. California—Politics and government—1951– I. Title.
JK8716.R67   1996
320.4794—dc 20   95-15779
                           CIP

This book is printed on acid-free recycled paper.

For Josiane,
who made it all worthwhile.

CONTENTS

Part Three
MAJOR INSTITUTIONS 137

PREFACE

C *alifornia: Its Government and Politics* is intended to serve three purposes: (1) Its readability makes it suitable for use in lower-division courses on American or California government; (2) its comprehensiveness makes it appropriate for upper-division classes in state and local government that emphasize California; and (3) it is directed to any reader trying to make some sense out of the buzzing confusion in Sacramento or in city hall. I have tried to make this book as flexible as possible by including political process, institutional, and public policy approaches. I hope that my analysis is clearly written, lively, and focused on issues. An issue approach is important because California is challenged by a wide range of issues that need to be resolved—these appear as problems to policy makers but as grist for the academic analyst.

A great deal has happened and continues to happen since the last edition. Chapter 1 shows that California politics is still an arena in which to experiment, often with mixed results, in areas such as school vouchers, single-payer health reform, emissions trading, toll roads, and electric vehicles. Chapter 2 raises one of the most explosive issues of recent times, immigration and Proposition 187, as well as NAFTA and GATT, which also have a federal–state dimension. Chapter 3 holds an expanded discussion of media campaigns and targeted messages, especially negative campaigning; the demographic differences between California voters and the California population; an initiative to repeal affirmative action laws; and the open primary and the 1996 earlier-than-ever presidential primary. Governor Pete Wilson and his policies play an important role in Chapter 6. Then Chapter 7 discusses the Assembly speakership and how it has changed with the adoption of term limits and the relative even balance of political party strength. We continue our focus on issues in Chapter 8 with the crime issue, "three-strikes" legislation, and prison construction. Finally, Chapter 10 focuses on "Big Five" budgeting, "the trigger" and the "hammer," and whether California has a structural deficit that persists even during good economic times. In these and other chapters, I have emphasized the power struggles, ideological controversies, and engaging personalities that now mold this state.

I wish to thank the numerous people who helped me write this book. Many instructors used the previous editions; their support has been very gratifying. The following reviewers were capable and discerning: Greg Andranovich, California State University, Los Angeles; Stanley E. Clark, California State University at Bakersfield; Joseph Moore, Fresno City College; Linda Norman, California State University at San Bernardino; and Greg Tilles, Diablo Valley College. Tammy Goldfeld was the sponsoring editor, and Steven Summerlight did the copy editing and production, which eased the manuscript down the bumpy road to publication.

The men and women who settled California long ago came with courage and hope in their hearts. May we live the same way.

Michael Ross
San Diego, California

Part One

SETTING OF CALIFORNIA GOVERNMENT AND POLITICS

*P*olitical issues touch nearly every aspect of our lives in California. We cannot get away from questions of public policy.

How can we create more jobs in California? What is being done about air pollution? Do we need urban mass transit? How is education to be financed? Are the needs of the state's poor and elderly being met? Does the state have an adequate energy supply? Will California be able to meet its future water needs? Are taxes too high?

In Chapter 1 we consider these and other issues. We also note that California state and local governments have attempted to resolve these issues in the wake of the belt tightening necessitated by the state's recent financial problems. In Chapter 2 we point out that California need not grapple alone with these matters. The federal government and other state governments (through interstate compacts) can lend assistance. We also point out that almost every major contemporary policy issue involves all levels of government: federal, state, and local. The federal government transfers substantial amounts of money to state government, counties, cities, and school districts: This is the primary reason for multilevel governmental involvement in most issues.

Decision makers address issues such as energy, transportation, and education in a series of overlapping stages that might be termed a *policy process*. At all levels of government, decision makers follow roughly five steps as they deal with policy issues. One step may begin before another is actually completed.

1. Problem identification: Public decision makers are presented with demands for action to resolve a problem.
2. Policy formulation: A course of action is chosen after various alternatives for dealing with a problem have been considered.
3. Adoption: A legitimate source of authority—for example, the state legislature or a city mayor—approves and often appropriates money for the course of action chosen.
4. Implementation: The policy, or plan of action, is carried out.
5. Evaluation: Decision makers determine whether the plan of action is accomplishing its objectives and whether adjustments need to be made in the policy.

This process of determination–implementation–evaluation is not static; it is dynamic. It is appropriate that a dynamic process should be used by a state that usually seems to be in motion—California.

Chapter 1
Policy Issues

O ver the years, California has meant many different things to different peo-ple. To millions of Americans, it has represented (and still represents) hope—a hope for something better than they have had—which is why they came here. To other Americans, California has stood for diversity, opportunity, and the chance to break out of the restrictive patterns of the past. This state has also stood for creativity and innovation. (For example, political scientists rate California's state government as one of the most innovative in the nation.) Carey McWilliams writes that restless California is the "giant adolescent [who] has been outgrowing its governmental clothes, now, for a hundred years. . . . Other states have gone through this phase too, but California has never emerged from it."[1]

Indisputably, California has meant growth. And until recently, Californians have welcomed growth as a blessing. A state of considerable size geographically (see Figure 1.1), it is first in population with more than 33 million people, which is equal to 12 percent of the nation's population. Therefore, California has the largest number of members in the U.S. House of Representatives (fifty-two) and the largest number of electoral votes (fifty-four). As a result of the 1990 Census, California received an increase of seven House seats. During the 1980s, California grew by 6 million people or 26.1 percent, which was more than twice the national growth rate of 10.2 percent.

Approximately 93 percent of all Californians live on just 5 percent of the state's land area, usually in areas near the coastline. However, in recent years, the population of inland areas has grown twice as fast as the population near the coast: The sparsely populated rural areas of the Sierra Nevada foothills are showing large percentage increases. People fleeing urban congestion and smog may head for El Dorado County or Placer County. Among more urban counties, Riverside and San Bernardino are experiencing rapid increases.

---

1. Carey McWilliams, *California: The Great Exception* (New York: A. A. Wyn, 1949), p. 17.

Figure 1.1 Map of California superimposed on the East Coast. Reprinted with permission from the *Los Angeles Times,* December 17, 1978, pt. I, p. 3

Approximately 45 percent of the statewide population increase resulted from natural increase (births exceeding deaths), 17 percent from migration from other parts of the United States, and 38 percent from immigration from other countries. The latter is particularly important because 28 percent of the state's population was born in other countries. The 1990 Census reported that almost one-third of the state's residents speak a language other than English at home. Californians include two of every five Asians nationwide, one of every three Latinos, and half of all Southeast Asian refugees.

The state's significant increase in immigration has dramatically changed the demographic mixture of the state. Whites, who have a lower birthrate and a higher median age than the rest of the population, constitute a decreasing percentage of the population. They will be a minority group before the end of this century. Latinos have a birthrate almost twice that of whites, and their numbers are increasing by high levels of both legal and illegal immigration. As indicated by Table 1.1, Asians are the third

Table 1.1 Racial and Ethnic Characteristics of Californians (as Percentages of Population) as Reported by the 1990 Census

	WHITES	LATINOS	ASIANS	BLACKS	OTHERS
ALL AGE GROUPS	57	26	9	7	1
UNDER AGE 18	46	35	10	8	1

largest group in California, and they have doubled in the last decade. The African-American percentage of California's population has been unchanging in recent years.

Demographer Peter Morrison predicts that California, which has one-eighth of the nation's population, will absorb three-eighths of the country's population growth through the year 2006.[2] Rapid population increase fosters rapid social change in other respects as well. California has been on the cutting edge of new trends, new beliefs, and new lifestyles. People often say that if you want to see the future, look at California. Whether you consider the results good or bad, the Golden State has often led the way in everything from tax revolts to Eastern mystical cults. One writer notes that "this state leads the nation in pornography, . . . suicide, home burglary, mind-meddling cults, and skateboard accidents. At the same time, perhaps for the same reasons, it leads the nation in microelectronics, solar energy, accredited law schools, Nobel Prize winners, women mayors, Olympic medalists, library use, salad lettuce, dates, figs, and nectarines."[3] The U.S. Bureau of the Census, which has the responsibility for gathering information on an amazing variety of topics, ranks California on several key indicators (see Table 1.2).

California is also characterized by highly **advanced industrialism.** The state relies on high-technology industry based on scientific expertise for the sustained application of theoretical knowledge for practical ends. The best example of such "knowledge-intensive" manufacturing is electronics. Sophisticated technology depends on research and development (R&D, as it is called), in which the state excels: California is a national leader in the creation of knowledge. Both government and private industry make substantial sums of money available to the state's universities and research institutes for R&D purposes. The key role of universities in generating the new knowledge and technology necessary to support advanced industries can be seen from the fact that Santa Clara's Silicon Valley grew up around Stanford University; other important "high-tech" centers are in Los Angeles, Orange, and San Diego counties. Industrialization has affected other areas of California's economy as well. Because of the high degree of automation in the state's farms and factories, fewer people are needed to work in these sectors, and more people can work in service

---

2. Peter Morrison "California's Future: More to Come," *Los Angeles Times,* December 3, 1991, p. B7
3. James D. Houston, *Californians: Searching for the Golden State* (New York: Knopf, 1982), p. 4.

Table 1.2 California's Rankings

ITEM	RANK
Total population (1992)	1
Land area in square miles (1990)	3
Percent of population in metropolitan area (1990)	2
Median age (1991)	44
Percent of population white (1990)	46
Percent of population Latino (1990)	2
Percent of population Asian (1990)	2
Percent of population black (1990)	23
Marriage rate per 1,000 population (1987)	32
Divorce rate per 1,000 population (1987)	26
Median household income (1991)	10
Percent of population in poverty (1991)	14
Home ownership rate (1980)	48
Median value of owner-occupied housing units (1990)	2
Violent crime rate per 100,000 population (1991)	3
Murder death rate per 100,000 population (1991)	6
Motor vehicle theft rate per 100,000 population (1991)	1
Police officers per 10,000 population (1991)	13
State correctional population as a percent of adult population	9
Percent high school graduates (persons 25 years old and older in 1990)	28
Percent college graduates (persons 25 years old and older in 1990)	9
Energy consumption per capita (1990)	43
Motor vehicle registrations per capita (1991)	35
Percent of workers commuting in car pools (1990)	18
Death rate per 100,000 population because of chronic liver disease and cirrhosis (1990)	3
Death rate per 100,000 population because of AIDS (1990)	3

SOURCE: Kathleen Morgan et al., eds., *California in Perspective, 1993* (Lawrence, KS: Morgan Quitno Corporation, 1993). Reprinted by permission.

jobs, which are increasing in number. Seven of ten Californians work in service industries—such as education, medicine, law, insurance, communications, banking, real estate, transportation, and government—rather than in the manufacturing of heavy durable goods.

Life in a highly developed industrial state such as California is becoming highly complex, its development characterized by rapid change and innovation. In this chapter, we consider the numerous policy issues facing the Golden State. We will also encounter three themes:

1. California state and local governments are low on **revenue** and are likely to remain so in the near future.

2. Special interests control California governments and the policies made by those governments.

3. The state's natural resources and physical resources (e.g., water, clean air, and open space) are limited or even becoming scarcer even while its population is increasing rapidly.

Many commentators assert that, because of these factors, the quality of life for many of the state's residents will decrease.

THE STATE'S ECONOMY

If California were a nation, its **gross national product (GNP)** would rank sixth in the world. If it is to flourish economically, California must retain its lead in aerospace, semiconductor, computer, biotechnology, and other high-technology industries. These industries provide jobs, and they pay significant amounts of taxes. States such as Texas, Illinois, Maryland, North Carolina, Florida, Kentucky, and Tennessee are trying to lure such employers away. Additional targets of job-hungry states are the furniture-making, apparel, and plastics industries. California is aided by its climatic and cultural advantages, the size and quality of its markets, its access to investment **capital,** the availability of many state-supported services, its location as gateway to the Pacific Basin, and its huge highway system. However, firms deciding to locate or remain in this state sometimes assert that it has liabilities: occupational safety and health regulations that surpass federal standards; delays and inconsistencies in the regulatory and permit process regarding construction and energy; high labor costs; high utility bills; the declining quality of the state's schools; crowding and congestion; unreliable water supply; a strong antigrowth political movement; excessive workers' compensation premiums; steep unemployment insurance taxes; and high corporate taxes. (Actually, tax considerations may not be paramount in an industry's choice of location.) Two key factors are the high cost of housing for employees and the availability and expense of land for employers to use for their facilities.

A 1992 study by the state's five largest utilities shed some interesting light on the problem. It found that only 2 percent of California manufacturers had left the state since 1980. This figure was far less than generally had been feared. The study also found that half of the factory jobs lost resulted from business failures or plant closings, rather than relocations to cheaper states or to Mexico. The worrisome part of the study indicated that 70 percent of the jobs leaving the state were in high-paying technology fields such as computers, aerospace, and other high-technology areas. One area not covered by the study was lost opportunities. For example, Intel Corp., the quintessential California high-tech company, decided to build a $1 billion factory in New Mexico rather than in its home state. Mercedes-Benz also decided to construct an auto plant in Alabama rather than in California. This is highly ironic because California surely has far more Mercedes per capita than does Alabama.

The study by the utilities noted that companies leaving California cited high labor and real estate costs, business taxes, environmental regulations, and permit restriction. According to the British magazine *The Economist,* "Without question, what is driving companies out of California is the frustration of having to comply with so many regulatory agencies at city, county, state, and federal levels. A company wanting to plant a tree in Los Angeles County has to get permission from 8 different agencies. To chop it down and make furniture from the timber requires 47 more permits."[4]

The foregoing analysis is strenuously disputed by two economists at Palo Alto's Center for the Continuing Study of the California Economy.[5] They argue that the main problems affecting the state's economy are *not* excessive business regulation, poor business climate, or cuts in defense spending (to be discussed soon). Rather, the maladies go deeper and are said to result from inadequate public spending on governmental programs such as education and pollution control, as well as government's low priority for full-employment policies and access to health care.

Many economists believe that the state's economic future depends on export jobs, each of which may create two nonexport jobs. California, which exports more than $70 billion per year (more than 15 percent of the U.S. total), is an important international exporter of computer equipment, office machinery, aerospace and telecommunications equipment, medical instruments, cotton, fruits, nuts, and crude oil. Its most important trading partners for both exports and imports are Singapore, Taiwan, Hong Kong, the Republic of Korea, Germany, Canada, Mexico, and especially Japan. As a result of this activity, California now has more foreign investment than any other state; foreign trade will increase as a result of the North American Free Trade Agreement (NAFTA) and the General Agreement on Tariffs and Trade (GATT), which are discussed in the next chapter.

High-tech manufacturing and international trade could be key sources of jobs in the future. But there may be an unfortunate mismatch between these jobs and the state's future workforce, which will increasingly include low-skilled immigrant minorities. These new workers are already concentrated in low-paying service jobs and light manufacturing, and the concentration may intensify.

4. "California Jobs," *The Economist,* July 17, 1993, p. 24. See also "California's Aggressive New Push to Lure Business," *Los Angeles Times,* October 31, 1993, p. D4.
5. Stephen Levy and Robert Arnold, "Restructuring the California Economy," in *California Policy Choices,* vol. 8, ed. John Kirlin (Sacramento: Sacramento Center of U.S.C. School of Public Administration, 1992), Chap. 3.

To sum up, the California economy is highly complex and diverse. Some of its salient characteristics are presented here:

CALIFORNIA ECONOMIC CAPSULE

- California is located on the edge of the Pacific Basin and Latin America, which afford good export markets for its products.
- One-fifth of all American aircraft-manufacturing jobs and three-fifths of American space- and missile-equipment production are in California.
- Tourism supports jobs for more than 515,000 Californians and generates more than $1.6 billion in tax revenue.
- The multibillion-dollar entertainment industry has an important "multiplier" or ripple economic effect.
- California is the nation's fourth-largest producer of oil, is second in amount of forested land (covering 40 percent of the state), and is richer in certain minerals, such as asbestos, boron, and tungsten, than any other state.
- California is the nation's foremost agricultural state, leading all states in the production of forty-nine crops and livestock products. Agriculture generates nearly 10 percent of all jobs in California.

Table 1.3 notes California's top dozen corporations.

California receives far more defense spending than does any other state. Counties heavily dependent on this money are Santa Clara, Los Angeles, Orange, and San Diego. Defense corporations not only are major employers, but also, with their employees, pay state and local taxes. These corporations also support numerous smaller subcontractors. Salaries paid to civilian and military personnel have immense ripple or secondary effects on the California economy in terms of enhanced commercial activity, housing prices, and so on. In the late 1980s, a reduction in Cold War tensions led the federal government to reduce weapons-systems procurement contracts and to close military bases. For budgetary reasons, the space program was curtailed. Between 1988 and 1993, California lost more than 180,000 jobs and suffered a decrease of 37 percent because of cuts in defense spending. "The disruption is felt in the eroding housing market, in oversubscribed U-Haul rentals, in a man laid off from his job as budget analyst at a big-name aerospace firm who had to find seasonal work filling out other people's 1040 forms at a storefront tax office."[6]

In addition to cutting weapons-systems contracts, the federal government is also closing military bases. Some of the bases on the closure list include Fort Ord; Alameda and Moffett Naval Air Stations; Castle, Norton, and George Air Force Bases; El Toro Marine Corps Air Station; Mare Island Naval Shipyard; and Long Beach Naval Station. More than half of the entire nation's military and civilian job losses are in California alone. The dislocations in the affected communities have been severe. But just as

---

6. "Payloads, Paydays, Palm Trees," *Los Angeles Times,* December 5, 1993, p. A1.

Table 1.3 California's Top Dozen Companies Ranked by Revenue

1. Chevron
2. Atlantic Richfield
3. Hewlett-Packard
4. Safeway
5. Bank of America
6. McKesson Corporation
7. Rockwell International
8. Pacific Gas & Electric
9. Lockheed
10. Pacific Telesis Group
11. Unocal Corporation
12. Occidental Petroleum

SOURCE: "The California Business 500," *California Business Magazine* (June–July 1993): 48. Reprinted by permission.

California profited the most from the post–World War II military buildup, so it will be hit hardest by the military build-down.

Many of California's U.S. House members with closed bases in their districts are liberal Democrats who made a career out of criticizing defense spending. Now they find themselves trying to preserve bases and weapons systems that the Pentagon admits it can live without. The House member in perhaps the most awkward position is Berkeley's Ron Dellums: The longtime pacifist and antiwar radical is now fighting to keep four bases in his district open. "I'm not arguing as a hypocrite," Dellums told the *Los Angeles Times*.[7] Dellums's supporters argue that the Pentagon's move is retribution for his many years of criticizing the military. Other California representatives are calling for cuts everywhere else, "but not in my district."

Interest in converting California's defense technology into civilian uses is keen, but there have been few solid successes to date. The brightest hope for defense conversion was once thought to be in producing trains and buses, but aerospace is poorly suited to move into the surface-transportation field because of the lesser number of workers needed, the different kinds of skills required, and the types of products produced. However, the electrical vehicle (EV) industry still remains a possibility. Other alternative nondefense industries in which the state's highly trained technical workforce might find skilled employment are high-technology communications, biomedical research, scientific measuring instruments, pharmaceutical research, optics, waste management, and other fields.

---

7. "Hit List Puts Pacifist on Offensive," *Los Angeles Times*, March 30, 1993, p. A3.

Woodward Payne / Photo 20–20

Rusting mothballed former Navy ships sit in Vallejo Bay.

The golden days of California's aerospace industry are clearly gone: Employment is expected to drop from 337,000 employees in 1990 to 153,000 by 1998. But the *Los Angeles Times* asserts that this is not a "death knell" for California but rather a "wake-up call."[8] The best hope for California lies in adaptive small- to medium-sized companies focused on world markets, the information industry (computers and computer parts), and EV technology.

ENVIRONMENT

Goals such as creating new jobs, supplying affordable housing, and providing sufficient food supplies are delicately balanced with the goal of environmental protection. A crucial aspect of this balancing process is the California Environmental Quality Act (CEQA). CEQA provides that if someone proposes a project that will cause significant physical change in the environment and which is either undertaken by a public agency or requires the permission of a public agency, then the person

---

8. "Diversity of Business in Region May Spell Renewal," *Los Angeles Times*, December 6, 1993, p. A1.

Doug Menuez / Reportage

Forty million discarded automobile tires could be an ecological nightmare, but in Modesto they are used to generate electricity.

proposing the project must prepare an environmental impact report (EIR). The EIR assesses all of the proposed project's environmental effects and describes measures that can minimize environmental harm or finds alternative sites for the project. If an initial study reveals that significant harm is not likely, then a city or county prepares a "negative declaration" saying that an EIR is not necessary. Government agencies may not approve projects that harm the environment unless the agencies also adopt mitigation measures that avoid or reduce the harm. However, if the agencies find "overriding circumstances" (for example, economic or social considerations such as the creation of jobs) that make mitigation infeasible, then they may still approve the project. A few conclusions about the CEQA process are clear: It is technical, lengthy, expensive, and political. CEQA is also a crucial weapon of antigrowth forces, who can delay a proposed construction project many years, making it more expensive and forcing the developer to scale back or drop a project.

Air pollution has been with us for the past half century. During World War II, people in Los Angeles noticed that the sky was more gray than blue, especially on hot days. Headaches, respiratory diseases (emphysema and bronchitis), deterioration of rubber products, and crop losses soon followed. In 1947 the first air-pollution-

Scott Willis / San Jose Mercury News

control district was formed. Since then, smog has been substantially reduced, in part because of the efforts of the state Air Resources Board (ARB) (described in Chapter 6). In Los Angeles, Orange, San Bernardino, and Riverside counties, second-stage smog alerts have decreased by 80 percent since 1978. During such an alert, large companies must require car pools for employees and curtail industrial emissions. Vigorous outdoor activity is discouraged. Third-stage alerts are the most serious, requiring people to remain indoors. So far, they are rare—the last was in 1974. The ARB recently reported that attempts to decrease freeway congestion actually increase air pollution. According to the report, nitrogen oxide pollution increases when cars go faster than 20 mph; carbon monoxide and hydrocarbon levels increase at 35 mph. Unfortunately, the report provides only small satisfaction to commuters trapped in stop-and-go freeway traffic. Governmental planners, on the other hand, may have to decide whether they want to reduce pollution or traffic congestion.

There are two comprehensive air-pollution programs in effect in all of California or in part of California: an ARB plan and a South Coast Air Quality Management District (SCAQMD) plan. The ARB program targets propellants used in pressurized deodorant and antiperspirant cans in order to reduce smog. Although the modified sprays may be increased in cost by approximately fifty cents a can, the ARB requirement is expected to reduce smog statewide by five tons per day, which is an amount equivalent to the emissions from a typical oil refinery. The ARB has also ordered that twenty-seven consumer products be reformulated to reduce hydrocarbons: These products include nail polish removers, perfumes, hair sprays, room air fresheners, auto windshield washer fluids, and furniture polish, among others. The reformulated items are expected to reduce smog by sixty tons per day.

The SCAQMD, covering Los Angeles, Orange, Riverside, and San Bernardino counties, has developed an extraordinarily ambitious air-pollution plan with 120 separate controls that will run in three phases until the year 2007. The plan increases long-standing controls on major sources of pollution such as oil refineries and utilities, but it also targets smaller industry sources such as dry cleaners, automobile paint shops, and bakeries. The inclusiveness of the plan is indicated by the fact that it also will require changes in individuals' lifestyles. People in the Los Angeles area will be driving a great deal less, and driving will be much more expensive. For example, the plan is intended to eliminate free employee parking as provided by employers. The 120-point plan also seeks to eliminate such familiar items as gasoline-powered lawn mowers, charcoal-lighter fluid, and drive-through restaurants. "Flexible-fuel" automobiles run on either methanol or gasoline: 33 percent of the cars sold in the Los Angeles area between 1995 and 2000 would be the so-called flex cars. Because the heart of the plan asks people to change their habits, how much are people willing to sacrifice to clean up their environment? The traditional approach to air-pollution control has been restraints on industries and major polluters, but the AQMD plan seeks to touch individual people directly. Another factor that calls into question the plan's viability is the **fiscal** constraints facing California state and local government: There simply are not sufficient funds for construction or for substantial public research that the plan may require.

An important part of the AQMD plan is emissions trading. The district sets an annual limit on how much nitrogen oxide and sulfur each company is allowed to emit. Those companies reducing pollution to levels below those required are allowed to buy and sell pollution credits with other companies. In addition, the annual limit is reduced 5 percent to 8 percent per year. The emissions-trading program relies on economic incentives for firms to eliminate pollution because economic self-interest dictates that the less they pollute, the richer they are (that is, it pays to be clean). The economic-incentive approach contrasts with the traditional technique favored by bureaucrats and lawyers of command and control, which employs threats and punishment to produce desired behavior. The Air Quality Management District argues that the command-and-control approach is overly rigid, has reached the limits of its effectiveness, and requires increasingly expensive controls on smaller and smaller businesses. Many environmentalists oppose emissions trading because they say that it is ethically wrong to create property rights in pollution, and they question whether the AQMD will be able to detect cheaters. An interesting twist to the plan would be if wealthy environmentalists—for example, socially conscious Hollywood personalities—bought up pollution credits in order to retire them from the market.

Hazardous wastes and dangerous chemicals generated by various industries also present a serious environmental problem. These toxic substances, which usually take the form of acids, caustics, corrosives, or solvents, may be flammable and explosive as well as poisonous. Perhaps most dangerous is their long duration in the environment. Toxic substances can be spilled in a highway accident on the way to a dump site or, at the site, can contaminate underground water supplies. In fact, toxic contaminants have been found in 18 percent of the state's wells, especially in industrial counties such as Los Angeles, San Bernardino, Riverside, and Santa Clara, and in agricultural counties in the San Joaquin Valley. The State Water Resources Control Board has estimated that 30,000 underground gasoline storage tanks leak benzene, which causes cancer. Cleanup may take fifteen years to complete and cost $5 billion. Toxic substances leaking into the water supply can cause birth defects, sterility, and cancer. More than 10 million tons of toxic waste are produced per year in California, approximately one pickup truckload per Californian.

Of the 70,000 industrial chemicals now in use, only 25 percent have toxicity data showing their effects on human beings and the environment. California has attempted to regulate the handling, processing, and disposal of those materials since 1972. Wastes are classified according to their danger, and disposal sites are graded in terms of geological security and their separation from water supplies. Still, disposal sites are becoming scarce, and many companies dump their chemical wastes at the site where they were produced. Actually, more than half of all wastes are disposed of in this manner. In an attempt to prevent clandestine "midnight dumping," the discarding of cargoes in remote areas, the state registers haulers and issues them permits. Drivers must carry a manifest of the toxic chemicals they are transporting and must have information on first-aid antidotes in case of an accidental spill. Unfortunately, this cradle-to-grave monitoring has not been vigorously maintained by the state.

Environmentalists' concerns that current environmental-protection laws are not strong enough prompted them to sponsor Proposition 65, a 1986 ballot proposition prohibiting release into a source of drinking water of any chemical in an amount known to cause cancer. Also forbidden is the release of an amount that exceeds 1/1,000 of the amount necessary for an observable effect on reproductive toxicity. Industries or farmers must warn the public before exposing it to such dangerous chemicals. The measure also provides for civil penalties and increases fines for toxic discharges, and it allows private individuals to sue violators and collect 25 percent of the penalties assessed.

The prospect of a law with such far-reaching effects prompted considerable political conflict. Arrayed on one side in favor were most Democratic Party candidates, environmentalists, actress Jane Fonda, and many other Hollywood personalities. On the other side were most Republican Party candidates, agricultural interests, the high-technology industry, and Chevron Oil. Proponents rejected the idea that environmental and health risks should be weighed on a scale against the economic benefits of the use of toxics. That is, they rejected the idea that policy making necessarily involves difficult value trade-offs. The proponents further argued that the burden of proof in toxics' use should be changed: Rather than requiring the government to prove that a chemical causes cancer before forbidding it, users of the chemical should prove that it does *not* cause cancer, a much more difficult task. Opponents such as the *Sacramento Bee* argued that "for some economic activity, the price between a very small risk and no risk—a price either in dollars or in health risks—can be astronomical."[9] The *Los Angeles Times* editorialized that the measure "deals with amounts of substances that are so minute they now can be detected in terms of parts per trillion. Unfortunately, the science of determining the health risk from these chemicals, or lack of a risk, is not as advanced as our ability to measure them." Amidst these vigorous assertions and counterassertions, the measure passed. In 1989 the maker of Liquid Paper correction fluid was threatened with a lawsuit under Proposition 65 and agreed to reformulate its product to remove ingredients known to cause cancer or birth defects. Other legal actions under Proposition 65 are described in Chapter 6.

In 1990 environmentalists placed on the ballot an initiative known as "Big Green," which was intended as a follow-up to Proposition 65. Covering thirty-nine single-spaced pages, the measure was defeated by the voters almost two to one. The initiative's comprehensive breadth and complexity contributed significantly to its defeat in an election year when the voters were already inclined to vote negatively. "Big Green" would have completely prohibited pesticide use on foods if the pesticides contained any ingredient that could cause cancer or reproductive harm; eliminated chlorofluorocarbons and reduced carbon dioxide emissions from fossil fuels by 40 percent; sold bonds to purchase old-growth redwood forests and prohibited clear-cutting of these stands; permanently banned new leases for oil and gas development in the state's coastal waters; established an oil-spill response fund; mandated water quality criteria; and created the office of a powerful elected environmental advocate to enforce all state environmental-protection and public-health laws. The wide-ranging nature of "Big Green" prompted a powerful coalition to oppose it and to wage an expensive media campaign against it. The measure also was weakened by having controversial legislator Tom Hayden as one of its authors. Opponents asserted that Hayden helped draft the measure and supplied large campaign contributions because he intended to run for the post of environmental advocate.

More than 160 million pounds of pesticides, herbicides, and fungicides are used each year by California agriculture. Although pesticides are helpful in dealing with crop infestations, environmentalists argue that these chemicals are poisoning the food eaten by the public. In addition, many farmworkers, pilots who fly crop dusters, and rural residents are harmed every year by pesticides that may cause cancer, nerve damage, sterility, birth defects, and other health hazards. Injuries to farmworkers are underreported because many of these people are in the country illegally and do not want to draw attention to themselves. Pesticide use became a much-discussed topic for urban residents during Southern California's sixteen-month struggle to eradicate the Mediterranean fruit fly in 1989 and 1990. State officials used helicopter spraying

---

9. "The Risks of Proposition 65" (editorial), *Sacramento Bee*, October 16, 1986, p. B-10. All other quotations are from "No on Toxics Initiative" (editorial), *Los Angeles Times,* October 29, 1986, pt. II, p.6.

of malathion for 100 nights over a 500-square-mile area of Los Angeles, Orange, Riverside, and San Bernardino counties. More than 52,000 gallons of malathion were sprayed, and nearly 6 billion sterile flies were released. Angry residents complained bitterly of health problems for themselves and their pets, as well as damaged car paint.

Solid-waste management, especially the disposal of garbage, is also a nagging problem. Californians have deposited garbage in landfills, covered it with soil, and forgotten about it. However, the dumps are filling up rapidly. Californians annually dispose of 1.5 tons of solid waste for each person in the state. Unless new landfills are opened, the state could run out of disposal ground around 1998. The state legislature responded to these problems by requiring cities and counties to reduce waste going into landfills by 50 percent by the year 2000. If recycling proves to be insufficient to meet the law's waste-reduction goals, then 5 percent of the garbage can be burned in incinerators. California currently has three waste-to-energy plants in Long Beach, Crow's Landing (in Stanislaus County), and the City of Commerce. These facilities not only reduce the total volume of garbage but also generate electricity. As will be noted later in the chapter, the nation is seriously dependent on foreign oil; garbage could well be considered an energy source, and there is plenty of garbage available. The "downside" to waste-to-energy facilities is that they pose air-pollution problems, emit small amounts of carcinogenic dioxin, and produce an ash residue.

For too long, California has tolerated such throwaway consumer items as containers. Between 1965 and 1986, fourteen bills and a ballot proposition to require deposits on all beer and soft-drink containers were defeated. Finally, in 1986 the legislature ended this two-decade struggle by passing a mandatory deposit bill covering aluminum, glass, and plastic containers. Retailers do not have to accept returned containers, which prompted them to end their opposition to mandatory deposits, because the law provides for a statewide network of thousands of recycling centers. Fourteen billion beverage containers are sold in the state each year, and this law and curbside recycling have gone a long way toward a cleaner California: 85 percent of aluminum cans are recycled, as are 75 percent of glass bottles and 60 percent of plastic containers.

Since the mid-1960s, California has sought to preserve open-space and agricultural lands, particularly around cities. The Williamson Land Conservation Act provides that cities and counties can enter into ten-year contracts with local farmers that provide that a farmer's land shall be assessed at a lower agricultural rate if it is not sold for development as houses, shopping centers, or factories. The intent of this law is to encourage landowners to preserve their land from development. The state government is supposed to reimburse cities and counties for most of the property tax revenue lost as a result of the program. Approximately one-third of the privately owned land in the state is covered by the law. Because only 3 percent of the acreage affected by the Williamson Act is farmland near cities, some critics argue that landowners are receiving a tax break on land that is not really threatened by development. The effectiveness of the law has been weakened by an **amendment** that allows leapfrog development; by the passage of Proposition 13 (described in Chapter

10), which has reduced the tax incentives under the Williamson Act by about 20 percent; and because the state government has not fully reimbursed counties for the revenue they have lost.

In the view of some commentators, environmental issues raise the question of a difficult trade-off between maintaining high employment and preserving environmental protection. Consider these recent bitter confrontations: reducing air pollution versus imposing significant costs on small shops or factories; restricting logging operations in the state's ancient forests versus saving the jobs of loggers and lumber mill workers; setting aside large areas of the California desert at the expense of mining and recreational uses; protecting endangered species such as the gnatcatcher or Stephens's kangaroo rat by stopping new home construction; using Sacramento River water to preserve chinook salmon and Delta smelt rather than supplying water to farmers. On one side of the issue are environmentalists or animal-rights activists who say that a higher value must be preserved or that the issue presents a false dichotomy; on the other side are a diverse array of economic interests who claim that their jobs are at stake.

ENERGY AND TRANSPORTATION

Coupled with the desire for a clean environment is the search for less polluting or nonpolluting sources of energy. California needs less polluting energy sources because if it were a country, it would rank ninth in the world in terms of total energy consumed. However, Californians use considerably less energy per capita for residential, commercial, and industrial purposes than do other Americans: We rank forty-second. Despite this state's "car culture," energy devoted to transportation per capita does not greatly exceed the national average. Petroleum provides 60 percent of the state's energy requirements; natural gas, 28 percent; coal, 3 percent; and hydropower, geothermal power, and nuclear power, 10 percent. In terms of end use, transportation receives 49 percent of the energy (primarily from petroleum), industrial and commercial uses receive 40 percent (mostly from natural gas and petroleum), and residential uses receive 11 percent (especially from natural gas).

No source of energy is without drawbacks. Oil is expensive, the supply is uncertain, and dependence on it subjects the country to foreign blackmail. This is a crucial issue: "California uses more gasoline than every country in the world except the United States and the Soviet Union. . . . California's continued overdependence on oil remains the state's fundamental energy problem."[10] Although today's cars are nearly twice as efficient as those built in the mid-1970s, we have not significantly reduced our dependence on oil. Half of the oil consumed in California is produced here, 8 percent comes from other countries, and 42 percent is from Alaska and the outer continental shelf.

---

10. California Energy Commission, *Fifth Biennial Report* (Sacramento: CEC, 1985), p. 32.

Methanol is a promising substitute for gasoline: It burns cleaner; it can be produced from oil, coal or natural gas; and it could be economically competitive if sold to a mass market. However, methanol is a victim of the "chicken-or-the-egg" dilemma. Automakers will not build methanol cars because gas stations do not have methanol pumps; on the other hand, station owners will not install methanol pumps because there are few methanol cars. Based on the principle of "practice what you preach," the federal, state, and local governments should convert their vehicle fleets to use primarily clean alternative fuels. One problem with methanol is that it is not as potent as gasoline: 1.7 gallons of methanol equal the energy in 1 gallon of gasoline. Cars powered by methanol would have to be equipped with significantly larger gas tanks to achieve the range of gasoline-powered cars.

Coal is heavily polluting; burning it releases sulfur dioxide and nitrogen dioxide. Furthermore, coal mining leads to black-lung disease in miners, or it is accomplished by ugly strip mining that devours the landscape.

The burning of fossil fuels such as oil or coal creates carbon dioxide, which leads to a warming of the atmosphere known as the greenhouse effect. In addition, chlorofluorocarbons (CFCs) used in refrigerators and air conditioners, as well as industrial solvents, also increase greenhouse gases and deplete the earth's protective ozone layer. The result will be climatic changes, but it is uncertain when they will occur or how severe they will be. The far-reaching air-pollution plan adopted by the South Coast Air Quality Management District, mentioned earlier, calls for phasing out chlorofluorocarbons and halon gas by the year 2000 at the latest. In addition, all air-pollution-control rules proposed in the future will first be examined to gauge their impacts on the greenhouse effect or on destruction of the ozone layer.

Nuclear-fission power has inspired a storm of protest. In 1981 a two-week demonstration at the Diablo Canyon nuclear power plant near San Luis Obispo resulted in the arrest of nearly 2,000 people and cost $3 million in law-enforcement expenses. Opponents of nuclear power seek to ban all nuclear power plants in California, fearing a reactor-core meltdown that would release dangerous radioactive materials, as happened at Chernobyl in the Soviet Union. In addition, atomic wastes (such as spent fuel rods) are toxic for centuries, and no safe disposal process has been developed. In 1983 the U.S. Supreme Court upheld a state law requiring that no new nuclear plants could be built in California until the state certifies that a demonstrated technology to dispose of high-level nuclear waste has been developed (*Pacific Gas and Electric Company v. Energy Resources Conservation and Development Commission*, 463 U.S. 1230 [1983]).

The "least-worst" calculations associated with all these energy sources have led environmentalists to trumpet various alternatives to meet a larger share of the state's energy needs. Interest in solar energy is keen, and California, with one-fourth of all American solar installations, is the national leader. Solar collectors are used principally for home water heating and swimming pool heating. A well-designed system can provide 80 percent of a home's water heating and cost 92 percent less than gas heaters in swimming pool heating. By means of "passive" solar building design, a home or office with large windows facing south, a slab concrete floor, and insulation can efficiently collect and store heat. The advantages of solar energy are that it is safe and nonpolluting and that it can supplant some of the state's natural gas use. Although installation costs are high, most systems pay for themselves after approximately fifteen years. As perhaps an indication of things to come, a large 43-megawatt solar facility has been built in the desert at Daggett (near Barstow). At Solar One, acres of mirrored reflectors focus the sun's rays on a pipe at the center, creating steam that turns a turbine to generate electricity.

Another alternative energy source is wind-generated electric power. California has 82 percent of the world's installed wind-energy capacity. The state's utilities have built gigantic windmills and wind turbine generators in San Gorgonio Pass near Palm Springs, in the Tehachapi Mountains, and in Altamont Pass east of San Francisco, and the utilities are considering building more facilities in other windy areas of the state. When these "wind farms" are supplying electricity, the utilities can scale back their use of oil-fired power plants. Wind power, too, has its drawbacks, though: Because these generators take the form of either enormous propeller blades or huge inverted eggbeaters, they could become collossal eyesores comparable to the offshore oil derricks near Santa Barbara.

Geothermal power is also in limited use. This process taps hot steam in the earth to drive turbines that generate electricity; it is used at the Geysers plant in the Napa–Sonoma area and in Death Valley.

The final energy resource that we will consider is conservation. By conserving energy, California can avoid having to build expensive new power plants. Devices such as storm windows, insulation, weatherstripping, caulking, water-heater insulation blankets, and low-flow shower heads can save a great deal of energy. The state's utilities also provide energy audits and interest-free loans to install such devices. The state government establishes minimum residential appliance-efficiency standards for appliances to be sold in this state—for example, standards for refrigerators. Refrigerators use 20 percent of the electrical energy consumed in the average California household; the conservation potential of the state's standards for refrigerators alone will save the state's consumers the cost of building a major (1,000-megawatt) nuclear or coal plant costing more than $3 billion. To encourage conservation, the California residential rate structure provides that as consumption goes up, cost per unit of natural gas also goes up. (However, lower-income people are protected by "lifeline" rates, which are minimal for the lowest levels of consumption.) Another way of lessening the need for new power plants is to decrease electricity demand at peak periods of use by transferring it to off-peak periods. This is facilitated by charging higher rates during peak periods.

Energy issues, environmental concerns, and transportation matters are all tied together: "California should aggressively work to increase the efficiency of its transportation system and the vehicles that use it since they consume three-fourths of the oil and half of all energy used in the state, and are the major source of air pollution in California."[11] The *inefficiency* of the current system is demonstrated by the fact that Californians waste as much as 400,000 hours per day in traffic delays; that traffic congestion is expected to increase by 200 percent by 2005, with average freeway speeds going down from 35 mph to 11 mph; that businesses have great difficulty transporting goods from one part of the state to another; and that employers are leaving the state because of freeway congestion. The best approach for increasing street and freeway efficiency is inducing more people to use fewer vehicles: mixing mass transit, car pools, van pools, group taxis, jitneys, as well as diamond lanes, toll roads, and metered on-ramps. The multimodal approach is vital because rush-hour freeways in many parts of the state have reached the point of saturation. Unless the vehicle occupancy rate can be increased through car pools or some other means, major freeways will simply become giant parking lots at critical times.

Clearly rail transit is the most efficient way to move people in and out of the central city at rush hours. Among the most prominent rail systems in California are the Bay Area Rapid Transit (BART) system; the Blue Line and Red Lines in Los Angeles; Metrolink, which joins Ventura County and Santa Clarita and San Bernardino County with downtown Los Angeles; and the San Diego Trolley.

Two much-debated transportation innovations are toll roads and electric vehicles. California state and local governments have little money to build new freeways. The toll road idea allows private companies to build and maintain roads, charge a toll, and then turn the roads over to the state after thirty-five years. Opponents of the toll road idea say that it is a form of aristocratic privilege by which wealthy people will travel on well-maintained toll roads while poor people will have to use congested and run-down public freeways. Antigrowth activists say that toll roads will encourage unneeded growth. The first California toll road built since the Depression is the Foothill Tollway in Orange County, which offers an AT&T "Smart Card" that is similar to a credit card and is mounted on the dashboard. Drivers can pass through toll plazas at freeway speeds while the toll road's computer reads the Smart Card. An interesting innovation is the idea that the tolls can vary according to the time of day that the toll road is used. Because higher tolls can be charged during the most congested times, this strategy is similar to load management and time-of-use electricity rates discussed earlier as part of energy pricing.

Electric vehicles are touted as a possible solution to both California's air-pollution problem and its dependency on petroleum products. Although these cars are pollu-tion-free, current models cost some $100,000 and have a range of only 100 miles; and if these cars are run at high speed or if the lights, windshield wipers, heater, or air conditioning are used, then the range is considerably less than 100 miles. Electric vehicles also need to be charged overnight (or for 8 hours) in order to run 100 miles. Whatever the limitations of electric vehicles may be, the ARB has ordered that they

---

11. California Energy Commission, *1991 Biennial Report* (Sacramento: CEC, 1991), p. 12.

Wide World Photos

City workers in Emeryville will use these electric vehicles to commute from work to a BART station.

will be 2 percent of all vehicles sold in California by 1998 and 10 percent by 2003. Because of these limitations, only the most committed and wealthiest Californians are likely to purchase them. Actually, the main purchaser may turn out to be the state government itself—which is to say, the state's taxpayers.

Freeway repair and construction is facing a serious crisis in California: Revenues are down sharply at the very time that the need for funds is increasing. Revenues are down because of lower gasoline-tax revenues resulting from more fuel-efficient cars, the defeat of state transportation bond issues, and declining federal funds. Ironically, the introduction of electric vehicles, which do not use gasoline, is likely to worsen this problem. At the same time, seismic repairs need to be completed to repair damage from the 1994 Northridge earthquake, old and deteriorating highways need to be reconstructed, new highway routes need to be added, new mass-transit projects completed, and normal bridge repairs made. The amount of money available is clearly insufficient—but the voters have made it clear that they will not stand for new taxes.

WATER AND AGRICULTURE

Water has always been a very sensitive issue in California politics, and recent conflicts over the Peripheral Canal, the protection of scenic wild rivers, and the Miller–Bradley bill are some of the latest skirmishes in a struggle that has been continuing for more than a century. The source of the problem is that 66 percent of the state's rain and snow occur in the northern third of the state, but 80 percent of the need for water is in the southern two-thirds. The potential for political conflict is obvious.

Runoffs from snowpacks in the High Sierras provide 70 percent of the state's water. The snowpack usually begins to accumulate in November and increases steadily through the winter, reaching a maximum depth and water content in April. If the water is not where the people are, massive aqueducts and dams and pumps are needed. The State Water Project and the federal government's Central Valley Project (CVP) constitute the world's largest water project. They are so huge that the astronauts who landed on the moon reported they could see the California project, the only item of human construction they could identify from that distance.

The 1959 Burns–Porter Act authorized the State Water Project, and in 1960 voters approved a $1.75 billion bond issue to help finance the project. It consists of a 600-mile-long series of dams, reservoirs, pumping plants, canals, and pipelines intended to move water from the Sierras as far south as the thirsty Southern California desert. One has to be amazed at both the engineering acumen and the political determination needed to undertake such an endeavor. The keystone is Oroville Dam in Butte County (the largest of eighteen state dams), which moves 1.6 million acre-feet of water per year (an acre-foot is 326,000 gallons, or the amount of water that will cover one acre of ground with one foot of water). After passing through the Sacramento–San Joaquin Delta and down the Governor Edmund G. Brown California Aqueduct, the water must be pumped 2,000 feet up the north slope of the Tehachapi Mountains to reach the Metropolitan Water District (MWD) of Southern California. Along the way, the North Bay Aqueduct supplies Napa and Solano counties, and the South Bay Aqueduct supplies Alameda and Santa Clara counties. San Francisco has its own Hetch Hetchy water project.

As a result of a bad drought in the late 1920s and early 1930s, the U.S. Bureau of Reclamation built the Central Valley Project. It consists of approximately thirty dams, the most important of which is Shasta Dam. The Bureau of Reclamation supplies 20 percent of the state's water needs; most of its customers are farmers in the Sacramento and San Joaquin valleys, for example, the Westlands Water District in Fresno.

The federal government also affects state water policy through its sale of low-cost water from federal reclamation projects. By means of the Newlands Reclamation Act of 1902, Congress tried to foster small farms in the arid West by selling federally subsidized water from its dams and canals. The 1902 act provided that a landowner could buy only enough water to irrigate 160 acres (320 acres in the case of a married couple). The act was never strictly enforced, but in the late 1970s, agrarian reformers persuaded the federal courts that this provision of the act should be enforced.

An aqueduct in San Bernardino County brings water from Northern to Southern California.

Congress responded in 1982 by rewriting the law and raising the amount of subsidized water that can be purchased to an amount sufficient to irrigate 960 acres. Water above this amount may be purchased at a higher price.

The Sacramento–San Joaquin Delta figures prominently in California water policy. This 740,000-acre area, where the Sacramento and San Joaquin rivers meet, discharges more than 40 percent of the state's natural runoff, hence it is a key link in the transportation of water from Northern California to Southern California. The Delta is an important fish spawning area and bird habitat. Its rich agricultural lands and wildlife habitats, such as the Suisun Marsh, must receive freshwater to repel the intrusion of saltwater from San Francisco Bay. Delta farmers fear that in a future drought too much water will be shipped to Southern California; environmentalists and recreationalists fear that Delta water quality thus would be lowered. All of these concerns came to a head in the emotional 1982 struggle over the Peripheral Canal. Southern California water interests argued that a forty-three-mile canal should be built around the periphery of the Delta to transport south useful water that was not needed to protect Delta water quality. Canal opponents rejected this position, arguing that Southern California does not need the water that the canal would deliver and that the canal would cost much more money than the state could afford. The interests on either side of the issue amounted to a roster of the state's major powers. For the canal were Getty Oil and Union Oil, the Metropolitan Water District of Southern California, the California Chamber of Commerce, the Association of California Water Agencies, the Irvine Company, and the *Los Angeles Times*. Opposed were the California Farm Bureau Federation, the California Cattlemen's Association, the J. G. Boswell Company, the Salyer Land Company, the Environmental Defense Fund, the Sierra Club, and the *Sacramento Bee*. The Peripheral Canal was soundly defeated, 62 percent to 38 percent.

In addition to the allocation of water, other key concerns are water quality, groundwater overdraft, and conservation. We noted recent attempts to prevent toxics in the water supply in our discussion of the environment, but California has long had water-treatment programs whose purpose is to remove suspended material and to kill harmful organisms. Water is filtered, treated chemically, and sterilized by chlorination or by exposure to ultraviolet light. To conserve water, California must also increase its reclamation of wastewater. Such reusable water can supply industry, irrigate crops and recreational areas, and recharge groundwater.

Approximately 40 percent of the water used in California is groundwater that has been pumped from below the surface. If farmers find that it is cheaper to draw water out of the ground than to purchase it from the federal or state government, then serious overdrafting occurs, especially because there are few governmental restrictions on this practice. Current overdrafts in the San Joaquin Valley amount to more than 1.5 million acre-feet a year. Although overdrafting lowers the water table and increases the costs of pumping, individual farmers continue to do it because they believe that if they do not pump heavily, other farmers will do so and will use the available water. This beggar-thy-neighbor situation is sometimes called the Tragedy of the Commons. California uses far more groundwater than any other state in the nation—and it also has the most serious **land subsidence** in the world because of overpumping. Land subsidence occurs when the ground sinks.

State water policy should be guided by the principle that water is a limited resource. Conservation must increase, especially on the part of agriculture, the chief water user. For example, water-intensive crops such as alfalfa and rice do not use water efficiently. These crops are more appropriately grown in other states. Needless to say, California farmers currently growing these crops are not overjoyed by this advice.

The supply of California's water is fixed by nature, yet the state's population is increasing. In fact, the state's supply of water can actually be considered to be decreasing because California has lost more than 550,000 acre-feet of water per year from the Colorado River because Arizona has completed its Central Arizona Project. Unless wild and scenic north coast rivers such as the Eel, American, Klamath, Trinity, and Smith are tapped, as farmers hope and environmentalists fear, then conservation must be pursued. Conservation is promoted when farmers or water districts temporarily sell surplus water accumulated through conservation without losing their legal right to the water. Approximately 170,000 acre-feet of water per year is saved by this process. It is sometimes said that California has no shortage of water, only a shortage of *cheap* water. Because water is frequently underpriced by the Central Valley Project and State Water Project, it is not used efficiently. If its price were to rise, then it would be put to its most efficient use. A good example of resource management is the "water bank" established in 1991 to deal with the drought then plaguing the state. This was a very successful voluntary program in which farmers sold their water to the California Department of Water Resources, which then resold the water at a higher price to urban water districts.

In the event of future droughts, Congress has provided for coordinated operation of the federal Central Valley Project and the State Water Project so that the former may use the latter's conveyance system of aqueducts, canals, pumps, and other facilities. In times of water shortage, more water can now be shipped to Southern California without allowing saltwater intrusion into the Sacramento–San Joaquin Delta. The possibility of future droughts should not be taken lightly, and the droughts of the mid-1970s, late 1980s, and early 1990s were probably not the last of this century. As we noted earlier, the state's economic system is complex and interdependent—and the thread of interconnection is water. Any shortage of water vastly complicates other problems, such as unemployment, pollution, and energy.

In 1992, Congress passed an important bill sponsored by Representative George Miller of California and Senator Bill Bradley of New Jersey that was intended to reform the Central Valley Project. For the first time, farmers receiving water under contract from the CVP could sell the water anywhere in California, for example, to the huge Metropolitan Water District of Southern California. This provision will surely become extremely significant during future droughts. The law also makes the restoration of threatened fish—such as smelt, salmon, and striped bass—and wildlife species a top water priority by guaranteeing 800,000 acre-feet of water for those purposes. As noted earlier, one acre-foot is 326,000 gallons; when we consider that the cities of San Francisco and Los Angeles use some 800,000 acre-feet per year, we realize that the Miller–Bradley bill made fish nearly as important as people.

The Miller–Bradley bill is also significant because it may presage a new alignment in California water politics. Past divisions featured a North-versus-South split, with farmers allied with the Metropolitan Water District against environmentalists. In the struggle over the Miller–Bradley bill, the MWD and business groups abandoned the farmers and allied themselves with environmentalists. Urban water interests may have reasoned as follows: The state's supply of water is fixed (or dwindling), the state's population is increasing, agriculture uses 85 percent of the water, and therefore the only way to get more water for urban uses has to be at the expense of agriculture. If this odd alliance holds together, California's farmers may face a future of diminished importance and influence in California.

Historically, however, agriculture has played a central role in the state's economy and politics. With gross farm income of $19 billion, California is the nation's foremost agricultural state, leading all states in the production of forty-nine crops and livestock products. Three crops are produced only in California, 90 percent of nine others is produced in the state, and more than half of twelve others is grown in this state. The leading agricultural counties in terms of value of production are Fresno, Tulare, and Kern, and the most important farm products by value are milk and cream, grapes, cattle and calves, and cotton. Agriculture generates nearly 10 percent of all jobs in California. An accurate picture of California agriculture should not omit marijuana. Although precise data cannot be secured, seasoned observers note that grower earnings of more than $1 billion would not be on the high side.

California's past success in agriculture can be attributed to many factors including mild climate, plentiful water supply, and research and development. Just as research has helped to make this state a leader in advanced industrialism, it has also contributed to our extraordinarily high value of crops per acre. Although the amount of land being farmed has fallen slightly in recent years, the number of farms has risen, especially the number of small farms under ten acres. California's acreage per farm is eighteenth in the United States and below the national average.

Some of the central issues of California farm policy have already been noted: the safe use of pesticides and ensuring an adequate water supply. Other pressing matters are the buildup of salt in the soil of the San Joaquin Valley and fair treatment for farm laborers. The fertile San Joaquin, one of the richest agricultural areas in the world, has seen the salinity of its water tables increase with each gallon of imported water. Water tables contaminated by salt that are close to the topsoil sterilize the soil and make it useless except for salt-tolerant crops. In addition to on-farm salt-purification systems, drainage canals need to be built that can effectively carry away subsurface salt.

California farmers once thought that their special advantages insulated them from the boom-and-bust cycles faced by farmers elsewhere in the country. Favorable weather and soil conditions allow this state's farmers to plant throughout the year. They can also diversify and hence cover their bets by planting anything from avocados to zucchini—they are not dependent on a single crop, as are Midwestern farmers. But in the 1980s, farm exports decreased, especially those of cotton, wheat, and rice. This development was crucial because one-third of all acres planted in California are for export. Overproduction, lower commodity prices, and shrunken markets led to foreclosures, bankruptcies, and a temporary decrease in land values.

The situation of California's farm laborers can be described as follows: Approximately three-fourths of these workers were born and raised in Mexico, and they move around California following the harvest in a generally south-to-north pattern, usually working at a particular farm for only two to six weeks. They are employed for approximately half the year.

Working conditions in the fields are deplorable, especially for children. Farmworkers toil in intense heat for long hours, bending, squatting, and lifting. If water is available for drinking or washing, then it may be of poor quality. Toilet facilities are meager. Workers are required to enter fields recently sprayed with dangerous pesticides before mandatory waiting periods have elapsed. Children, often as young as 10 years old or even younger, work to help support their impoverished families.

Wide World Photos

Farmworkers from Mexico work long hours in the hot sun for very little pay.

In the 1980s, forty-seven children younger than 15 were killed in farm accidents, especially those caused by machinery. Pesticide exposure is particularly hazardous for children because federal Environmental Protection Agency (EPA) regulations establishing how long workers must wait before entering a field after it has been sprayed are based on toxicity levels for adult men.

Living conditions are as inhumane as those in the fields: Farmworkers live amidst poverty and squalor in lean-tos, storage sheds, abandoned trailers, and ramshackle camps. Proper sanitation and nutrition are serious problems. Medical care is inadequate, especially for pregnant women and new babies. Many farm laborers are illiterate, even in their first language, and the children of migrant workers often must work in the fields themselves, thus furthering the illiteracy problem. Those children who do go to school must frequently move from school to school, receiving only a sporadic education—most eventually drop out of school entirely.

Growers bear much of the responsibility for these sordid conditions, because in recent years they have attempted to maintain the legal fiction that the farmworkers are not really their employees but rather the employees of labor contractors. These unscrupulous exploiters, who are frequently former farmworkers themselves, are supposed to supervise the workers and to pay their wages, taxes, unemployment insurance, and workers' compensation premiums. The labor contractors cheat the workers out of their wages and then fail to pay the required taxes and premiums. The farmworkers are afraid to protest this situation because the contractors can keep them from working at all. State and federal government inspectors tolerate this situation and, if they are finally moved to action, the labor contractor has vanished in a beat-up truck.

As the labor contractors have flourished in recent years, farm labor unions have waned. The United Farm Workers (UFW), founded by the late César Chavez, once had 100,000 members but now has only 15,000. Unionizing workers hired by contractors is virtually impossible. There is also a huge oversupply of farmworkers. These factors, along with grower hostility and internal strife within the UFW, have weakened the union.

Many years ago, John Steinbeck wrote about the sorry condition of the Joad family in the *Grapes of Wrath*. Not much has changed, although the Joads, who were native-born Anglos, have been replaced by Latino illegal aliens. The basic problem is that the farmworkers are viewed as somehow not fully human. One farmworker activist was asked by the *Sacramento Bee* how such conditions could persist, decade after decade: "It's almost as if farmworkers aren't human. They're just doing farm work and they're just picking the crops, so that's all they deserve. And you have these tractors, and plows, and farmworkers, and rakes, and shovels, and tanks of pesticides. Farmworkers are just one more tool."[12] And when tools are no longer useful, they are thrown away.

EDUCATION

Education is an important and expensive state activity: Approximately 30 percent of the state budget is spent on elementary, secondary, and community college education, and an additional 11 percent is spent on four-year colleges. Proposition 13 of 1978 substantially reduced local property tax revenues and forced school districts to rely heavily on state aid. The state pays approximately 67 percent of local school costs, some three-fourths of which are for salaries and benefits. In 1988 the California Teachers Association (CTA) sponsored Proposition 98, which was approved by the voters. This far-reaching measure guarantees that a fixed percentage of the state budget must be spent for elementary, secondary, and community college educa-tion—thus making education the only governmental function in California with an

---

12. "Thousands Live in Squalor," *Sacramento Bee,* December 10, 1991, p. A1.

assured level of funding. Despite the assurances of Proposition 98, California's spending for elementary and secondary education is forty-second in the nation and well below the national average. Because of the state's fiscal problems, the state is unlikely to provide significant amounts of new money for elementary and secondary education. However, at the local level, school districts are finding it exceedingly difficult to muster the two-thirds vote needed to raise local property taxes. A 1993 ballot proposition to lower the percentage to a majority was soundly defeated by the voters.

State funding of elementary and secondary education is guided by the California Supreme Court's ruling in *Serrano* v. *Priest*. In that case, the court declared unconstitutional the manner in which the property tax was used to finance public schools. The court decided that because certain school districts had a higher tax *base* (in terms of industrial, commercial, or residential real estate), they were able to set a lower tax *rate* and still generate *higher* revenue for schools. The court ruled that this method of financing schools violated the equal protection clause of the California Constitution. (Because the U.S. Supreme Court has ruled that this method of school funding does not violate the equal protection clause of the U.S. Constitution, the *Serrano* decision is an example of the "independent-state–grounds" doctrine described in Chapter 8.) The reasoning of the state's highest court was that the property tax, as then administered, made the quality of a student's education (expressed in terms of the amount of money spent per pupil) dependent on the presence of nearby industry or high-priced homes. The California Supreme Court ordered the governor and the state legislature to devise an acceptable plan to pay for the education of elementary and secondary school students.

One of the stated goals of Proposition 98 was reducing pupil–teacher ratios in California, which are the highest in the nation. However, this is an extremely expensive endeavor, and school districts are already hard-pressed just to keep up with rapidly rising increases in enrollment. Furthermore, reducing class sizes would exacerbate the classroom shortage problem, which requires that nineteen new classrooms be built every day until the turn of the century.

The demographic composition of California is changing in significant ways, as indicated earlier. Whites became the minority in the schools during the 1988–1989 school year. Many Latino and Asian students are from immigrant families and have English difficulties. Approximately one-third of the state's 5.2 million students speak a primary language other than English. More than 100 languages are spoken by students in the Los Angeles Unified School District. These students need early English-language instruction to prevent them from falling behind in early grades.

Measurable indicators of the performance of California's elementary and secondary students are discouraging. In 1993 the U.S. Department of Education conducted the National Assessment of Educational Progress in forty-three states and U.S. territories. California fourth-graders tied Mississippi fourth-graders for last place in reading and were next to last in mathematical skills. In 1994, the state established the California Learning Assessment System (CLAS), which for the first time measured students not against each other but according to rigorous performance standards set by educators, school board members, business leaders, parents, and testing experts. The tests were also designed to measure students' thinking abilities rather than their responses to multiple-choice questions. More than one-third of all students demonstrated "little or no basic understanding of mathematics," and 20 percent to 30 percent of the students showed only a "superficial or worse" understanding of what they read. Furthermore, only 7 percent to 10 percent of the students showed "substantial mathematical understanding," and only 26 to 38 percent of them read with "thoughtful understanding."[13] Although the mathematics and reading portions of the test yielded disappointing results, it was the writing portion of the test that sparked the most controversy. Because students were asked to read a passage and respond to it in writing, some parents contended that CLAS delves too deeply into the private lives of students by requiring them to call upon feelings and beliefs to answer questions about personal relationships or family situations. In the face of invasion-of-privacy lawsuits, the State Department of Education allowed parents to exempt their children from the exam.

Dissatisfaction with performance results led to 1993's ballot Proposition 174, which sought to establish school vouchers in California. Under the plan, any school-age child could receive a school voucher of $2,600 if he or she were to enroll in a private school that accepts vouchers. Proponents of school vouchers argued that public schools do a poor job of educating students because they currently have a guaranteed clientele as a result of compulsory attendance laws. If public schools had more competition for students, proponents said, public schools would have a strong incentive to improve. Voucher advocates charged that public schools are now dominated by school bureaucrats, teacher unions, and overly burdensome and inefficient regulations. For example, the state's Education Code is more than 11,000 pages long and regulates every conceivable matter, including the kind of paint that must be used on bathroom walls. Arguing along the lines of consumer choice, proponents said the plan would empower parents, not educational bureaucrats, and it would finally make private education accessible to poor people. Those who favored Proposition 174 said that the plan would save money for the state because the value of the $2,600 voucher is one-half of the $5,200 that the state spends to educate a child in a public school. In fact, as more public school students who use vouchers transfer to private schools, the more money the state saves. Finally, proponents noted that many public school teachers, the people who know the most about public schools, send their own children to private schools.

Opponents of school vouchers, led by the CTA, described the plan as radical and dangerous. They said that voucher schools would accept public money but would be unregulated and unaccountable. For example, voucher schools would not be required to hire teachers with degrees or credentials, would not be required to have

---

13. "State's Pupils Score Poorly," *Sacramento Bee*, March 9, 1994, p. A1.

graduation standards or to teach specific courses or to have a minimum length of the school day or the school year. A self-described coven of witches in Concord said that it would use vouchers to start a school for pagans. Voucher schools could legally discriminate against prospective students on the basis of income status, ability level, or gender. Opponents also noted that the voucher plan would subsidize the 550,000 California children already in private schools at a cost of $1.35 billion. In what may have been a telling admission, opponents also said that if numerous private schools were established, too many students would leave the public schools, thus devastating the latter.

The school-voucher issue dominated the **special election** of November 1993, and the measure was decisively defeated. Opponents spent an extraordinary $24 million, with almost all of the money coming from the teachers unions; proponents spent $3.6 million. The *Los Angeles Times,* which opposed school vouchers in its editorials, analyzed the election results in terms of the distribution of power in state politics: "The CTA emerged from the campaign as perhaps the most powerful special interest in California, proving it can quickly raise millions of dollars and mobilize thousands of savvy union representatives and teachers for a grass-roots campaign."[14]

California's higher education was traditionally guided by the Master Plan for Higher Education of 1960, which envisioned a system of widespread student access and low financial cost to students and their families. The Master Plan also specified the functions of the University of California, the California State University System, and the community colleges. (The governing boards of California higher education will be discussed in Chapter 6.) The University of California, with 165,000 students at nine campuses, provides higher education in the fields of liberal arts and the sciences, and in professional fields such as law and medicine. It awards the Bachelor's, Master's, and Ph.D. degrees, and it conducts a substantial amount of basic research. Those who seek undergraduate admission must be in the top eighth of the state's graduating high school classes. The California State University System, with 350,000 students at twenty-one campuses, also provides higher education in the liberal arts and sciences, and it trains many of the state's elementary and secondary school teachers. The CSU System awards the Bachelor's and Master's degrees and, jointly with private universities and the University of California, the Ph.D. degree. Entering undergraduates must have graduated in the top third of the state's high school classes. The California community college system, the nation's largest two-year system, offers postsecondary instruction leading to the A.A. (Associate of Arts) degree. Some 1.5 million community college students attend 107 colleges in 71 districts, which makes their enrollment almost three times as large as the combined UC and CSU enrollments. More than three-fourths of all community college students attend part-time; approximately 4 percent transfer to four-year institutions to finish their education. The community colleges are open to all high school graduates or to persons eighteen

---

14. "Vouchers: Voters Reject Plan to Use Tax Funds for Private Schooling," *Los Angeles Times,* November 3, 1993, p. A27.

years of age or older who can profit from the instruction offered. Community colleges are heavily dependent on state aid, receiving a higher percentage of their revenue from the state than do elementary and secondary schools.

The state government's financial crunch, which has affected all aspects of state government, has been particularly severe on higher education. The governor and the legislature have decided to appropriate less money for higher education and to shift a far higher proportion of the cost of this service to the recipients of the service. This decision reflects the "benefits-received" principle of public finance described in Chapter 10. Elected officials, perhaps without realizing it, have also abandoned the wide-access–low-charge goal of the Master Plan for Higher Education. But the California of 1960 was much less populous, much less diverse, and arguably more capable of funding the public sector than it is now. The clear result of the state's cost shift has been rapidly rising student fees (which the state has finally admitted are the same as tuition), layoffs of part-time faculty members and some full-time faculty and staff, course cutbacks, and the squeezing out of many students, particularly those from less-affluent families. Only 6 percent of CSU students and 31 percent of UC students graduate in four years. In the midst of all of these difficulties, press reports revealed that the UC Regents had secretly raised the pensions and perquisites of high-ranking University of California administrators. Future prospects indicate increased cost shifting to students, which will continue at least as long as or longer than the state government's financial difficulties continue. Private colleges and universities in California, which grant one-third of all four-year degrees in the state, could relieve some of the pressure, but their tuition is currently much higher than that of public universities.

WELFARE, HEALTH, AND HOUSING

After education, the next most important component of the state budget is welfare and health, which constitutes approximately 26 percent of the budget. The major welfare programs are Aid to Families with Dependent Children (AFDC), Supplemental Security Income/State Supplementary Program (SSI/SSP), general relief, and food stamps. Aid to Families with Dependent Children is the largest assistance program, and it provides grants to poor families in which one parent is missing or involuntarily unemployed. Most AFDC families are headed by a woman, and approximately 70 percent of AFDC recipients are children. Half of the program is financed by the federal government, with the state paying almost all of the rest and the counties paying a small portion. Standards of eligibility and the level of benefits are set by the state government, and AFDC recipients also use many of the other programs, especially Medi-Cal (described later). Supplemental Security Income benefits aged, blind, and disabled persons with low incomes and few assets; because of the characteristics of SSI/SSP recipients, this program does not prompt bitter political disputes in the state legislature, as does AFDC. Many recipients of the latter program are minority-group members, many are unwed mothers, many are illegitimate children, and some are able-bodied men. General relief is financed entirely by the counties and provides income for people who cannot qualify for either of the previous programs; for example, male transients or alcoholics. County governments determine eligibility rules and frequently impose work requirements. Payments vary widely from county to county. Food stamps are a federal program in which the state and counties pay half of the administrative costs: Low-income individuals are given coupons that serve as money at grocery stores. The Social Services Program is intended to promote social goals, such as keeping families intact and preventing child abuse, promoting family planning, and allowing elderly or disabled persons to live in their own homes rather than in institutions. For example, the program furnishes day care for children and homemaker-support services for senior citizens. In sum, California provides a wide range of social welfare services.

In 1992, Governor Pete Wilson sponsored ballot Proposition 165, which was intended to cut spending drastically on welfare. Claiming that welfare was bankrupting the state budget, Wilson said that welfare spending was increasing four times as fast as the state's population and that California has 12 percent of the nation's population but 26 percent of its welfare recipients. He asserted that welfare grants are too high and thus reduce the incentive to work. The situation was described by the *Los Angeles Times* as follows:

> Many poor mothers find that welfare can provide more income for their families than if they were supporting them on low-wage jobs. In California, public assistance pays a mother and two children maximum food stamp and welfare benefits of $10,200 a year, while a 40-hour-a-week minimum wage job pays $8,840 a year.
>
> The prospect of going off welfare also presents recipients with the loss of another significant benefit: free health care, which is lost one year after a recipient leaves the rolls. In the private sector, most low-wage jobs come without health benefits.[15]

Hence, Wilson wanted to reduce AFDC by 25 percent over an 18-month period. Other provisions of Proposition 165 said that the maximum grant would not increase if a welfare mother had more children while on welfare, that unwed teenage mothers must live with a parent or guardian, and that welfare families moving into California could receive AFDC benefits no higher than those of their former state for their first 12 months in California.

Opponents of Proposition 165, principally public employee unions and Democratic Party officials, counterattacked by saying that reducing benefits by 25 percent would hurt children, the most vulnerable Californians, because 70 percent of AFDC recipients are children. Table 1.4 shows Wilson's claims and the opponents' rebuttals.

---

15. "Welfare: Disagreement Over Wilson Plan," *Los Angeles Times*, August 11, 1992, p. A22.

Table 1.4 **Arguments For and Against Proposition 165 (1992)**

GOVERNOR WILSON'S ARGUMENTS	OPPONENTS' REBUTTALS
1. Welfare spending is increasing four times as fast as the state's population.	1. Between Fiscal Year 1983 and Fiscal Year 1992, AFDC as a percentage of the general fund budget increased only slightly from 6.3 percent to 6.5 percent.
2. California has 12 percent of the U.S. population, but 26 percent of the welfare recipients.	2. The adjacent states of Oregon and Nevada have lower AFDC payments, but their welfare rolls are growing at a higher percentage than are California's rolls.
3. Do not increase grants for welfare for mothers who have more children.	3. This provision will only increase abortions.
4. Do not increase welfare benefits for families moving to California.	4. This provision is clearly unconstitutional according to two U.S. Supreme Court decisions.

Proposition 165 was defeated by the voters, but the defeat was due in part to another section of the measure that would have significantly increased the governor's control over the state budget and reduced the legislature's control. In any event, the rejection was a major setback for Governor Wilson.

Another welfare-related area is collection of child-support payments. Critics allege that California is not particularly forceful in enforcing its child-support laws—other states are much more likely to send nonpaying parents to jail. Approximately 350,000 children in California are receiving welfare because a parent is not paying court-ordered child support; 93 percent of the delinquent parents are fathers. Wisconsin has an innovative program of automatic income withholding for persons subject to a court's child-support order. California has recently established a nation-wide computer search using Social Security numbers to locate delinquent parents and garnish their wages. The state can also deny business and professional licenses to persons who are late in their child-support payments.

The most costly element in California's welfare and health benefits system is the Medi-Cal program, which is financed half by the federal government and half by the state. Minimum levels of services are established by the federal government, which California supplements, as well as optional categories of coverage whose cost the national government will share with California. Thirty-two services fall into the latter category; California provides thirty of these services, with the national average among states being eighteen optional services provided. Federal law requires that all people receiving AFDC or SSI/SSP also receive Medi-Cal.

One out of five Californians has no health insurance, and many of these people are medically indigent adults (MIAs) or their dependents. The MIAs are employed persons whose employers provide no health coverage. These people are not poor enough to qualify for Medi-Cal, but they do not make enough money to pay for health insurance or to see a private physician. As California's postindustrial economy becomes increasingly service-oriented, the number of poorly paid service workers is expected to increase. When MIAs become ill, they go to an emergency room. Because they have postponed routine medical problems until the problems have become acute, the conditions are much more expensive to cure. The problem is particularly severe for uninsured children who do not receive treatment and then later develop complications that require costly hospitalization.

Medically indigent adults have been at the center of the health-care disputes that have raged in California and nationally: managed care, health-insurance–purchasing cooperatives (HIPCs), and the single-payer plan. Managed care is a recently established program of Governor Wilson. Under the previous fee-for-service system, Medi-Cal patients chose their own doctors, hospitals, and level of care, but they had to find physicians who would accept the state's relatively low reimbursement rates. Through managed care, the state contracts with health-maintenance organizations (HMOs), county health organizations, and clinic chains, with the state paying these providers a set monthly fee for each patient. The Wilson plan rests on the hope, which may be unfounded, that managed care will produce substantial cost savings.

Health-insurance–purchasing cooperatives are a reform proposal also adopted by Governor Wilson, the nation's first government-run purchasing pool designed to use market forces to deliver health-insurance coverage to small businesses at reasonable rates. Small businesses can join together in purchasing pools to gain the leverage that large corporations have traditionally had when bargaining for health coverage. The Wilson plan does not compel any employer to join. Workers may choose from eighteen health-care providers, each of which uses managed care. Providers offer the same benefits, but costs to the employee differ from one provider to another. The employer pays at least half of the cost of the lowest-priced plan; the coverage is "portable," which means that a worker remains covered if he or she switches jobs to another employer participating in the cooperative. Annual price increases are capped.

In 1994, California voters were presented with Proposition 186, the single-payer initiative, which would have established a Canadian-style health plan in which the State of California would finance and administer health coverage, thus abolishing all private health-insurance companies in California. Proponents promised universal health care for all legal residents of California. Taxes and government funds would replace Californians' current insurance premiums, medical bills not covered by insurance, and bills for prescription medicine. The program would have been financed by a tax increase on all taxpayers, a payroll tax on employers, and a cigarette tax increase of $1.00 per pack. The plan was bitterly opposed by small businesses, which now are usually not providing medical coverage for their employees and which did not want their taxes raised as well. The single-payer plan would have added at least $70 billion per year to the state budget, thus more than doubling in a single stroke the current state budget of $57 billion. This mammoth increase in the size of state government, along with the potential for seriously increasing the state's deficit, caused Proposition 186 to be defeated by a margin of 73 percent to 27 percent.

Because the median age in the state is rising, private health-care costs and Medi-Cal costs will become an even larger responsibility in the future. Reports by the state's "Little Hoover" Commission (see Chapter 6) have shocked Californians with descriptions of conditions in the state's 22,000 private board-and-care facilities for the elderly, mentally ill, and retarded. The commission has found instances of patients strapped to their beds and lying in their own excrement, and of elderly people covered with ants. Overcrowding, lack of food, poor toilet facilities, and inadequate fire escapes were widespread. Board-and-care facilities provide only custodial care, but conditions were not significantly better in the state's 1,200 nursing homes, which additionally provide medical care. The legislature has passed bills to increase the penalties for neglect or abuse of patients and to improve the training of inspectors employed by the state. However, a 1988 report by the federal government found that more than half of California's nursing homes fail to provide their residents with proper daily care to ensure personal cleanliness, and nearly half of the facilities do not meet sanitary standards for food storage and preparation. The report also noted that approximately 40 percent of the state's homes fail to administer medicine according to doctors' orders, to provide rehabilitation care so that residents will not lose their ability to walk, and to follow correct isolation techniques to prevent the spread of infection among a fragile population whose average member is more than eighty years old.

The field of health care is replete with tragic and heartrending situations, but perhaps none is more so than care of the mentally ill. California has long sought humane treatment in this field, going back to the Short–Doyle Act of 1957 (which provides state financial assistance to counties for mental-health treatment in local facilities). Counties may either run their own programs or contract with private providers, but in any event they are governed by state standards and regulations. The Lanterman–Petris–Short (LPS) Act of 1967 sought to end the practice of warehousing senile persons and chronic alcoholics in mental hospitals:

> To assure that the state hospitals were not arbitrarily incarcerating the mentally ill, LPS placed restrictions on the power of the courts to commit people to mental hospitals. A disordered person may be involuntarily detained for evaluation and treatment for 72 hours if he shows signs of being a danger to himself or others, or is unable to provide for his personal needs. After medical certification, this period may be followed by 14 days of intense treatment. If the person shows signs of being dangerous during this period, he may be incarcerated for up to 90 days in a treatment facility. For those persons who meet the standard of being "gravely disabled," the court is authorized to appoint a conservator, who may place the mentally ill person in a hospital for a period of one year. The conservatorship automatically expires after one year, but the court may renew it if the person is

certified as needing continued treatment by medical personnel. LPS also assures certain civil rights to conservatees in state hospitals. They have the right to confidential correspondence and phone calls, and may refuse shock treatment and lobotomy operations.[16]

The Lanterman–Petris–Short Act sought to reserve state mental hospitals for only those who are a danger to themselves or to others, or who suffer severe psychological disabilities, with senile people and alcoholics being directed to less restrictive local facilities. The act was certainly well-intentioned when enacted, but it has made meeting the needs of today's homeless people (described below) more difficult.

The theory that has governed California's mental-health policy for more than three decades is **deinstitutionalization.** This has meant getting mentally ill people out of large, isolated institutions, which have staffing problems, into smaller community care facilities closer to their homes; these are believed to be more economical, effective, and humane in treatment. Hence the number of patients in state mental hospitals has dropped from 37,500 in 1959 to 5,000 today.

Critics of deinstitutionalization now argue that community programs are inadequate to meet the need because counties are unable or unwilling to establish comprehensive mental-health treatment programs, and that community programs are actually more expensive than state hospitals. These critics declare that because of economies of scale, hospitals can have sufficient staff, pay less per patient for the physical plant, and have a higher occupancy rate. They also claim that deinstitutionalization has seriously contributed to the large numbers of people "in the skid rows of cities, where former mental patients are numerous among the homeless and semi-homeless who wander the streets, dine in soup kitchens, [and] sleep when they can afford it in fleabag hotels."[17] According to a mental-health professional who helped draft LPS:

> In our zeal to move people out of very restrictive, very inhumane places, we forgot that there were a whole variety of supports that were provided [by institutions]. . . . We had a simplistic notion that basically what you could do is take people out of institutions, move them into the community and provide outpatient mental health care. But what we forgot is that institutions provide people with shelter, food, health care, and a whole variety of other basic human needs.[18]

Psychiatrists in the 1950s supported deinstitutionalization because they had great faith in tranquilizers and other drugs as a way of helping people live outside

16. T. Anthony Quinn and Ed Salzman, *California Public Administration,* 2d ed. (Sacramento: California Journal Press, 1982), pp. 65–66. In 1988 the legislature extended the fourteen days of intensive treatment to forty-four days for gravely disabled, mentally disordered persons who are unable to stabilize within the fourteen-day period or whose previous discharges have resulted in frequent rehospitalizations.
17. Walter T. Anderson, "Thousands Released; Few Treatment Facilities," *California Journal* (June 1984): 215.
18. Quoted in Sherry Bebitch Jeffe, "California: Good Aims, Bad Results," *Los Angeles Times,* March 22, 1987, pt. V, p. 3.

institutions. Now, how well the drugs work or even whether they help or harm the patient is not clear. Drugs may be used merely to make troublesome patients more manageable or to get people through the bureaucratic system as quickly as possible without really doing anything for them.

The California Department of Housing and Community Development has estimated that between 50,000 and 75,000 people are homeless in California. Contemporary homeless individuals are younger than previous "skid-row" populations, which were dominated by people in their fifties or sixties: The average age is approximately 37.[19] Some 20 percent are women. Although former skid-row populations were at least 90 percent white, less than half of the current Los Angeles homeless population is white; 32 percent is black, 10 percent is Latino, 6 percent is Native American, 1 percent is Asian, and 2 percent constitutes members of some other group. The homeless population contains all of the following people, plus others: transients moving through an area; elderly alcoholics; "bag ladies"; young, single men who are recently unemployed; mentally ill adults; women and children fleeing family violence; unemployed heads of households and their families; young persons aged 12 to 16; and Vietnam War veterans. Contemporary journalistic accounts stress the large number of chronic alcoholics, regular drug users, and severely mentally ill persons. The effects of deinstitutionalization and Lanterman–Petris–Short have already been noted. LPS may have resulted in fewer of these people ever having received extensive care because the thrust of the law is to make it more difficult to institutionalize people and easier for patients to win release.

Yet another vexing public policy issue is supplying affordable housing for middle-income people or those of modest means. Sunday editions of major California newspapers regularly publish an "affordability index" showing how much income is necessary to purchase a local home: Most Californians are priced out of the market, especially first-time home buyers. State residents have to spend 48 percent more of their income on housing than do residents of other states, but their salaries are only 8 percent higher than the national average, hence it is not surprising that California is ranked forty-eighth in home ownership rate as shown in Table 1.2. Will California's economic growth be throttled by high housing prices? Various companies have indicated that they do not want to stay in or relocate to California, because housing costs force them to pay their employees more here than elsewhere. The slow-growth policies of many California cities (see Chapter 9) restrict the number of housing units that can be built. Developers' fees (also Chapter 9) eliminate moderately priced housing. Stringent environmental regulations and building codes cause delay, string out the permit-approval process, and ultimately increase housing costs. In any event, quick solutions are nowhere to be found. Providing affordable housing may be one

19. Demographic information on homeless people is from Richard Ropers, "The Rise of the New Urban Homeless," *Public Affairs Report* (University of California at Berkeley) 26 (October–December 1985): 1–6; League of California Cities, "The Homeless: Who Are They and Why Are They on the Streets?" *Western City* (March 1986): 3–6.

of those issues that state policy makers, or government policy makers at any level, are unable to solve at reasonable cost.

One solution that has been attempted at the local level, with mixed success, is rent control. In fact, approximately half of California's population lives in communities with rent control. Proponents point out that it saves money for renters by preventing rent gouging by landlords. Opponents counter that rent control aids renters in the short run but seriously harms them in the long run because it reduces the supply of rental housing. Investors would rather spend their money on more profitable office buildings or invest in cities without rent control. (However, all rent-control ordinances enacted in California so far exempt new rental housing.) Rent control is also said to lead to "housing gridlock" because renters are afraid to move from a rent-controlled apartment because they may not be able to find a comparably priced substitute. Finally, opponents argue that under rent control, landlords will not perform needed maintenance and will let units deteriorate; they will also spend less for heating and lighting. All these points were carefully examined in a study of the Los Angeles rent-control law: Its findings surprised both sides and pleased neither side.[20] The law not only had little effect on the rate of increase in rents compared to nearby cities with no rent control but also reduced only slightly landlord profits compared to those of landlords in adjacent cities. Rent control neither saved tenants much money (only $7 per household per month) nor had much effect on owners' incentives to maintain apartment buildings.

OTHER ISSUES

According to historian James S. Holliday, emeritus director of the California Historical Society, California's most important export has always been images: The streets are paved with gold, anything is possible, this state does not require anyone to conform. Note that California's founding fathers were the gold-seeking forty-niners, and consider how this contrasts with having the Mayflower Pilgrims as founders.[21] California novelist James Houston argues that the California Dream—this is a land of promise, a land of milk and honey—is in many respects the California Myth, but that the Myth has not been diminished by earthquakes, raging fires, and persistent drought.[22]

At the beginning of this chapter we indicated that one of the key characteristics of California is diversity. Consider the variety of climate, terrain, and natural features exhibited by this state's mountains, deserts, and coastal areas. Mt. Whitney, at 14,494

---

20. "Report Finds Rent Law's Impact Has Been Slight," *Los Angeles Times*, April 24, 1985, pt. I, p. 3.
21. James S. Holliday, "California—Images and Realities" (Paper presented at the Second Conference on Research Needs in California Government and Politics, Institute of Governmental Studies, University of California at Berkeley, May 2–3, 1986).
22. James Houston, "California: Earth, Air, Fire, Water" (Paper presented at the Fourth California Studies Conference, Sacramento, February 8, 1992).

Dennis Renault / *The Sacramento Bee*

feet, is the highest point in the United States outside Alaska, but only sixty miles away is Death Valley at 282 feet below sea level, the lowest point in the Western hemisphere. However, the diversity is not merely in the land; it is in the people as well. One sympathetic observer of the California scene has written:

> Half the people living here have arrived from somewhere else. If California has a working history, it really consists of this intersection of pasts from every direction, from Arkansas and Sonora and Vietnam and Bengal and Armenia and Canada and

Italy. This is what California is, an intersection, a world crossroads of extraordinary and sometimes maddening diversity. There is enormous interchange and energy and vitality and motion and flux.[23]

One out of every four residents of the state is a Latino, and 7 percent of the state's people are black. Another 10 percent are Filipinos, Chinese, Japanese, Vietnamese, Native Americans, and of many other ethnic or racial backgrounds. Will these various people reach an amicable understanding with the white majority and with one another? The white majority currently stands at 57 percent of the state's population, but it will soon be a minority group; various other minorities will then form a majority, making California a "minority-majority" state. Will this situation increase intergroup tensions? Will competition between racial and ethnic groups become a zero-sum game in which one group's gain can only come at another group's expense? Coalition building is usually suggested as a way out of a zero-sum situation, but coalition building assumes some common ground among groups.

Transcending economic and racial diversity is ideological diversity: Clearly, philosophical consensus is lacking on the ends of California government or even the means to reach different ends. Liberals point California in one direction, conservatives in another, and middle-of-the-roaders have their own agenda. Many observers have said that the challenge of California as it reaches the year 2000 is to govern diversity. But first we must ask ourselves: *Can* diversity be governed?

What can we conclude about bustling, restless California? Some observers note that the symbol of the State of California is the mighty California grizzly bear—but the grizzly has been extinct since 1911. Men and women of goodwill might take note of the state flower, the golden poppy, which is said to be found blooming somewhere in California at any time of year:

> It was the lure of high Sierra gold that triggered the rush to California in 1849. In those days the American economy was based on dollars redeemable in gold. Today the economy and its currency are based on the natural riches of the land and the productivity of the people. The rush to California continues.
>
> The Golden State possesses vast natural resources—water and trees, wind and sun, geysers and gas. It also possesses the intellectual and spiritual energies of people who still are pathfinders and pioneers, dreamers and builders.[24]

In this introductory chapter, we have introduced three themes that will recur in many places in the book: the financial problems of government in California, the degree to which special interests control public decision making in this state, and the tension between declining natural resources and increasing population. The latter point means that policy making requires difficult value trade-offs in the face of economic and demographic changes. Consider the many vexing policy issues on the state's political agenda: economic prosperity, environmental protection, transporta-

---

23. Houston, *Californians*, p. 272.
24. California Energy Commission, *Fifth Biennial Report*, p. 44.

tion congestion, an adequate supply of water, poorly educated elementary and secondary students, racial conflict, political reform, and other issues of vital concern. Although these problems are serious, close attention to them can keep them from getting out of hand. With a vigilant citizenry, dedicated public officials, and perhaps a little bit of luck, we can fulfill the expectations of those first hearty souls who came to California looking for a better life.

DISCUSSION QUESTIONS

1. What characteristics make California a highly advanced industrial society?

2. Name some of the environmental problems confronting California and indicate what is being done about these conditions.

3. What are California's sources of energy? Evaluate them in terms of such factors as availability, reliability, expense, safety, and amount of pollution generated.

4. The private automobile is the chief means of transporting Californians. Name other modes of transportation now used or proposed for the future.

5. Why is water policy such an explosive issue in California politics?

6. California, which is a heavily urbanized advanced industrial society, is also the nation's leading agricultural state. Explain this seeming contradiction.

7. In addition to a lack of money, what are some of the issues facing public elementary, secondary, and higher education?

8. What are the major welfare programs in California?

9. Medi-Cal is the most costly element in California's system of welfare and health benefits. How has the state sought to increase access to medical care for poor people and for low-income workers?

10. What are some of the ways that defense spending has been reduced in California? How have defense contractors and impacted local communities responded to the reduction?

Chapter 2

California in the Federal System

Before considering such topics as California politics, the California legislature, or local government in California, it will be helpful to take a look at the constitutional framework in which these activities and institutions are found. We will describe the state Constitution and how changes can be made in it. Because California is only one of fifty states, we will also discuss its relationships with the other forty-nine states, especially neighboring ones, and its role as a member of the federal system.

THE CALIFORNIA CONSTITUTION

In 1849, the year of the great gold rush, California drew up its first constitution. A year later, California was admitted into the Union as one provision of the historic Compromise of 1850 (September 9, 1850). The Constitution of 1849 proved to be inadequate, and just thirty years later, a new constitution had to be written to meet the needs of the time. The Constitution of 1879 is the current state constitution, although it has been amended (changed in some manner) almost 500 times.

The California Constitution is long (more than one hundred pages of standard print) and very detailed. Some of its twenty-two articles are devoted to matters that might better be left to ordinary legislation. Many authorities contend that a constitution should be a basic document that briefly outlines the division of powers among a state's executive, legislative, and judicial branches and between state and local governments; sets forth a bill of rights specifying citizens' basic liberties; and describes a means for amending the document or calling a **constitutional convention.** The Constitution of 1879 as originally written was rather stingy in its grants of power to public officials, especially in financial matters. It severely and narrowly limited official discretion because its writers feared the corrupting influence over legislators that

California's multicultural heritage is evident in its first Constitution, published in 1849 in Spanish and English. Article XI decrees that all future laws be translated into Spanish. The 1879 Constitution does not include this provision.

could be wielded by large corporations, particularly the railroad. The Constitution contained strong restrictions against the legislature passing special laws to benefit favored corporations. Because of the state Constitution's specificity and restrictiveness, and because it was designed to regulate so many different subjects, it has had to be amended hundreds of times, and the amendments have made it even longer. (The use of the initiative by interest groups has contributed to this vicious circle. See Chapter 5.) In contrast, the United States Constitution is less than one-fourth as long as the California Constitution and has been amended only twenty-seven times, even though it is twice as old.

One interesting aspect of the California Constitution is that it may grant more civil liberties than does the U.S. Constitution. The Declaration of Rights (Article I) proclaims that Californians have "inalienable rights" of "acquiring, possessing, and protecting property" and of privacy. In addition, Article I broadly asserts that "[e]very person may freely speak, write and publish his or her sentiments on all subjects." Other articles (such as IX and XVI) have special provisions relating to religious expression and to gender discrimination. Some rights protected by the California Constitution are found in no other state constitution: Newspersons have shield protection against contempt for not revealing confidential sources, noncitizens have the same property rights as citizens, and the public has the right to fish on public lands and waters. State courts are still in the process of giving a definitive interpretation to these clauses and many others, but the effort can have important consequences because of the doctrine of independent state grounds described in Chapter 8.

CHANGING THE CONSTITUTION

Constitutional change can be accomplished in California by any of three processes: constitutional amendment, constitutional revision, and the drafting of a wholly new constitution by a constitutional convention. Constitutions in general can also be changed more subtly as they are interpreted by courts.

Constitutional Amendment

Most changes in the state Constitution have come through constitutional amendments, which must initially be approved by a two-thirds vote of the state legislature. After legislative approval, these proposed amendments must be finally approved by a **majority vote** at the next statewide election. Citizens may also amend the constitution by circulating a proposed amendment to obtain voter signatures and then placing it on the ballot. This initiative route has the same effect as if the legislature had originated the proposal.

Constitutional change by means of amendment is generally piecemeal and ad hoc—that is, an article or section is added here or another is dropped there. Individually, these changes may not amount to much. But over the years, the amendments that

J. D. Crowe

appear and win approval at statewide primary elections and general elections may cumulatively alter the Constitution in basic ways.

Constitutional Revision

A **constitutional revision commission** is used to change substantial amounts of the state Constitution at one time. This blue-ribbon commission of distinguished citizens and legislators is selected by the legislature and meets at length to revise whole sections of the Constitution. The recommendations of the revision commission must be forwarded to the legislature for its approval by a two-thirds vote before being submitted to the voters. From the early 1960s to the early 1970s, a constitutional revision commission headed by Judge Bruce Sumner substantially modernized and streamlined California's constitution. Another revision commission began work in 1994.

Constitutional Convention

If major alteration of the Constitution or a wholly new document is necessary, a constitutional convention is called. On five occasions the legislature has asked Californians if they want to have a constitutional convention. Only once—during the tumultuous Great Depression—have the voters answered affirmatively, and then a surprised legislature refused to carry out the order. Currently, the calling of a constitutional convention is not likely. Constitutions are important and basic documents; although some people are mildly dissatisfied with the current Constitution, few want to discard it entirely. Furthermore, many special interests benefit from the existing Constitution and might not want a convention tampering with their favorite provisions. In any event, a convention to write a new fundamental law for a state as diverse and factious as California would be a major and conflict-ridden undertaking.

Role of the Courts

"No constitution interprets itself"; that is, no constitution says what its words mean in every situation. This crucial function is performed by the courts in a common-law country such as the United States. In applying the words of a very old document to a modern situation, judges must of necessity use their own judgment and beliefs concerning what is good public policy for California.

RELATIONS WITH OTHER STATE GOVERNMENTS

Every state government must have relations with other states; even an island state such as Hawaii is not exempt. California has certain obligations to other states. For example, the U.S. Constitution (Article IV, Section 1) requires that "full faith and credit shall be given in each state to the public acts, records, and judicial proceedings of every other state." The purpose of this provision (the **full faith and credit clause**) is to prevent a person from escaping his or her civil obligations (for example, debts) by moving to another state. Mortgages, leases, contracts, and wills that are enforceable in a civil proceeding in another state are enforceable in California. Moreover, according to the U.S. Supreme Court, the governor of California can be required by a federal court to return fugitives from justice in another state upon request of that state's governor. We shall discuss extradition in Chapter 6.

No state may discriminate against the citizens of other states in favor of its own citizens—that is, California cannot deprive citizens of other states of what the U.S.

Constitution calls the "privileges and immunities" of U.S. citizenship. The exact nature of these privileges and immunities has not been spelled out by the U.S. Supreme Court, but California may constitutionally charge higher tuition to out-of-state students or require teachers certified in another state to obtain a California credential. In addition, the commerce clause of the U.S. Constitution (Article I, Section 8) forbids states from discriminating against the businesses and products of other states in an attempt to advance their own commercial interests.

States may undertake joint ventures by means of interstate compacts, which usually require approval by Congress. For example, California and Nevada belong to the Tahoe Regional Planning Agency (TRPA), which attempts to provide planning and regulations to protect the environment of the Lake Tahoe area. Unfortunately, the agency has had only limited success in preventing overdevelopment, pollution, and smog around the lake, but a development plan is now in force that may protect the lake.

NATION–STATE RELATIONS

California deals not only with the other forty-nine states, which are its constitutional equals, but also with the federal government, which is California's constitutional superior. The U.S. Constitution and all federal laws or treaties made under its authority are "the supreme law of the land" (Article VI, Section 2). Any state constitution, state statute, or state executive action violating federal law must yield. However, federal power is not limitless. As the U.S. Supreme Court has said, "Congress may not exercise power in a fashion that impairs the states' integrity or their ability to function effectively in a federal system."[1] The constitutional relationship between the federal government and the states is as follows: The states possess all powers that have not been delegated, either by express provision or by implication, by the U.S. Constitution to the federal government.

The advantages of federalism are that it fosters diversity within unity by allowing the many heterogeneous states to resolve their own problems in their own way. Within the limitations set forth by the United States Constitution, states can become the "laboratories of federalism." This flexibility encourages innovation—and Chapter 1 indicates that California has shown no reluctance to be innovative. Federalism encourages the states to experiment with different policies: If California adopts a policy that works well, the federal government can adopt it—and all Americans will benefit. If a state adopts a policy that is an abject failure (and Chapter 1 provides some examples of this as well) only the residents of a single state will suffer. Because of their smaller size, state governments are presumably more easily controlled by their citizens than is a larger and more remote federal government, which is on the

---

1. *Fry v. United States*, 421 U.S. 542 (1975).

other end of the continent from California. Finally, the proponents of federalism assert that state governments are more attuned to popular sentiment than is the federal government. Ironically, this book will argue that California—with its weak political parties, political campaigns requiring substantial campaign contributions, and direct democracy devices—is really most responsive to powerful interest groups.

The U.S. Constitution places certain restrictions, in addition to the supremacy clause, on the states. States may not make treaties with foreign nations, coin money, or tax foreign imports. The vitally important Fourteenth Amendment declares that no state shall "deprive any person of life, liberty, or property, without due process of law, nor deny to any person within its jurisdiction the equal protection of the laws." The U.S. Supreme Court has ruled that according to the Fourteenth Amendment, nearly all of the Bill of Rights (the first ten amendments to the U.S. Constitution) applies to state and local governments.[2] Of special note is the fact that should California and the federal government have a dispute, the arbiter will be an organ of the federal government, the Supreme Court of the United States.

Because of U.S. Supreme Court decisions since 1937, there is hardly any subject matter that the federal government cannot regulate. Two students of federalism have argued that the Court no longer views federalism as a "constitutional bulwark against tyranny."[3] The U.S. Supreme Court had generally rejected the doctrine of dual federalism, which held that the federal government and the states operate in independent and autonomous spheres of influence or centers of power, with each making its own decisions about public policy.[4] The states suffered a serious setback when the Court ruled that the Tenth Amendment to the U.S. Constitution is not a barrier to Congress's legislating on the traditional or integral functions of state and local governments (*Garcia v. San Antonio Metropolitan Transit Authority*, 469 U.S. 528 [1985]). The Court decided that it is too difficult for federal judges to determine which are the traditional functions of state and local governments; therefore, if the latter dislike laws that Congress has passed to regulate them, then their recourse is through the political processes of lobbying Congress or of electing new House members and senators. According to Daniel Elazar: "The Court did exactly what the Constitution pledged not to do, that is to say, make one of the parties to any intergovernmental controversy the arbiter of the results."[5] However, the states later won a victory when the Court ruled that the Tenth Amendment requires that Congress may not directly compel states to enact and enforce a federal regulatory program such

---

2. Although the subject is a matter of scholarly debate, the following parts of the Bill of Rights presumably do not limit the states: the Second and Third Amendments; the Fifth Amendment right to a grand jury indictment for capital or infamous crimes; the Seventh Amendment right to a jury trial in civil cases; and the Eighth Amendment right to be free from excessive bail. In any event, states may protect these rights either by means of the state Constitution or by statute.

3. Michael Reagan and John Sanzone, *The New Federalism*, 2d ed. (New York: Oxford University Press, 1981), p. 15.

4. Raoul Berger has presented a forceful argument that dual federalism was actually the constitutional arrangement intended by the framers of the U.S. Constitution. Berger, *Federalism: The Founders' Design* (Norman: University of Oklahoma Press, 1987), Chap. 3.

5. Daniel Elazar, "Opening the Third Century of American Federalism," *Annals* 509 (May 1990): 12.

as disposing of low-level radioactive waste generated within their borders (*New York v. United States,* 112 S. Ct. 2408 [1992]).

In conclusion, the U.S. Supreme Court has long since discarded the dual-federalism principle that the functions of government can be neatly parceled out among the federal, state, and local levels of government. The current view is that all levels must jointly implement important public policies in a dynamic partnership. For example, in Chapter 1 we noted extensive federal–state–local involvement in AFDC, SSI/SSP, and Medi-Cal. But if all three levels of government are involved in implementing key public policies, then who is to be held accountable when something goes wrong or when the objectives of the programs are not being met? This constitutional partnership can also lead to governmental buck-passing.

Under current legal theories, the federal government's constitutional power to undertake some activity is seldom challenged successfully. Instead, those who question federal authority may assert that some other level of government can perform an activity more effectively or that the activity is not necessary in the first place. As the constitutional aspects of federalism have declined in importance, the fiscal aspects of the relationship have moved to center stage.

FISCAL RELATIONSHIPS

Through more than 550 grant-in-aid programs, the federal government annually funnels more than $22 billion to California state and local governments. However, in terms of federal grant spending per capita, California ranks twenty-seventh among the states. Federal grants usually include restrictive requirements intended to further social objectives favored by federal officials. Whatever the intent of a grant program may be, Congress might attach any of sixty requirements, such as the protection of endangered animal species, the protection of historic sites, and special provisions for handicapped or elderly persons, among others. Moreover, California state and local governments may even be penalized in one grant program for failing to take action desired by the federal government in a different area. For example, any state with a minimum drinking age of less than twenty-one years of age receives less in federal highway funds. Former governor Victor Atiyeh of Oregon is highly critical of the federal government's attitude toward the states. Noting that other countries receive billions of dollars in foreign aid with no strings attached, he says that state and local governments are treated "as if we are crooks who must be watched like hawks."[6]

As a result of the 1994 elections, the Republican Party gained control of both chambers of Congress for the first time in forty years. Federalism was an important part of the "Contract with America" crafted by Rep. Newt Gingrich, now Speaker of the House, as a governmental reform program for the nation. The Republicans passed

6. Quoted in "Mandates Without Money," *National Journal,* October 4, 1986, p. 2369. See also Michael J. Ross, *State and Local Politics and Policy: Change and Reform* (Englewood Cliffs, NJ: Prentice-Hall, 1987), Chap. 2.

landmark legislation to restrict unfunded federal mandates, which are requirements that the national government has dictated to states and local governments without providing the money to pay for the requirements. This reform is a historic shift of power from the federal government to state and local governments and reverses a half-century of ascendancy by the national government. The law covers both new and existing unfunded mandates, as well as mandates imposed on private industry. For *new* mandates, the reform provides that if Congress establishes a program that would cost state and local governments more than $50 million annually or private industry more than $100 million annually to carry out, then Congress will have to provide the necessary funds or will have to vote explicitly to waive the unfunded mandates law. If neither is done, the new mandate is void. The theory is that if Congress believes that something is so important for state and local governments to do, then it ought to provide the money to pay for the program. Critics of the unfunded mandates reform, who are almost always Democrats, say that the federal government's fiscal and deficit problems mean that it will be nearly impossible to find new money and that this will discourage Congress from setting future national standards in areas such as the environment, public health, labor, and safety.

As for *existing* unfunded mandates, the reform law would apply if Congress makes major changes in current laws that increase the regulatory burden on state and local governments. Hence, nearly all of the federal–state–local environmental, health, and labor laws would be affected. However, if Congress merely reauthorizes the existing laws without major changes, then the unfunded mandates reform does not apply. When one considers the importance and the large compliance costs involved in certain current laws—the Clean Water Act and wetlands legislation, the Safe Drinking Water Act, solid-waste disposal laws, and the Clean Air Act—one is struck by the revolutionary nature of the unfunded mandates law.

The unfunded mandates law has truly far-reaching implications for those who wish to maintain or expand, as well as curtail, legislation in the environmental and social welfare areas. However, there is a striking irony in the new law: State (and local) officials were among those who most loudly called for the unfunded mandates law, but state governments have shown no reluctance about imposing unfunded mandates on local governments. As Chapter 9 notes, the California legislature has been shameless in forcing unfunded mandates on California cities and counties.

Total federal spending in California includes not only **grants-in-aid** to state and local governments but also federal salaries, payments to individuals (Social Security, Medicare, federal retirement benefits, aid to farmers, and so on), and especially defense spending. Total spending in California by the national government is more than $150 billion, which places the state twenty-third on a per capita basis. At least two conclusions can be drawn: First, because California has the largest representation in Congress, the Golden State should receive very high per capita spending, but it does not. Second, because California's defense-spending income far exceeds that of other states, it receives an insufficient amount of payments to individuals and grants-in-aid.

FEDERALISM ISSUES: IMMIGRATION, NAFTA, AND GATT

Three of the most contentious issues of the 1990s grew out of California's role as a state in the federal system: immigration, the North American Free Trade Agreement (NAFTA), and the General Agreement on Tariffs and Trade (GATT). The matter of illegal immigration to California was a "back-burner" concern throughout the 1980s, but it definitely moved to the "front burner" as the state's economy took a serious nosedive around 1990. The issue reached a boiling point in the 1994 election as Governor Pete Wilson made immigration a key part of his campaign for re-election, and Proposition 187, which would deny some public services to undocumented persons, appeared on the ballot. Wilson argued that the federal government should pay for the health, education, and other costs that it requires the state to provide, that a tamper-proof identification card be required for all persons, and that the Fourteenth Amendment to the U.S. Constitution be changed to deny American citizenship to children of illegal immigrants. (The Fourteenth Amendment currently provides that every person born in the United States is an American citizen, even if his or her parents were in the country illegally.) Perhaps most important, Wilson claimed that the state's fiscal problems make the state budget a "zero-sum" game: To provide services for undocumented persons, money must allegedly be taken from other areas of the budget. Wilson sought to eliminate prenatal care for pregnant illegal immigrants, arguing that he would not reduce services to people legally in the country in order to provide services to people who have no legal right to be here. Wilson's Democratic opponent in the election, Kathleen Brown, and nearly all Democratic elected officials and Latino and Asian activists rejected the zero-sum analogy as false and demagogic. They castigated Wilson's stance as racist and as attempting to use immigrants as scapegoats for the state's miserable economy. They noted that California has a long and unfortunate history of immigrant bashing, especially in hard economic times. (As mentioned earlier in this chapter, the writers of the 1879 Constitution were anticorporation. But they were also anti-immigrant, and an important element at the convention was the Workingmen's Party, whose motto was "The Chinese must go!" During the depression of the 1870s, many Californians supported the anti-immigrant positions of the Workingmen's Party.)

The purpose of Proposition 187 was to deny education, welfare, and nonemergency medical services to illegal immigrants. Opponents of the measure made at least six arguments:

1. Denying elementary and secondary education to any children throws them out in the street (where they may become involved in crime or drugs).

2. Denying nonemergency medical care exposes the public at large to the risk of contagious diseases, for example, tuberculosis from food service workers.

3. It would turn teachers and doctors into Immigration and Naturalization Service workers.

4. The measure does not directly address jobs, which are the real magnet drawing undocumented workers to this country.

5. It does not do anything about the porous U.S.–Mexico border.

6. It would cost the state more than $15 billion in federal aid for education, welfare, and Medi-Cal because it conflicts with federal law.

The measure was approved by the voters by 59 percent to 41 percent, despite the fact that opponents outspent supporters by more than two-to-one. According to a *Los Angeles Times* survey of 5,000 voters leaving polling places, Republicans favored Proposition 187 by three-to-one, Independents favored it by three-to-two, and Democrats opposed it by two-to-one. An Associated Press exit poll found 64 percent of whites in favor, 57 percent of Asians in favor, 56 percent of blacks in favor, and 69 percent of Latinos in opposition. Surprisingly, the measure did not increase Latino voter turnout. Proposition 187 was immediately challenged in court, and it is likely to take years before the measure's final legal status is determined.

At the same time that the political debate over immigration raged, an academic debate took place among professors, researchers at public policy institutes, and analysts at think tanks over whether undocumented immigrants are a net benefit or a net detriment to California's economy.[7] Those arguing the "benefit" side said that immigrants come to California seeking work, to be with family members already here, or to escape persecution—they do not come to get government services. Furthermore, immigrants take jobs that few Americans want. Both employers and the consumers of the goods and services produced by immigrants benefit because immigrants provide cheap labor. Some industries could not survive without cheap labor—for example, the garment industry, restaurants, and agriculture. Immigrants keep these important industries competitive. A key study by the Urban Institute in 1994 found that both legal and illegal immigrants to the United States since 1970 have contributed $12 billion more in taxes each year than they cost in schooling, health care, and other government services. Other researchers have noted that immigrants pay Social Security and unemployment taxes but may not receive benefits from those programs. Finally, these researchers oppose national identity cards because these cards could be used to monitor all Americans, just as is done in totalitarian countries. In addition, "tamper-proof" cards cannot be effective in proving citizenship unless the integrity of the underlying documents used to generate the identity cards (such as birth certificates) has also been secured.

On the net detriment side, Donald Huddle of Rice University published a hotly disputed study of illegal immigration to California arguing that the net cost (public assistance received by illegal immigrants minus the taxes paid by them) is $5.1 billion per year. Richard Parker and Louis Rea of San Diego State University studied the costs

7. Summaries of the many reports and counter-reports in this debate can be found in the *Los Angeles Times*, August 13, 1993, p. A1; November 5, 1993, p. 3; November 15, 1993, p. A1; November 21, 1993, p. A1; November 30, 1993, p. A1; February 23, 1994, p. B4.

Large anti–Proposition 187 rally in Los Angeles.

of providing services to undocumented immigrants in San Diego County subtracted by the taxes paid by undocumented persons. Parker and Rea projected their results statewide, and found net costs of $3 billion per year. Other researchers have asserted that only in a growing economy can immigrants be absorbed without displacing native-born workers. The displacement problem is said to be found in construction and in lower-paying occupations such as building janitors, hospital orderlies, and hotel maids. Because of an oversupply of immigrant labor, the wages of native-born workers are depressed, thus pushing many low-income workers onto unemployment compensation or public assistance. George Borjas of UC San Diego reported that recent immigrants are younger, are less educated, and have fewer skills than previous immigrants or native-born workers, hence he argues that they are more likely to rely on public services. Many immigrants come to California in their peak childbearing years—their children are said to be overburdening the state's schools. The Los Angeles County Department of Health Services has revealed that two-thirds of all mothers giving birth in public hospitals are undocumented. The underlying theme of many of these studies was expressed by the Carrying Capacity Network, which commissioned the Huddle report noted earlier. The Carrying Capacity Network includes population-control advocates such as Paul Erlich and officials of environmental groups such as the Wilderness Society and the Sierra Club. The Network asserts the position that, in a context of fixed or decreasing physical resources, California is supposed to have reached its carrying capacity and cannot absorb more immigrants.

Many have said that the solution to the illegal immigration problem is to penalize employers who hire illegal aliens. However, seventeen documents may be used to verify work eligibility; many of these can be easily falsified. If employer fines were strictly assessed, employers might be reluctant to hire anyone appearing "foreign." Latino and Asian groups do not favor employer sanctions, fearing that sanctions increase unemployment among Latinos and Asians who are legal workers. On the other hand, black civil rights groups strongly favor sanctions because they believe that blacks have been displaced by undocumented workers in construction jobs, janitorial positions, and other types of employment.

Governor Wilson has sued the federal government and sought reimbursement of the money the state has paid because the federal government requires California to provide elementary and secondary education to the children of illegal immigrants, to incarcerate undocumented felons in state prison, and to provide emergency medical care for undocumented persons, including childbirth services. If all of these matters were not difficult enough, the federal government has failed to live up to its obligations to reimburse California for the costs of providing health, education, welfare, and other costs of newly legalized immigrants since 1986. Approximately 55 percent of the nation's newly legalized immigrants live in California and are eligible under the State Legalization Impact Assistance Grant (SLIAG) program. California's large congressional delegation has been unsuccessful in getting the state its fair share of the money. President Bill Clinton, who claims to be a special friend of California, will not push for full reimbursement to the state.

NAFTA took effect in January 1994. It eliminated nearly all tariffs and allows for the free exchange of goods, services, and investments among the United States, Canada, and Mexico, thus creating a single market of 360 million people. The broad sweep of NAFTA means that virtually no aspect of the California economy will be untouched. As noted in Chapter 1, California already was a major exporter before NAFTA, sending some $70 billion overseas annually—15.4 percent of the U.S. total. Foreign trade was at least one-half of the economic growth that California experienced immediately before NAFTA went into effect, and foreign trade will increase as a result of NAFTA. As with any major change of policy, there are some gainers and some losers. The gainers are thought to be high-technology businesses, especially manufacturers of aircraft, computers, telecommunications equipment, and electronics. In agriculture, the winners are expected to be growers of apples, pears, and nuts, as well as the beef and dairy industries. Losers may be companies that formerly relied on low-skilled, low-wage, and mainly immigrant workers, such as the garment industry, furniture making, and food processing. These industries are said to be unable to compete with even lower-wage Mexican competition. Many of the industries employing the largest concentration of illegal immigrants may also be the ones most adversely affected by NAFTA. Losers in the agricultural sector could be growers of asparagus, broccoli, cauliflower, and canning tomatoes.

NAFTA was approved by the U.S. Congress only after a bitter and hard-fought struggle. The main opponents were labor unions who feared that American jobs

Greg Gawlowski / Photo 20–20

International trade is vitally important for California's future. A cargo ship sails under San Francisco's Golden Gate Bridge.

would move south to low-wage Mexico. Environmentalists also opposed NAFTA, fearing that Mexico would become a safe haven for American polluters seeking to escape U.S. and especially California's strict environmental laws. Although Mexico has some tough antipollution laws, environmentalists feared that Mexico has neither the resources nor the determination to enforce them. Supporters of NAFTA said that this was merely paternalistic thinking.

GATT is another free-trade measure with important implications for California. GATT is a 22,000-page agreement that cuts tariffs by an average of 38 percent and eliminates them entirely for steel, pharmaceuticals, paper, and medical equipment. Supporters assert that it will create 500,000 jobs nationwide as a result of increased commerce with other nations. California winners under GATT are farmers (especially rice growers, who may boost exports by one-third), beer and wine, furniture, medicine, medical equipment, semiconductors, computer software firms (who benefit from strengthened intellectual property rights), and the movie industry (which would benefit from expanded copyright protection). Losers include the garment industry, which also lost under NAFTA. Critics of GATT included an unusual assortment of liberals and conservatives led by Ralph Nader who claimed that the World Trade Organization (WTO), an international bureaucracy created by GATT, could negate American laws protecting consumers, worker safety, or the environment if the WTO found them to be restricting trade. California laws in the areas of pesticide regulation, food purity, and fuel efficiency were said to be in jeopardy. GATT supporters said that WTO would not have the power to overturn state or federal laws but only to impose sanctions in the form of higher tariffs.

CALIFORNIA IN THE U.S. CONGRESS

With fifty-two House members and two senators, California has the largest congressional delegation, but its low rankings on per capita federal grants-in-aid, per capita federal spending, and SLIAG reimbursement indicate that its delegation has not converted size into clout. The ineffectiveness of the California delegation in garnering increased federal spending was most unfortunate during the severe recession that began in 1990 and which hit California harder and lasted longer than in the rest of the country. Californians chair only one House committee, and a quite minor one at that. However, Californians are the ranking minority party members on five committees, four of which are important. Despite the importance of defense spending for the state's economy, only six of the fifty-five members of the House National Security Committee are from California. The state's House members cannot work as a team because they are polarized between extreme liberals and extreme conservatives. The problem is caused in part by gerrymandered districts (described in Chapter 7), which make it nearly impossible to defeat an incumbent no matter how extreme he or she may be. (On the other hand, safe districts allow Californians to amass seniority that someday may lead to numerous committee chairmanships.) In addition, the sheer size and diversity of California mean that there are just too many actual or potential conflicting interests for the state's House members to work together cooperatively. The California House delegation has not only liberal versus conservative splits, but also geographic splits such as north versus south, coastal versus inland, and urban versus suburban versus rural. The conclusion seems inescapable that California's delegation in the House is much more polarized and ideological than effective.

On the Senate side, Dianne Feinstein and Barbara Boxer are both liberal Democrats who can work together well. Feinstein has proved to be an important exception to the general rule that California's representation in Congress is usually ineffective. In 1994, Feinstein prevailed in the struggle stretching back nearly a decade to pass a federal Desert Protection Act for California covering more than one-third of California's desert. The act creates a new national preserve in the eastern Mojave near Barstow and designates 7.5 million acres as wilderness in Death Valley and Joshua Tree. The latter two were elevated from national monuments to national parks, which affords them greater protection. The area has significant ecological diversity: several mountain ranges, waterfalls, huge sand dunes, the world's largest forest of cactus-like Joshua trees, approximately 2,000 plant and 600 animal species, more than 100,000 archaeological sites, and even dinosaur tracks. Feinstein was able to get general agreement on numerous serious issues that had held up the legislation for years: how to

The California desert is a beautiful but fragile ecosystem.

compensate any private landowners who were restricted in the use of their property because of environmental rules; whether to allow hunting, mining exploration, and livestock grazing; and whether it was wise to increase the National Park system at the same time Congress is cutting its budget appropriation and reducing the number of ranger positions. Debates on the bill took a particularly ugly turn as all four California House members representing parts of the desert opposed the bill and described the bill's supporters as people who did not live in the area trying to preserve it for upper-class Sierra Club backpackers and closing it off to blue-collar hunters, off-road vehicle users, and workers dependent on the desert for their livelihood. In the end, Feinstein's determination and legislative skill prevailed.

A good example of the ineffectiveness of the state's representation in Congress is the inability to secure major scientific projects, despite California's reputation as a high-technology center. Particularly galling was the decision by Congress to locate the National Earthquake Center in New York. The size and wealth of California has encouraged an "ABC syndrome" in Congress: "anywhere but California" is the place to locate important federal projects. This sentiment is likely to increase because California got more House seats and electoral college votes as a result of the 1990 Census. California has by far the largest House delegation and one-fifth of the electoral votes needed to choose a president. (Whatever the shortcomings of the state's congressional delegation may be, California's interests are also protected by paid lobbyists for thirty-three cities, fourteen counties, twenty special districts, and at least fourteen other public organizations. All of the following have employed lobbyists: the governor, the state Assembly, the state Senate, the University of California System, the California State University System, and the California community colleges.)

In 1992, California voters expressed a rather low opinion of the California congressional delegation by imposing term limits for House members (six years) and Senators (twelve years). (Chapter 7 has a discussion of the arguments for and against term limits.) The voters rejected the claim of opponents of congressional term limits that, if California adopted term limits but other states did not, this state's influence in Congress would decline. In 1995, the U.S. Supreme Court ruled that the imposition of congressional term limits by state-level action is unconstitutional: U.S. House members and Senators are federal officials whose terms cannot be altered by state law. The establishment of term limits for the presidency was only accomplished by an amendment to the U.S. Constitution.

SUMMARY

At least since the end of World War II, American politics has increasingly focused on the national government's resolution of issues. This development has resulted from the increase in the power of the federal government, U.S. Supreme Court decisions, the position of the United States as a world power, presidential visibility, the national emphasis of the electronic media generally, and rapid social change, among other factors. More than four decades ago, Leonard White, an eminent political scientist, wrote that "if present trends continue for another quarter century, the states may be left hollow shells, operating primarily as the field districts of federal departments and dependent upon the federal treasury for their support."[8] White's dire prediction has fortunately not come true, although California government limps along with problems of shrunken revenues, special-interest domination, and dwindling natural resources.

The California Constitution of 1879 remains the basic law of the state. By means of nearly 500 amendments and the work of two revision commissions, it has been altered to meet the needs of the times and the ever-changing balance of political forces. But whatever the California Constitution may provide now or in the future, one factor will remain constant: The U.S. Constitution, federal laws and treaties, and decisions

8. Leonard D. White, *The States and the Nation* (Baton Rouge: Louisiana State University Press, 1953), p. 3.

of the U.S. Supreme Court take precedence over the state Constitution. This is the nature of our federal system. The constitutional or legal relationships between the federal government and California state and local governments are complemented by fiscal relationships, such as grants-in-aid. In this regard, this chapter has stressed the dynamic interaction among all three layers of government and between our state government and other states in providing services for the public.

DISCUSSION QUESTIONS

1. What are some of the characteristics of the California Constitution, and how have these characteristics stimulated alterations in the document? Of the three processes for changing the Constitution, which is most commonly used?

2. Does it seem peculiar that the federal government should raise large amounts of money in California (by means of the income tax) and then return it to California (through grants)? Would it be wiser for the federal government just to keep the money or not to raise it in the first place?

3. Some commentators on the federal system view the future of federalism as the federal government raising the money but states and communities spending the money. Other observers stress the "golden rule of politics": "He who has the gold makes the rules." Can these two views be reconciled?

4. How was the illegal immigration issue argued out in the political arena and also in debates among public policy specialists? What do you conclude about the claims and arguments presented?

5. What is NAFTA? Draw up a scorecard of NAFTA winners and losers.

6. Congressional delegations from other states, even when they have equal numbers of Democrats and Republicans, appear to work together more effectively than does California's delegation. What is the matter with this state's legislators, especially House members, and what have been the effects on California's welfare?

Part Two
POLITICAL
ORGANIZATIONS
AND PROCESSES

*C*alifornia government, like the national government, is government "of the people" and "for the people." Popular wishes should be reflected in public policy, or the public may soon be looking for new policy makers: "The only really effective weapon of popular control in a democratic regime is the capacity of the electorate to throw a party from power."[1] What ultimately keeps politicians responsive to public opinion is the presence of another group of politicians waiting in the wings to seize their jobs. "Ambition must be made to counteract ambition" was good advice once, and it still is.[2]

In Chapter 3 we examine the selection and retention or rejection of California politicians. Keep in mind the matter of competition, because in competition lies responsiveness. Statewide races (for example, for the office of governor) are generally more competitive than legislative races (for example, for membership in the Assembly or Senate). Some regions of California are also more competitive than others. Two legacies from the past characterize California's politics: antipartyism and the spirit of reform.

In Chapter 4 we consider interest groups. Californians can influence their government not only by participating in elections but also by joining together in interest groups. However, nearly all interest groups tend to be self-seeking. We make note of different kinds of interest groups.

---

1. V. 0. Key, Jr., *The Responsible Electorate* (Cambridge: Harvard University Press, 1966), p. 76.
2. Alexander Hamilton, James Madison, and John Jay, *The Federalist Papers* (New York: Mentor Books, 1961), p. 322. Madison's famous quote is from Federalist 51.

Finally, in Chapter 5 we discuss direct democracy. Should Californians become fed up with politicians and their interest group allies, they can take matters into their own hands through the initiative, referendum, and recall. But, paradoxically, evidence also shows that these direct democracy devices can be the tools *of* (not against) interest groups.

Chapter 3

Politics, Parties, and Elections

*I*n the first chapter we noted numerous California policy issues. The means for resolving these issues is at hand: Politics flourishes in California. Candidates and parties eagerly press their claims of being best able to provide the needed leadership. A change of policy makers (officeholders) often means a change of policy, although voters make their decisions not only on the basis of issues but also on the basis of candidate characteristics and party affiliation.

This chapter describes the robust, no-holds-barred politics of the Golden State. Californians are frequently independent-minded voters who refuse to hew to a party line. Such antipartyism is a major theme of the chapter. Paradoxically, this independence may be more prevalent in statewide races, such as the election of the governor, than in local legislative-district races, in which members of the Assembly and state Senate are selected.

Other factors that affect the electoral behavior of Californians are the type of election—**primary election,** general election, or special election—and the local traditions of the voter's area (political region). In addition, Californians have shown a long-standing preference for political reform, especially when they feel that politicians have become corrupt or unresponsive.

In politics, as in many other fields, California often acts as the pacesetter. Trends and styles gaining acceptance here are frequently adopted throughout the nation. California has a political style, or political culture, that was once thought unique but is now increasingly becoming the national norm.

ANTIPARTYISM

The key element of California's political style is antipartyism—that is, California parties are weak as organizations, and they prompt few stirrings in the hearts of their members. The state's voters like to say that they vote for the person and not the party. Californians are chronic **ticket splitters,** often to the dismay of newspaper columnists, political scientists, and losing candidates. They divide the ticket, choosing here a Democrat, there a Republican. In 1994, for example, Californians overwhelmingly re-elected Republican Governor Pete Wilson but also re-elected Democratic U.S. Senator Dianne Feinstein. The form of the California ballot facilitates, if not encourages, ticket splitting. As we shall see, an office-block ballot is the form used.

Another aspect of the California political landscape is intraparty factionalism. Within each party are groups, or factions, contending for power and for the right to define party principles. These factions may consist of the personal supporters of an ambitious politician, or they may be dedicated to a political philosophy such as liberalism or conservatism, or they may represent a combination of the two. Among the Republicans, conservatives usually vie with middle-of-the-roaders, or *moderates,* as they prefer to call themselves. Up and down the state in Republican circles, followers of Ronald Reagan square off against those who carry on the tradition of Hiram Johnson (governor, 1911–1917; U.S. senator, 1917–1945) and Earl Warren (governor, 1943–1953). Among the Democrats, liberals battle moderates for the right to say what the Democratic Party stands for. In each party, tension exists between those who work for the party as volunteers because they have strong beliefs about today's controversial issues, and the party's elected officials, who have the responsibility to legislate on these issues and then face the judgment of the **electorate.** Party activists are especially important because of the tireless effort they put into campaigns and because they sustain the political party as an organization between elections. Republican and Democratic activists tend to be middle-class professionals for whom issues or ideology are vitally important. The activists reject compromise and bargaining, and they believe that advocating correct principles takes precedence over winning elections. Party activists may be not only at odds with their party's elected officials but also unrepresentative of rank-and-file members of the party.

Bitterness is often greater *within* parties than *between* them. Pent-up antagonisms burst forth during primaries when factions struggle to secure the party's nomination for their own candidates. In recent years, the Republican Party has been split between self-styled moderates led by Governor Pete Wilson on one side and evangelical Christians on the other. All Republican elected officials and party activists in California support fiscal conservatism, a strong law-and-order position, and high defense spending. But the two factions part ways on abortion and homosexuality, which evangelicals see as "moral" or "family" issues. In addition, the Christian Right is opposed to nearly every tax increase. In the 1992 Republican primaries for the state legislature, Governor Pete Wilson supported and funded his own "moderate" candidates. The result was extreme acrimony, which helped the Democrats capture many

R. moderate

formerly Republican seats in the general election. Such intraparty hostility and factionalism not only weaken California parties but also do little to endear the parties to an electorate that already views them with a jaundiced eye.

In addition to voter independence and intraparty factionalism, weak party organization is another aspect of antipartyism. Organizational weakness is a key characteristic of the California political style. Heavy immigration and the mobility of the state's population hamper stable, locally based party organizations. Faced with such mobility, parties cannot maintain the kind of frequent contact between organization and voter that enables the local party organization to turn out the faithful on election day. The political party organization is weak at its base, so not surprisingly the whole structure is shaky. But organizational frailty did not just happen; it was planned.

Until the early part of this century, the Southern Pacific Railroad dominated California politics. This virtually complete control was ensured by the company's manipulation of both political parties. To break Southern Pacific's control over the state's politics, the **California Progressives,** a group of reform-minded Republicans, decided to break the state's parties. They succeeded, and the wreckage is still strewn across the state (the Progressive heritage is described in detail later in the chapter). Party organizations that might wield significant power in other states, such as the Republican or Democratic state central committees or the parties' county central committees, have little influence in this state. Here these party organizations either have few functions prescribed by law or, as in the case of the state central committees, they may be so large (approximately 1,200 to 1,700 members) as to be ineffective. Until recently, official party organizations were not allowed to make preprimary endorsements; that is, prior to the election in which party members choose the party's nominee, the state committees or county committees could not indicate which person running in the primary they would prefer to have receive the party's nomination. In 1989 the U.S. Supreme Court ruled that the California law prohibiting preprimary endorsements by official party committees violated the First Amendment of the U.S. Constitution (*Eu v. San Francisco County Democratic Central Committee,* 489 U.S. 214 [1989]). The ruling may make both state and county party committees more powerful because having the power to make preprimary endorsements gives them something valuable to award or withhold. Moreover, members of party committees are much more liberal (in the case of the Democrats) or much more conservative (in the case of the Republicans) than are members of the state legislature. This could make state politics more ideological, but official party organizations generally have not used this significant power available to them.

Unofficial party organizations have long made preprimary endorsements because these entities are not regulated by the state's election laws. Currently four of these organizations exist: California Republican League (CRL), California Republican Assembly (CRA), United Republicans of California (UROC), and California Democratic Council (CDC). Each of these private organizations promotes a point of view (CRL, the Johnson–Warren Republican tradition; CRA, conservative; UROC, very conservative; CDC, very liberal). They endorse party candidates prior to the primary as a way of identifying for party voters the "true" bearer of party principles. They also back their endorsements with modest campaign contributions and campaign workers. Because these volunteer organizations are to some degree immoderate, they add a little color to state politics and often increase its temperature.

The ultimate in antipartyism would be elections free from party affiliation, or **nonpartisan elections,** which are what California holds at the city and county levels. There are also nonpartisan elections for governing boards of special districts, judges, and the state superintendent of public instruction. Holding nonpartisan elections does not mean that political parties cannot be found endorsing candidates or working behind the scenes; it simply means that a candidate's party affiliation is not revealed on the ballot itself. However, because most voters do not know the party affiliations of candidates running for the city council or county board of supervisors, or do not take the time to find out such affiliations, considerations of party are kept to a minimum. Another aspect of nonpartisanship is that, by removing party labels from the ballot in local elections, voter turnout is reduced, especially among lower-income groups or less educated voters. These voters often need the pull of political party appeals to attract them to the polls.

Another aspect of state government that contributes to antipartyism and weak parties is California's civil service system. A civil service system in which state employees are selected and promoted on ability and merit may go a long way toward promoting more efficient public service, but such a merit system also substantially eliminates one of the best means for building a strong political party—**patronage.** The promise of a state job as a reward for working for a party can be a potent ingredient in making vigorous parties. In New York, the governor has 40,000 jobs at his disposal; in Illinois, 14,000; but in California, only 3,000.

Antipartyism is also fostered by the way campaigns are conducted. California candidates seldom stress their loyalty to party while campaigning, nor do a party's candidates run as a team. Instead, each candidate has his or her own precinct workers, fund-raisers, and strategy. Campaigns are run independently of the party and other party candidates. In fact, many a candidate has run for office by running *away from* his or her party. Republicans running for statewide office frequently downplay their party affiliation. Much of the electoral success of Earl Warren and Ronald Reagan was due to their images as citizen-politicians, rather than as partisan politicians. In legislative districts with high registration of one party, the voter will search in vain through the campaign literature of the minority party candidate for any mention of his or her party.

Because little help may be forthcoming from the official party organization, candidates run personalized campaigns. Instead of saying, "Vote for me because I am a Democrat (Republican)," the candidate simply says, "Vote for me." This tactic, made necessary by the tendency of California voters to vote for the person, not the party, in turn encourages that tendency. Such a lone-wolf strategy is fostered by two indispensable tools that go hand in hand, the media campaign and campaign-management firms.

All statewide election candidates depend on television and radio in their campaigns. With little party machinery on which to rely, the aggressive candidate has to take to the airwaves to get his or her message across. The electronic media are well-suited to the California political style of antipartyism. The candidate can use the media to emphasize self, personality, and the most effective issues, a tailor-made appeal. Radio, moreover, can reach millions of voters made into a captive audience twice daily by the state's morning and evening snarled freeway traffic. Statewide media campaigns are facilitated by the fact that approximately 85 percent of Californians live in four major media markets: Los Angeles, the San Francisco Bay Area, Sacramento, and San Diego.

Television and radio can also be targeted toward specific audiences whose votes the candidate is seeking; for example, a candidate might believe that he or she could score well with people who view sports events, or listen to Spanish-language stations, or like country-and-western music. Certain audiences may be reached more effectively during the day rather than at night, or vice versa. Certain regions of the state could get a message tailored for them. For example, coastal areas are thought to be particularly receptive to proenvironment messages. Statewide candidates also use focus groups to test possible campaign themes. Focus groups are small groups of carefully selected persons who are exposed to different political messages and then asked their reactions. Themes that "sell well" to the focus group are then used statewide or targeted to specific groups or regions.

Another example of campaign targeting is the use of direct mail by both statewide and local candidates. When a person registers to vote, he or she is required to give the Registrar of Voters information about one's age, address, occupation, and so on. Candidates feed this information into a computer that cross-references it with census data, public-opinion polling data, and past election returns. Campaign consultants can then craft a carefully tailored glossy, multicolored, direct mail piece that is targeted to a specific audience. The target audience has been preselected in terms of income level, occupation, age, gender, race, ethnic group, or even sexual preference. Different messages can be sent to different groups. In fact, the wily candidate can send direct mail to one preselected group that describes the candidate as an advocate of lower taxes and frugal government, while sending direct mail pieces to ten other groups saying the candidate favors full funding for each of their favorite spending programs.

Another example of campaign targeting is the use of slate mailers sent to specifically selected demographic or occupational or political groups. Slate mailers are cards that contain the names of candidates (from president all the way down to the local school board) who supposedly favor law enforcement, abortion, high education spending, or some other issue of importance to the targeted group. The candidates on the slate mailer may actually have little in common with one another regarding law and order, abortion, and so on: The candidates for high office may not know that they are on the slate mailer, while candidates for low-visibility offices have *paid* to be on the mailer. In fact, places on the slate are sold to the highest bidder. Slate mailers are partly intended to affect election outcomes, but they are primarily commercial ventures to make money. In 1990, a slate mailer titled a "Democratic Voter's Guide" was sent to Democrats with a record of high turnout in previous elections. The card urged votes for Democratic candidates Dianne Feinstein and Kathleen Brown as well as for candidates Dan Lungren and Matt Fong. Feinstein and Brown were Democrats who got on the mailer for free, but Lungren and Fong were Republicans who paid to get on the card. Slate mailers have minimal effect on races at the top of the card because voters already have enough information on these races, but they can provide the margin of victory in a city council or school board race lower on the ballot.

Television and radio spots, those nuisances that seem to be necessary for the conduct of modern democratic politics, require expertise in their making. Campaign-management firms supply this expertise. These private corporations, which provide the services that California's feeble parties cannot supply, can do almost everything for a candidate from writing the press release announcing that the candidate has entered the race to planning the election-night party. The firms can even do the fund-raising that helps to pay for their services. However, a local candidate may want to purchase only a few services rather than contract for complete campaign management. He or she may want some of the following: advice on strategy, speech preparation, direct mailing, phone banks, polling, press relations, media arrangements, get-out-the-vote drives, or other services. California campaign-management firms could be described as virtual political parties for hire or "rent-a-parties." In any event, candidates for offices such as governor or U.S. senator search out the most prestigious firms and rely heavily on their direction, especially regarding television and radio.

The vast size of the state, as well as its mobile and rapidly growing population, make campaigning primarily by mass media a practical necessity for candidates for statewide office. In addition to purchasing television time to air the "spots" produced by campaign-management firms, statewide candidates also use staged media events or pseudoevents. A media event is a contrived event that is made to appear spontaneous in order to catch the attention of the mass media. Events such as a speech, a handshaking tour, a parade, or airport arrival can directly reach only a relatively small audience. But if the electronic media report the event on prime-time news, a vastly greater audience is reached. The beauty of the media event is that the candidate can reach a large audience without having to buy costly air time.

Media consultants and campaign-management firms operate on the premise that candidates seldom lose an election by underestimating the intelligence of the voter. California media campaigns are long on image and personalities but short on substance. On the other hand, considering that this state is characterized by substantial population immigration, weak voter party loyalty, and little electoral support from party organizations, this is perhaps the only effective strategy. Moreover, the more specific a candidate is about issues or public policies, the more likely it is that he or she will say something that someone opposes. Campaigns stress negative advertising—attacking the opponent's supposed weaknesses without stating one's own platform and positions on key issues. Unfortunately, this strategy is effective because voters respond to this kind of advertising. Californians are mistrustful of politicians in general and disenchanted with politics: They may be looking for reasons to vote "against" rather than "for" a candidate. The 1994 U.S. Senate campaigns of Dianne Feinstein and Michael Huffington relied almost exclusively on negative advertising.

Campaign-management firms are astute at using public opinion polls to identify "switchers," or voters who back the opposing candidate but who might switch to their candidate or who are undecided. The bulk of television, radio, and direct mail advertising is then targeted at these people.

Do the campaign-management firms win elections for the candidates? Important races will find professionals on both sides. Candidates in less visible races would be well advised to purchase as much expert advice as their budgets allow. However, not all authorities are convinced that the campaign-management industry with all its wizardry can replace the time-honored winning mix of the right candidate, the right issues, and the right year.

We have now considered the party in terms of its members and as an organization. What about the party in office? Do party members vote as a bloc in the state legislature? Members elected as Democrats generally are like-minded people (predominately liberal with a few middle-of-the-roaders), as are the members elected as Republicans (predominately conservative with a few middle-of-the-roaders). This common ideology within each party and the reliance of legislators on legislative leaders for campaign contributions foster a substantial amount of party cohesion, especially in the Assembly.

THE PROGRESSIVE HERITAGE AND RECENT ELECTIONS

The California Progressives

In the California Progressives of the early 1900s we can see many of the characteristics of current state politics: antipartyism, liberal economic legislation, and even anti-Asian prejudice. The Progressives were an insurgent political movement, primarily within the Republican Party, seeking to overthrow the pervasive power of the Southern Pacific Railroad over California government. Railroad control was so extensive that historian George Mowry has written that the state had only "the shadow of representative government, while the real substance of power resided largely in the Southern Pacific."[1] The railroad, which was the largest landowner and employer in the state, dealt ruthlessly with anyone—farmer, merchant, shipper, employee, or elected official—who crossed its path. Setting the highest rates the traffic could bear, the SP employed arbitrary charges (with rebates to favored shippers) and threatened to bypass cities that would not pay it tribute. Reminding the Los Angeles City Council that the city's vitality depended on the railroad, Charles Crocker, one of the Southern Pacific's founders, announced, "I will make grass grow in the streets of your city."[2]

Who were the California Progressives and what was their political philosophy? They were young men primarily in their thirties, "largely Protestant and small-town in origin, upper-middle-class, university-trained professionals [especially lawyers and journalists], forward-looking and reform-minded, yet at the same time slightly nostalgic for a lost myth of American self-reliance and individualism."[3] The Progressives viewed government as "a public trust almost beyond politics, a stewardship of high-mindedness and efficiency in the public interest."[4] In a manner similar to many of today's political activists, the Progressive pictured himself as "wholly divorced from particular economic as well as class interests, ready to do justice in the name of morality and the common good."[5] The Progressives placed their greatest trust in "the people" (conveniently leaving the term vague and undefined), always believing them to be fundamentally wise and public-spirited. The California Progressive of the early 1900s was truly a person in the middle: concerned about the power of large

---

1. George E. Mowry, *The California Progressives* (Berkeley and Los Angeles: University of California Press, 1951), p. 9. See also p. 11.

2. Crocker, quoted in Carl Brent Swisher, *Motivation and Political Technique in the California Constitutional Convention, 1878–79* (Claremont, CA: Pomona College, 1930), p. 47.

3. Kevin Starr, *Inventing the Dream: California through the Progressive Era* (New York: Oxford University Press, 1985), p. 236.

4. Ibid., p. 274.

5. Mowry, *California Progressives*, p. 101.

corporations on one side but also fearful of the contemporary rise of socialism and labor unions on the other.

In national politics, the Progressives looked to President Theodore Roosevelt, the crusading nemesis of the trusts, as their source of inspiration. At the state level, they followed the leadership of Dr. John Haynes (an early proponent of direct democracy and leader of the AntiSaloon League), Fremont Older (editor of the *San Francisco Bulletin* newspaper), and especially Chester Rowell (general manager of the *Fresno Republican*). But the commanding figure of California Progressivism was Hiram Johnson, governor from 1911 to 1917 and U.S. senator from 1917 to 1945. Such political longevity is unmatched in state history; only death in office ended Hiram Johnson's career.

Johnson first gained fame in the San Francisco graft trials of 1907 when he took over for the trial's prosecutor, who had been shot in open court by a prospective juror. A trial lawyer with a combative personality, Johnson was a "fighter in every ounce of his body. . . . [H]is attack upon a problem was never subtle or diplomatic. . . . [Johnson was] righteously cocksure. In a struggle, his outward attitude belied all doubt. He stood for the forces of light, and the opposition was obviously allied with the devil."[6] Hiram Johnson was the perfect person to carry the fight to the Southern Pacific. The fact that Johnson's father, with whom he had quarreled bitterly for many years, was a politician working for the Southern Pacific adds an interesting Freudian aspect to the story.

The immediate background to Hiram Johnson's 1910 challenge to the Southern Pacific lies in the fateful 1906 Republican nominating convention held at Santa Cruz. Nominations were made for all state offices at a single convention, from the governorship down, and were tightly controlled by the political bureau of the Southern Pacific. Nominations were shamelessly bartered, including those for justices of the California Supreme Court. The resulting public embarrassment persuaded the legislature to change the nominating rules for the next **gubernatorial** election. Thenceforth, candidates for governor would be nominated by *primary*, an election in which all registered party members select the party's candidate for the general election. It was no longer possible for the railroad to manipulate party nominations and thereby control elections. The first gubernatorial candidate to benefit from the new rules was Hiram Johnson.

After securing the Republican nomination, Johnson campaigned hard against the Southern Pacific. Traveling up and down the state in a bright-red open-topped car (to show his independence of the railroad by not taking the train), Johnson assailed the SP at every stop. In his shirtsleeves and standing on the backseat of the car, the pugnacious trial attorney told crowds in towns throughout the state that if elected, he would "kick the Southern Pacific out of California politics." As a result of Johnson's relentless assaults, the people of California returned an astounding verdict for Johnson and the California Progressives and against the railroad.

---

6. Mowry, *California Progressives*, pp. 113–114. See also Starr, *Inventing the Dream*, p. 253.

Firmly ensconced in power in Sacramento, the Progressives embarked on a legislative program that was monumental for its time and that intimately affects California today. In the area of elections and governmental reform, the Progressives' program included a civil service system of merit selection for state employees (to replace the previous patronage system based on political loyalty), the council–manager form of local government, women's suffrage, and a secret Australian ballot. The reform program was guided by two key Progressive beliefs: trust in the people, and a determination to remove any procedural or structural impediments to expression of the public's will. For example, the Progressives instituted direct popular election of United States senators (rather than election by the state legislature) and initiative, referendum, and recall. We shall discuss the last three reforms in detail in Chapter 5, but the initiative is law made by voters (rather than law made by the legislature), the referendum is law repealed by voters, and the recall is the removal of an undesirable official from office by voters before the end of the official's term. Recall was particularly controversial because it applied to judges as well as all other elected officials. It was the opinion of prominent Progressive John Haynes that of the three branches of state government, the Southern Pacific's control over the judiciary was most complete.

The Progressives' trust in the people was complemented by a distrust of political parties and political party organizations. In response to the Southern Pacific's manipulation of judgeships at the 1906 convention, the Progressives established nonpartisan election of judges. Because the Progressives believed that there is no partisan way to run counties, cities, and school districts, they made these offices nonpartisan as well. Some Progressives believed that political parties are inherently evil; therefore they passed a law in 1915 establishing nonpartisanship for state offices (a law soon repealed).

Perhaps the Progressives' most famous political reform was **cross-filing**, which allowed a candidate to run in the primaries of two or more political parties without having to reveal his or her real party affiliation. This reform, which was clearly intended to weaken parties, lasted until the 1950s. Because there were five political parties (Democrats, Republicans, Progressives, Socialists, and Prohibitionists) at the time, a candidate could garner the nomination of more than one party; an enterprising candidate in 1914 actually got the nomination of all five parties. In 1916 the Progressives established an open primary in which a registered voter could vote in the primary election of any political party. However, the Progressives' opponents used one of the Progressives' favorite tools, the referendum, to repeal the open primary.

The Progressives also had a program of economic and social reform that early in this century established California as a liberal state. We noted earlier that the Progressives feared both concentrated corporate wealth and also labor radicalism. To prevent a violent confrontation between these two forces, which they feared would tear apart California society, the Progressives favored both increased business regulation and programs such as workers' compensation. The Railroad Commission (forerunner of today's Public Utilities Commission) was given complete power to set uniform rates, thus ending the Southern Pacific's practice of both extortionate rates and rebates to favored shippers. The commission also received power to regulate utilities such as electricity, gas, telegraph, and telephones unless these utilities were municipally owned. Industrial employers were also required to make payments to a state-operated workers' injury compensation fund. Laws were passed that mandated the periodic payment of wages, curtailed child labor, and established minimum wages and an eight-hour day for women industrial workers.

The Progressives also encouraged the reform of state mental hospitals, provided textbooks at no charge to public school children, established mandatory kindergartens, and required pensions for teachers. Dealing with an issue that remains a problem today, Hiram Johnson sought money for new prison construction to reduce the number of prisoners in each prison cell.

Although they were characterized by courage and public-spiritedness, the California Progressives were also anti-Asian. In this unfortunate aspect they were characteristic of their time: The Republicans, Democrats, and labor unions were also anti-Asian. Small farmers feared competition from Japanese immigrants. Johnson drafted the Alien Land Law, which provided that aliens ineligible for citizenship could neither own land in California nor lease land for more than three years. Federal law at that time made all Asians ineligible for naturalization. Since passage of the Federal Exclusion Act of 1882, there had been no legal immigrants from China for more than thirty years, hence the law was really aimed at the 45,000 Japanese noncitizen immigrants living in the state. Not until 1952 did the California Supreme Court declare the Alien Land Law invalid as a violation of the equal protection clause of the Fourteenth Amendment to the U.S. Constitution.[7]

There are many reasons why the Progressive movement eventually declined in California. Its contentious leaders fought fiercely among themselves, and many (especially Johnson) demanded unquestioning loyalty from supporters. The movement was unable to deal with the foreign policy issues raised by World War I, such as isolationism, which split it internally. The rise of communism in Russia (1917) and American labor radicalism (1916–1920), particularly the violent tactics of the International Workers of the World (IWW), caused the Progressives to adopt a more conservative posture. The relatively short duration of the Progressives' ascendancy can also be traced to the fact that they never cemented enduring ties to labor unions. As a middle-class movement, Progressivism was unable to commit itself wholeheartedly to the cause of the economic underdog. On the other hand, because the Progressives feared concentrated wealth, they also refused to align themselves with corporations. Finally, by 1920, the conservative wing of the Republican party had reasserted control of the party, both nationally and in California.

---

7. *Fujii v. California*, 38 Cal. 2d 718 (1952). See also Royce Delmatier et al., *The Rumble of California Politics, 1848–1870* (New York: Wiley, 1970), p. 185, and Walton Bean, *California*, 3d ed. (New York: McGraw-Hill, 1978), p. 287. Spencer C. Olin, Jr., writes that "California Progressives were practically unanimous in their support of the measure, and all shared responsibility for its passage." *California's Prodigal Sons: Hiram Johnson and the Progressives, 1911–1917* (Berkeley and Los Angeles: University of California Press, 1968), pp. 177–178.

According to George Mowry, a close student of the California Progressives, the greatest achievement of the movement was that during its day it gave the state honest and decent government, and that it established a tradition of judging political practice by an ethical yardstick rather than by crude power and political self-interest. Although the Progressive movement led a brief life near the beginning of the twentieth century, its heritage is still a vibrant part of California government and politics as the state nears the end of the century.

We will note the influence of the Progressives many times later in the book, but it is significant to mention now that many of their reforms have had unintended consequences or have even been reformed again. For example, Chapter 4 raises the issue that by weakening political parties, the Progressives may have actually strengthened interest groups. Chapter 5 will show clearly that the initiative process did not work out as the Progressives intended. In Chapter 9, we note that the Progressives favored the council–manager form of city government but that most large cities continue to have direct mayoral election. The Progressives gave California city government **at-large election** of city council members, but a new wave of liberal reform now wants to return local governments to district elections. On the other hand, some of the Progressives' ideas are needed in local government now more than ever. The Progressives favored the **short ballot** (having fewer elected executive officials, with other executive officials being appointed rather than elected); Chapter 9 will show how this reform is vitally needed in local government, especially in county government. Chapter 6 shows that state government could also greatly benefit from this improvement. Although Hiram Johnson and his Progressive followers are long dead, it is interesting to consider how recent elections reflect the influences of those political pioneers.

The 1990 Election

As the 1990 primary season opened, the Republicans had no heir apparent for retiring Governor George Deukmejian, and they were fearful of a partisan Democratic **gerrymander** (see Chapter 7) after the 1990 election. Almost in desperation, Republican leaders persuaded Pete Wilson, who had been elected U.S. senator only two years before, to run for governor. On the Democratic side, Attorney General John Van de Kamp became the early leader for the nomination, but he was soon eclipsed by former San Francisco Mayor Dianne Feinstein. Using a dramatic television commercial that showed how she calmly became mayor after her predecessor was assassinated, Feinstein was able to catch the attention of the voters. She also stressed her support for abortion and for capital punishment; the latter was especially important because polls at the time showed that more than three-fourths of the state's voters favored the death penalty. In contrast, Van de Kamp said that although he was "personally opposed" to both abortion and capital punishment, he would enforce the state's laws supporting both if elected: Van de Kamp's position of private opposition but official support reduced his credibility with the voters. Feinstein also stressed that all previous California governors had been men and asserted, "It's time we had a woman governor." Feinstein defeated Van de Kamp by more than 10 percent.

In the general election for governor, Wilson narrowly defeated Feinstein, 49 percent to 46 percent. The closeness of the race can be explained in large part by the similarity of the two candidates: Both were fifty-seven years old, were environmentalists, favored abortion and the death penalty, and were members of the "moderate" wings of their respective parties. Wilson and Feinstein had even been good friends when both were mayors of important California cities. When candidates are so much alike, voters may find it difficult to choose. However, significant differences also were found between the two contenders: Feinstein strongly supported, and Wilson opposed, the "Big Green" environmental initiative described in Chapter 1. Feinstein's narrow loss cannot be clearly attributed to any unmistakable factors, but she failed to solidify her Northern California base, winning only fifteen of fifty northern California counties; she also received only 43 percent of the votes of white voters, according to a *Los Angeles Times* statewide poll of those leaving precinct stations. The final Field Poll before the election showed Wilson leading Feinstein by 6 percentage points among women voters.

In the vitally important race for attorney general, former U.S. House member Dan Lungren defeated San Francisco District Attorney Arlo Smith by less than 30,000 votes out of 6.7 million votes cast. The outcome was not known until two weeks after election day, when all absentee ballots had been finally counted. Although the Lungren–Smith contest was even closer than the Wilson–Feinstein race, the attorney general candidates were far apart on the issues. The conservative Lungren is strongly opposed to abortion and would also allow oil drilling off the California coast in the event of a reduction in oil from foreign sources; the liberal Smith took the opposite positions.

The voters in the 1990 general election were clearly disgruntled about taxes, the looming economic recession, recent corruption scandals involving incumbents, and the large number of measures appearing on the ballot. The voters defeated twenty-two out of twenty-eight ballot propositions presented to them, including noncontroversial constitutional amendments placed on the ballot by the legislature and bond issues that previously had enjoyed strong support. The only "high-profile" measure that did pass was a strict plan to limit the terms of incumbents (see Chapters 6 and 7).[8] In a truly odd twist, the voters re-elected a convicted felon to the powerful State Board of Equalization. Paul Carpenter was an incumbent board member who had been convicted of four counts of felony extortion and racketeering after he had been nominated in the June primary.

8. Further information on the 1990 election may be found in the *Los Angeles Times,* November 7, 1990, p. A1; Mark DiCamillo, "The Gubernatorial Election as Covered by the California Poll," in *California Votes: The 1990 Governor's Race,* ed. by Gerald Lubenow (Berkeley: Institute of Governmental Studies, 1991). Further information on the 1992 election may be found in the *Los Angeles Times,* April 22, 1992, p. A3, May 13, 1992, p. A20, June 8, 1992, p. A3; and the *Sacramento Bee,* February 7, 1992, p. A3. Further information on the 1994 election may be found in the *Los Angeles Times,* April 18, 1994, p. A1, June 8, 1994, p. A1; the *Sacramento Bee,* November 13, 1994, p. A32; the *California Journal* (May 1994): 11; and the *California Journal Weekly,* November 14, 1994, p. 3.

The 1992 Election

Both of California's seats in the U.S. Senate were on the ballot in 1992, which was a very unusual situation. Veteran Senator Alan Cranston did not seek renomination for a fifth term because he had been tarnished in an influence-peddling scandal and because he was in poor health. The Senate seat vacated by Cranston carried a six-year term and was called "the long seat." In contrast, there was also a contest for the "short seat," which was the final two years remaining in the term of Senator Pete Wilson, who had resigned after being elected governor in 1990. Wilson appointed John Seymour as his interim replacement, and Seymour then had to run in his own right. In 1992, the primary elections raised more issues and sparked more interest than did the general elections. Both the Democrats and the Republicans had spirited primary races for each seat, but the Republican primaries were especially bitter because they raised the issue of who was "legitimately" a Republican and what the future direction of the party should be.

The Republican primary for the long seat pitted conservative Los Angeles television commentator Bruce Herschensohn against U.S. Representative Tom Campbell, the candidate for the self-styled "moderate" wing of the party. A former Democrat, Campbell favored reduced military spending; took a strong environmentalist posture, including support for a ban on offshore oil drilling; supported abortion rights; and argued that homosexuality is not a threat to traditional family values. Herschensohn took the opposite position on each of these issues. He also strongly supported a low flat-rate income tax with no deductions, not even the extremely popular home-mortgage deduction. Herschensohn claimed that Campbell's strong environmental record gave "more importance to rats and fish than to your jobs." Despite the presence of singer and Palm Springs Mayor Sonny Bono, who gave the Republican primary a light touch, the campaign was extraordinarily intense, and Herschensohn was nominated by only 56,000 votes out of 2.3 million cast. Newspaper columnist Dan Walters described the race as "a microcosm of partisan and ideological conflict in California in the 1990s." As the Republican party increased its share of party registration in the 1970s and 1980s, it drew in more moderate members and younger members. The struggle between moderates and traditional conservatives is a fight to "redefine the Republican party in California."

The redefining struggle was also fought out in Republican legislative primaries throughout the state. Incumbent California governors usually have not involved themselves in state legislative primaries, but Pete Wilson took the step of intervening in sixteen Republican primaries on behalf of "moderate" candidates aligned with his wing of the party. In legislative districts from the Oregon border to the Mexican border, Wilson and the moderate wing locked horns with evangelical Christian groups opposed to abortion, gun control, and tax increases.

In contrast to the divisiveness in the Republican party, the Democratic primary for the long U.S. Senate seat provided an uncharacteristic amount of unity. Each of the candidates was a strong liberal, so debate centered on personalities and campaign tactics. Lieutenant Governor Leo McCarthy was the early leader, but he quickly faded in favor of the eventual primary winner, Barbara Boxer, a liberal member of the U.S. House from the San Francisco area. Running as a feminist candidate in an election year that was heralded as the "Year of the Woman," Boxer ran as an outsider because of the strong anti-incumbent feeling in the electorate. However, her opponents noted that Boxer was hardly an outsider because she was a five-term veteran who bounced 143 checks in the House of Representatives banking scandal. Deriding Boxer as "Barbara Bouncer," Mel Levine was a liberal House member from Santa Monica and a staunch supporter of Israel. Levine staked out two issue positions that were unusual for a California Democratic politician: He had supported the use of military force against Saddam Hussein in the Persian Gulf war, and he condemned the recent Los Angeles riots as "mob rule." But most important about Levine's campaign was his strategy: He was trailing far back in the opinion polls but sitting on the largest campaign war chest of any U.S. Senate candidate in the country. Levine's campaign managers were the legendary West Los Angeles firm of Berman and D'Agostino (BAD) Campaigns, which had a long record of impressive election victories. After making few personal appearances on the campaign hustings, Levine unleashed a $4 million television blitz late in the campaign that was timed to sway voters right before the election. The television barrage did not work, and Berman and D'Agostino suffered a rare election defeat. Boxer won the nomination with 44 percent of the vote.

In the Republican primary for the short seat, John Seymour was Pete Wilson's handpicked successor to serve the remainder of Wilson's Senate term. The lackluster Seymour was handicapped by the fact that appointed senators rarely win in their own right, by his own lack of accomplishments and public visibility during his brief time in the Senate, and by having even less sparkle and charisma than his mentor, Pete Wilson. Seymour's primary opponent was William Dannemeyer, a House member from Orange County who was the most conservative member of Congress from the state—and possibly from *any* state. The conservative-versus-moderate dogfight within the Republican party erupted in this race as well, with Seymour carrying the Wilson banner and with Dannemeyer supported by the same group of evangelical Christians who battled Wilson in sixteen state legislative primaries. As a member of the state legislature, Seymour had argued that abortion and homosexuality are morally wrong and that offshore oil drilling is necessary for the nation's energy independence. As a U.S. senator, Seymour switched positions on all of these issues. Dannemeyer, whose campaign consisted primarily of short slogans, said that Seymour had "flip-flopped so often on so many issues that he is the candidate cast in Jello." Dannemeyer's campaign had strongly religious overtones, and he hammered Seymour's position on gays by asserting that "God's plan was for Adam and Eve, not Adam and Steve." Although Seymour won the short seat primary handily, he clearly was in serious trouble because his Democratic opponent for the general election was the person who had nearly been elected governor only two years earlier. Dianne Feinstein easily won the Democratic nomination for the short-term Senate seat by making a strong gender-based campaign pitch. Noting that only two of one hundred U.S. senators were women, Feinstein urged Californians to double that number by sending herself and Barbara Boxer to Washington. Feinstein argued that the need for women senators was shown by the fact that male senators did not believe the sexual harassment allegations made by Anita Hill against Clarence Thomas during the latter's confirmation hearings for a U.S. Supreme Court position. Feinstein's playing of the "gender card" was effective in the Democratic primary, because a majority of voters usually are women. Among the women who voted in the primary, 41 percent selected both Feinstein *and* Boxer, while 30 percent voted for either Feinstein *or* Boxer. Another 29 percent of the women voted for neither candidate.

In the Democratic presidential primary, Bill Clinton easily defeated former governor Jerry Brown, who was making another run for the presidency as an outsider and antiestablishment candidate.

The general election campaign proved to be somewhat anticlimactic: Each expected winner (Clinton, Boxer, and Feinstein) did emerge triumphant. The California economy was in a serious recession with widespread unemployment, and angry voters blamed President Bush and Republicans in general for their plight. Bush made an early decision to concede California to Clinton as a lost cause, and Clinton easily became the first Democratic presidential candidate to carry California in nearly a quarter of a century. Herschensohn made a strong last-minute surge against Boxer, but her early lead in the polls and her large advantage in campaign spending enabled her to escape with a much-closer-than-expected victory. Feinstein defeated the hapless Seymour by 17 percent.

1994 Election

In 1994, two experienced California officeholders sought re-election: Pete Wilson as governor, and Dianne Feinstein as U.S. senator.

Pete Wilson entered the race with perhaps the most unfavorable prospects of any sitting California governor in the last half-century. Wilson was burdened by the state's anemic economy, its recurrent budget crises, and his own lack of personal magnetism. Concerning the latter, pundits have frequently said that Pete Wilson launching into a joke is no laughing matter. Despite giving him statewide victories in 1982, 1988, and 1990, Californians had never really taken Pete Wilson to heart. Wilson's weakness was clearly revealed when he lost 34 percent of the primary vote to political newcomer Ron Unz and an additional 5 percent to various entirely unknown candidates. Unz was a 32-year-old owner of a computer software company who had never run for any office before, and he spent millions of his own money to wrest the nomination from an experienced veteran. The upstart Unz was perfectly situated to hit Wilson where Wilson was weakest in a primary: He was clearly an outsider who bore no responsibility for the ongoing ills of state government, he was a self-made millionaire businessperson who had risen from humble beginnings, and he was a strong conservative who could appeal to the conservative wing of the Republican Party, which has never embraced Wilson. Calling the governor a "closet Democrat" for having raised taxes, Unz touted himself as "*the* Republican for Governor." He downplayed bilingual education and affirmative action as "ethnic separatism." Wilson, in turn, tried to ignore the pesky Unz by sharpening issues such as crime and illegal immigration to use in the fall campaign against the Democratic nominee. Wilson stressed his unqualified support for "three-strikes-and-you're-out" legislation (see Chapter 8) and for the position that illegal immigrants are a net economic detriment to the state's economy and budget deficit (Chapter 2). Wilson aired a controversial television commercial showing a dozen illegal aliens running across the border at the San Ysidro checkpoint, dodging cars as they were running. In the background an announcer ominously said, "They keep coming."

In the Democratic primary for governor, California Treasurer Kathleen Brown was clearly the front-runner: As the daughter of one former governor and the sister of another, she had strong name recognizability. She also showed substantial fund-raising ability, pulling in far more money than either of her opponents, Insurance Commissioner John Garamendi or State Senator Tom Hayden. Finally, most Democratic primary voters are women, and Brown frequently noted that both of her opponents were men. Garamendi campaigned hard against Brown, faulting her for personal opposition to the death penalty and pointing out that she had raised more than $1 million from employees of bond firms doing business with the treasurer's office. Hayden ran as a reform candidate who was not tied to special interests: He refused to accept campaign contributions greater than $94, and he criticized both Brown and Garamendi for having too close ties to wealthy interest groups: "We cannot bring about change by business-as-usual politics, by relying on contributions from the same lobbyists who already dominate Sacramento." Hayden (and Unz on the Republican side) were clearly protest candidates. Brown won the nomination, but she failed to receive a majority of the vote, and her campaign relied too heavily on slogans and vague promises of change rather than on a focused plan for governing. Perhaps most troubling for the Brown camp was an exit poll of more than 5,000 voters conducted by the *Los Angeles Times* that showed she did not run strongly among older or white or Asian voters or among moderate-to-conservative Democratic voters or those concerned about crime or immigration. Wilson would surely target these Democrats in the general election.

If both Wilson and Brown were nominated by their parties without enthusiastic support, the same can also be said about senate nominees Dianne Feinstein for the Democrats and Michael Huffington for the Republicans. Feinstein received less than three-fourths of the primary vote against unknown opponents who spent no money on their campaigns. This result is very surprising, because Feinstein had raised more money than any other member of Congress since her election in 1992. Money, lots of money, was the key to Huffington's success: He spent nearly $7 million of his own money to propel himself from being an obscure one-term House member to being the Republican senate nominee. The son of a Texas oil tycoon, Huffington had moved to California from Texas only two years earlier—and he immediately ran for a U.S. House seat and won. Spending $5 million of his personal fortune in that 1992 House race, Huffington defeated a twenty-year veteran in the Republican primary and set a spending record. It was this House seat that Huffington abandoned at the very next election to challenge Feinstein.

The fall campaign between Huffington and Feinstein promised to be a spending extravaganza like Californians had never seen: The *California Journal* estimated Huffington's personal wealth to be approximately $75 million, while Feinstein's was a mere $50 million.

In the fall campaign for governor, Pete Wilson scored a resounding re-election victory, defeating Kathleen Brown by 15 percent of the vote (1.2 million votes), carrying 53 out of California's 58 counties—including Los Angeles County, which usually votes Democratic in statewide elections.The most surprising aspect of the Wilson victory is that he won after coming back from 23 points behind in statewide public opinion polls; after being written off as politically dead by nearly all political analysts, Wilson rose from the dead and returned to win with a vengeance. The keys to Wilson's victory are that he constantly repeated two campaign themes—crime and immigration—that were highly salient for voters and that he was running in a year in which national political trends clearly favored the Republicans. Wilson emphasized his support for tough "three-strikes-and-you're-out" legislation and pointed to Brown's opposition to the death penalty, while campaigning hard for Proposition 187 which would deny some public services to illegal immigrants (see Chapter 2 for more information on Proposition 187). Wilson won 56 percent to 41 percent, and Proposition 187 passed 59 percent to 41 percent. According to the Field Poll, Wilson got the votes of 62 percent of whites, 51 percent of Asians and women, and 25 percent of Latinos. In general, Wilson's support of Proposition 187 was extremely unpopular in Latino communities.

In the general election for U.S. senator, Dianne Feinstein defeated Michael Huffington 47 percent to 45 percent. Huffington spent an amazing $30 million (almost all of it his own money) on television, radio, and newspaper advertising; Feinstein spent $12 million. The garish amounts spent on campaign advertising produced what *California Journal Weekly* called "the most squalid, invective-filled, mud-splattered dismal excuse for a political campaign" seen in many years. The bitterness of the campaign probably explains why approximately 9 percent of the voters selected someone other than the major party candidates. The tragic aspect of the campaign is that, with $42 million spent by the candidates in getting their "message" out, the electorate received little substantive discussion of significant issues. For example, genuine issues separated the candidates on the role of government: Feinstein told an interviewer "I have been in government all my life. I believe in government." In contrast, Huffington was decidedly antigovernment, believing that it spends too much and saps private initiative. Nor was there much discussion of such relevant issues as the effect of the defense build-down on California, the future of the aerospace industry, or even California's export–import role in the world economy. The 1994 election featured the most expensive U.S. senate race and the

Dianne Feinstein and Michael Huffington, 1994 U.S. Senate candidates, square off during "Larry King Live."

most expensive gubernatorial race in American history; in terms of furthering public understanding of contemporary issues, the money was almost entirely wasted.

REGISTRATION AND VOTING

A person who wants to become a voter and who meets the citizenship, residence, and age requirements must register with the county clerk or county registrar of voters at least twenty-nine days before an upcoming election. This may be accomplished by filling out a voter-registration postcard and dropping it in the mail. In 1993, Congress approved "motor voter" registration, which allows citizens to register at their states' motor vehicles department (in California, the Department of Motor Vehicles, or DMV) or at welfare offices. Preliminary estimates indicate that 15 percent more people will be registered by using the increased registration opportunities.

Once registered, a person stays on the voter rolls until he or she moves to another county, has a name change, becomes ineligible because of insanity or conviction of a felony, or fails to vote in a general election. In a decision of interest to college students, the state Supreme Court has ruled that a voter may continue to vote at a former permanent residence until he or she has established a new permanent residence (*Walters* v. *Weed*, 45 Cal. 3d 1 [1988]). Dissenting justices warned of vote fraud, noting

Table 3.1 Voters Using Absentee Ballots (Percentage)*

1982	6.5
1984	9.3
1986	9.0
1988	14.1
1990	18.4
1992	17.2
1993	21.9
1994	22.0

*All elections are general elections except 1993, which was a special election.

that a person could continue to vote indefinitely in a community he or she had abandoned simply by declaring that no new permanent residence had been established.

To keep voter rolls current, California once conducted a **positive purge** of the rolls. Those who were registered to vote but did not were notified by mail, and if they did not respond, their names were removed from the list. In 1975 the state changed to a **negative purge**, in which nonvoters are contacted by mail and removed from the voting list only if the post office returns the cards as undeliverable or if the cards are returned by the person now living at the address. In many respects, the accuracy of the state's election rolls depends on the efficiency of the U.S. Postal Service, a somewhat unnerving thought. Mervin Field of the Field Poll believes that the current registration system carries on the rolls the names of phantom voters or deadwood amounting to 1 million to 2 million of the approximately 14 million registered voters. Moreover, the cost of mailing election materials to those who have died, moved, or no longer care to vote is quite expensive. Campaign specialists generally agree that persons incorrectly remaining on the voting rolls are overwhelmingly Democrats. Finally, the frequent assertion that too low a percentage of the state's registered voters turn out to vote needs revision.

Another administrative aspect of politics that can be completed by mail is **absentee voting.** Before 1978 if someone wanted to vote by absentee ballot, then he or she had to cite illness, absence on election day, conflicting religious commitment, or residence at a long distance from a polling place as a reason for a mail ballot. The requirements were dropped in 1978, and candidates soon started urging the public to "vote in the convenience of your own home" and began to send absentee-voter applications along with campaign literature. As indicated by Table 3.1, the percentage of people voting by absentee ballot has increased dramatically in recent years.

Reasons for the increase in absentee voting include the convenience of being able to vote anytime during a three-to-four-week period rather than during a thirteen-hour period on a single day. Furthermore, voters can take as long as they want to complete the ballot, and they do not feel pressured to finish in ten minutes while other voters wait impatiently at the precinct. In addition, a voter neither has to wait in line nor get off work to vote. An absentee voter also can seek information and advice from others while in the process of voting. Finally, political parties, candidates, and interest groups all encourage their supporters to use absentee ballots. Absentee voters are more likely to be older and more politically conservative.

The current use of absentee ballots raises serious concerns in election administration. For instance, in addition to distributing absentee ballot applications, political party workers take absentee ballots to the voter and can even be present when the voter marks the ballot. In such a situation, no poll judge is present to ensure the integrity of the ballot; moreover, the voter can be coerced into voting a certain way by relatives, friends, employers, union leaders, interest group officers, or, of course, party workers who happen to be on the scene. In these circumstances, who actually marks the ballot cannot be ascertained for certain. In some instances party workers have even asked for absentee ballots on behalf of people who were unaware of the request and then forged the voter's signature. In other words, the potential for fraud is great; former Secretary of State March Fong Eu has described the situation as a "time bomb waiting to explode."[9] On a less serious level, the possibility of human error is genuine. People often sign absentee-voter applications without knowing exactly what they are requesting. When the absentee ballot arrives, they throw it away thinking that it is campaign literature. These unfortunate people then cannot vote at the polls because the poll record indicates that they have received an absentee ballot.

When we combine registering by mail and absentee voting by mail, we have the potential for vote fraud on a widespread scale. Votes could be cast for years without election officials ever seeing a specific flesh-and-blood person.

ELECTIONS

Primary Elections

In a primary election each party selects a person to represent it for each office in November's general election. California primaries are "closed," which means that only registered Democrats may vote in the Democratic party primary, only registered Republicans may vote in the Republican party primary, and so forth. If a person has indicated "decline to state" when registering to vote, then he or she will receive on primary day a ballot containing only initiative and referendum propositions, the names of candidates for nonpartisan offices such as judgeships and for county offices, and the names of candidates for the office of California superintendent of public instruction (this four-year office was on the ballot in 1994). Approximately 9 percent

---

9. "Is Liberalized Absentee Ballot Fraud-Prone?" *San Diego Union*, December 12, 1984, p. C6.

of the state's voters are registered as "decline to state" a party preference: This rather high percentage is another indicator of the antipartyism discussed earlier.

In 1996, California voters will decide whether the state should return to the open primary that was briefly established by the California Progressives. Under this arrangement, all parties appear on a single consolidated primary ballot. The voters can choose to nominate a Democrat for governor, then a Republican for the Assembly, then a Democrat for the state Senate, and so on. The voter is allowed to participate in nominating candidates from all five of the parties that have qualified for the California ballot. The top vote-getter for each party for each office would run again in November. This is "buffet-style" politics that takes a similar procedure used in special elections (described later) and applies it to all offices on the primary ballot. Proponents of the consolidated primary ballot argue that it maximizes the choices available to the voter and that it increases the power of independent and middle-of-the-road voters who can pick and choose between parties for each office. Opponents assert that the consolidated ballot weakens political parties (which we have already noted are rather weak in this state) and maximizes the campaign contributions of interest groups. If this primary procedure is adopted, then *crossover voting* may occur—that is, one party's members may vote in the other party's primary because it has a more exciting or hotly contested race. *Raiding*—voting in another party's primary to nominate the weakest candidate—also is possible. In states with the open-primary arrangement, few, if any, instances of large-scale raiding have been documented because most voters are not strongly partisan enough to engage in this kind of political sabotage.

Turnout (the percentage of people who actually vote) is lower in the primary than in the general election. This low turnout is unfortunate because, in California's noncompetitive one-party districts, the primary is often more important than the general election. As a result, party factions (liberal, middle-of-the-road, conservative) are encouraged to fight it out in the primary. However, most primaries are not particularly dramatic. Incumbents (persons already holding the office) have a distinct advantage. Especially for the minority party, the primary campaign is brief, the candidates are not well known, and the issues are unclear.

As an experiment and to increase California's influence in presidential politics, the legislature changed the 1996 primary from the usual June date to March. In the past, California's presidential primary had come long after each party's presidential nomination had been locked up, so California's vote rarely mattered. With the largest group of convention delegates now up for grabs relatively early in the process, the California presidential primary could become a major event. In previous presidential years, candidates spent little time campaigning in California, only coming to the state to raise money that could be spent on the really important primaries. This situation contributed to California's image as the "ATM [automatic teller machine] of national politics." The earlier primary could force presidential candidates to address issues of particular interest to Californians such as reduced defense spending, conversion to nondefense employment, and illegal immigration. The change, which is a one-time-

Table 3.2 Timing of General Elections

OFFICE	YEAR				
	1990	1992	1994	1996	1998
FEDERAL					
President	—	Yes	—	Yes	—
Senators	—	Yes[a,b]	Yes[a]	—	Yes[b]
Representatives	Yes	Yes	Yes	Yes	Yes
STATE					
Governor and all state constitutional officers	Yes	—	Yes	—	Yes
Assembly members	Yes[c]	Yes	Yes	Yes	Yes
State senators	1/2	1/2	1/2	1/2	1/2

[a]Seat "A" held by Dianne Feinstein.

[b]Seat "B" held by Barbara Boxer.

[c]Congressional and state legislative districts redrawn after this election.

only event and which includes all federal and state-level primaries, could become permanent if the legislature views the 1996 results as worthwhile.

Although our discussion has concerned party, or partisan, primaries, California also has nonpartisan primaries for all officials elected on a nonpartisan basis. Municipal (city) officials usually have their primaries in March or April. County officers, all judges, and the state superintendent of public instruction have their primaries on the same day as the partisan primaries. This part of the ballot is the same for everyone, whether registered as a party member or as a "decline to state." All candidates who receive a majority vote in the primary are elected outright. Should no one gain a majority, then a runoff must be held between the two top vote-getters.

General Elections

Politics comes alive for most people at the time of the general election. Names of political heroes may be on the ballot, issues are discussed (often heatedly), and politics is in the air and on the airwaves. California's elections for governor and state constitutional officers, such as controller or treasurer, are held in the even-numbered years in which no presidential election is held (see Table 3.2). All state Assembly members and one-half of the state Senate are elected every two years. As for federal officials elected

Table 3.3 Hypothetical Special Election

CANDIDATE	PARTY AFFILIATION	VOTE PERCENTAGE
A	Democrat	26
B	Republican	11
C	Democrat	31
D	Libertarian	2
E	Republican	17
F	Democrat	7
G	Peace and Freedom	5
H	Green Party	1

from the state, all members of the House of Representatives are elected for two-year terms; U.S. senators serve six-year terms.

The **office-block ballot** form is consistent with the spirit of antipartyism and independence discussed earlier. Such a ballot groups candidates according to the office sought, rather than listing party members in columns as a party-column ballot does. The California ballot and punch-card voting machines force the voter to make a new decision before voting for *each office.* With a **party-column ballot,** the voter is initially given an opportunity to vote for an entire party by simply marking the circle at the head of the list of party candidates. The office-block ballot, if only by the way it appears to the eye, suggests picking and choosing between candidates of different parties.

Special Elections

Should a vacancy occur in the state legislature or in the state's congressional delegation because of death, resignation, or another reason, the governor must call a **special election.**[10] In a special election all candidates of all parties are listed on a single ballot, and the voter votes for one candidate. The candidate who receives a majority of the votes cast is automatically elected. If no one receives a majority, the top vote-getters of *each* party face each other in a runoff. This procedure, however, may result in a curious situation. If the percentages of the vote are as shown in Table 3.3, then the runoff ballot will list Candidates C, D, E, G, and H, although more voters in this district clearly favored Candidate A than E.

The adoption of term limits has caused many officeholders to quit their present seat and seek higher office or a career in the private sector, thus leading to many

---

10. An example of a different kind of special election was the 1993 balloting on extending the sales tax and the school-vouchers ballot proposition.

Table 3.4 Turnout of Registered Voters by Type of Election

	PRESIDENTIAL ELECTION	GUBERNATORIAL ELECTION	PRESIDENTIAL PRIMARY	GUBERNATORIAL PRIMARY
1994	—	60.1	—	35.0
1992	75.3	—	47.4	—
1990	—	58.6	—	41.5
1988	72.8	—	46.1	—
1986	—	60.0	—	38.6
1984	73.9	—	49.3	—
1982	—	69.7	—	52.9
1980	76.5	—	64.2	—
1978	—	68.7	—	74.1
1976	81.1	—	71.2	—
1974	—	62.6	—	51.7
1972	80.4	—	68.9	—

special elections. Special elections have become so common that the state government is now paying for them, rather than county governments paying for them as has been traditional.

ELECTION TURNOUT

Over the last twenty years, election turnout has generally been lower than turnout in the latter part of the 1970s. As Table 3.4 indicates, the drop in voter turnout has been greater in presidential or gubernatorial primaries than in presidential or gubernatorial general elections. Because primary election turnout has almost always been lower than general election turnout, the drop in primary turnout is particularly severe.

Mervin Field and Mark DiCamillo studied the characteristics of voters and nonvoters: Voters are more likely to be Anglos who are older, more educated, have a higher income, and are homeowners rather than renters.[11] Nonvoters generally do not share these characteristics and can be classified as political passives (40 percent), contented apathetics (30 percent), politically alienated (20 percent), and system disenfranchisees (10 percent). *Political passives* are the most common nonvoters: They pay little or no attention to politics and government and devote most of their daily

11. Mervin Field and Mark DiCamillo, *California Poll No. 1547,* June 5, 1990, and *No. 1741,* November 8, 1994.

energy trying to survive economically or pursuing purely personal affairs. Many political passives are racial or ethnic minorities, low-income, poorly educated, or are young adults. *Contented apathetics* do not vote because they believe that their lives are progressing well enough and that they have no need to pay any attention to politics. The *politically alienated* are turned off by the political process and frequently are former voters. They believe that it does not matter who gets elected or that their lives will change for the better if they do vote. The smallest group is *system disenfranchisees,* who have voted in the past and would like to vote in the upcoming election but cannot do so because they are not registered to vote. These people get the desire to vote in the closing weeks of a campaign but have missed the deadline requiring people to register twenty-nine days before the election. Some system disenfranchisees may have recently moved.

The drop in voter turnout (especially in primaries) is clearly undesirable, but keep a few points in mind. All of the people studied by Field and DiCamillo were adults and not incompetent children, many had made a conscious choice not to vote, and no legal barriers prevent any of them from registering and voting in the future. Data on low voter turnout can also be somewhat misleading because of the "deadwood" problem discussed earlier and because of high legal and illegal immigration to the state. If 10 percent of all registered voters have died, moved, or remain on the rolls because of the inefficient negative purge (i.e., are deadwood on the voter rolls), then turnout figures on *registered* voters could be misleading by nearly 10 percent. On the other hand, many writers provide turnout data in terms of all Californians above the age of 18. Those data also can be misleading because many Californians 18 and older are immigrants not legally entitled to vote. Field and DiCamillo prefer to express turnout in terms of citizen-eligible adults. The low-turnout problem is disturbing, but it should not be blown out of proportion.

CAMPAIGN-SPENDING ISSUES

Campaign spending in California is increasing at a dizzying rate, with each election year's total far surpassing the last, especially for state legislative races. The largest item in legislative campaign budgets is direct mail—for example, computer-written letters and full-color brochures. The most expensive item in statewide races is television and radio. The prohibitively high cost of campaigns has discouraged new candidates from running and presenting their ideas to the public. Incumbents usually outspend their challengers by overwhelming amounts—in 1990, eight to one; in 1992 and 1994, five to one. It is not surprising that 98 percent of all incumbents are re-elected. Incumbents raise tremendous amounts of money for many reasons: to deter potential challengers from running against them; to hedge against the possibility of a personally rich opponent or one who received large contributions from interest groups or party sources; and to protect themselves against a last-minute surprise blitz.

*Put me down for "no comment" on that one . . . I really haven't
read enough polls on the subject to have an opinion!*

Two particularly troublesome issues are off-year fund-raising and out-of-district
contributions. Off-year fund-raising occurs during a year when the incumbent is not
running for re-election and usually takes place in Sacramento. Legislators solicit
lobbyists for contributions, frequently scheduling fund-raising events such as recep-
tions on the eve of important votes that affect substantial economic interests. This
activity receives little public scrutiny because it takes place when fewer contribution-
disclosure reports are required, the incumbent does not have an announced opponent, and the attention of the press may be diverted to the more visible business of
government, such as hearings and legislative votes. Off-year fund-raising must be
contrasted with fund-raising during an election year. In the latter case, money is given
to candidates, often because the contributor likes the candidate's ideology or point
of view on many issues or because the contributor dislikes the opponent's ideology.
The purpose is to support a point of view and to win a specific election. In contrast,
off-year contributions go to incumbents, but this time to gain access or influence for
the contributor. The purpose now is not to influence an election but to influence
pending legislation. Two important off-year contributors are the California Trial
Lawyers Association and the California State Employees Association (CSEA). Off-year
contributions are almost always out-of-district money: The interest groups and
Sacramento lobbyists who give the money are usually not located in the legislator's
district. These out-of-district forces lessen the importance of the legislator's own
constituents. Both off-year fund-raising and out-of-district contributions figure in
Reading 3.1 (page 92).

READING 3.1

Money and Power

SACRAMENTO—The tobacco industry, which won major protections from lawsuits in a "tort reform" bill that was rushed through the Legislature on the last night of its 1987 session, contributed $23,750 to 16 lawmakers immediately after the vote, according to figures released Friday by Consumers Union.

The money was contributed by the Tobacco Institute on Monday, Sept. 14, the first working day after the bill was brought to a vote in both houses of the Legislature, the consumer group reported. Among those who received the contributions were top Democratic and Republican leaders who played key roles in assuring approval of the last-minute deal.

In addition, the study found that the Tobacco Institute and three other special-interest groups that helped draft the measure contributed a total of $635,000 to lawmakers during 1987, a non-election year. The three groups—manufacturers, physicians and trial lawyers—traditionally are among the largest contributors to legislative campaigns. . . .

The tort reform bill provides broad protections for private industry and individuals against personal injury lawsuits and exempts manufacturers of alcoholic beverages, cigarettes and other "inherently unsafe products."

The final compromise was struck in a series of closed-door meetings that culminated the night before the session ended. The Legislature's top leaders shuttled between tables at a Chinese restaurant to forge the agreement that eventually was outlined on a white, linen napkin. The next day it was presented to the Legislature and passed exactly as written.

Supporters had argued that many of the measure's provisions had been heard by various legislative committees over the years. But the provision exempting tobacco products was never fully discussed before the final night of the session. Tobacco industry lawyers who flew to Sacramento from Washington to help write the measure were credited by other participants with heavily influencing the final product. . . .

But [Common Cause spokesperson Bob] Shireman said the fact that the money was contributed during a year when no elections were scheduled is evidence that tobacco interests had an ulterior motive.

"This is what I call policy money," Shireman said. "It has nothing to do with supporting people for public office and everything to do with power."

SOURCE: "Tobacco Industry Gifts After Vote Reported," by L. Wolinsky, *Los Angeles Times*, January 9, 1988, pt. 1, p. 32. Copyright 1988, Los Angeles Times. Reprinted by permission.

Just as the public is not aware of off-year fund-raising and out-of-district contributions, neither is it aware of the prominent role played by partisan contributions. Partisan contributions include those from legislative leaders, party caucuses in the state legislature, and state party committees. Democrats stress money transferred from legislative leaders such as the Assembly Speaker and Senate president pro tem (as long as the Democrats control the state legislature), while Republicans emphasize money from the Assembly Republican Caucus, the Senate Republican Caucus, and the Republican State Central Committee. The California Commission on Campaign Financing notes that transfers from party leaders and party caucuses and committees have disrupted the electoral process in several respects. First and perhaps foremost, transfers inject a psychologically destabilizing element into campaigns. Candidates know that at any moment their opponents may suddenly receive as much as $200,000 in last-minute money. This threat encourages candidates to stockpile large cash reserves. Transfers thus contribute to an "arms race" mentality between candidates.[12] Extremely large single contributions by individuals or interest groups could have the same effect; these are influential when they occur, yet they are infrequent.

The California system of privately financed elections has many unfortunate consequences. Off-year fund-raising, out-of-district contributions, and partisan contributions all have the profound effect of making the legislator beholden to someone *other than* the legislator's constituents. If the legislator can stockpile enough money from these sources, then he or she can vote against the interests or wishes of constituents *and may get away with it,* especially if the media do not blow the whistle on the legislator. Yet another unfortunate consequence is that locally made decisions are frequently overruled. For example, a city government may turn down the building request of a wealthy developer or enact a zoning ordinance that the developer does not like. The developer then asks the state legislature to overturn the city's decision while at the same time making generous campaign contributions to influential legislators. In 1993, when cities throughout the state passed antismoking laws, tobacco interests went to the state legislature to get a state law overturning the local laws. Decisions that should really be made at the local level are increasingly being made in the state legislature.

The California Commission on Campaign Financing has suggested expenditure ceilings, contribution limits, and limited public financing of campaigns to reform the state's election finance system. Expenditure ceilings reduce some of the destabilizing elements mentioned earlier, such as the fear of last-minute contributions, and they also lessen the fund-raising advantages of incumbents. Candidates accepting matching funds and expenditure ceilings would not need to be constantly searching for ever-increasing amounts of money in an attempt to ensure an election victory. Contribution limits reduce special-interest influence over the legislative process and encourage candidates to seek a larger number of smaller contributions. Limited matching funds would be provided until the expenditure ceilings are reached; within-district contributions would be matched at a ratio of five to one, but out-of-district contributions would be matched only at a ratio of three to one. Matching

---

12. California Commission on Campaign Financing, *The New Gold Rush: Financing California's Legislative Campaigns* (Los Angeles: Center for Responsive Government, 1985), p. 102. See also pp. 2–14, 47, 56, 102–104, 115–120, 134–135, and 143. The California Commission on Campaign Financing is a distinguished group of private citizens.

funds are derived from a voluntary individual state income-tax checkoff of $3. The commission's reform package is a comprehensive one that also prohibits transfers by candidates or incumbents to other candidates, prohibits non–election-year fund-raising, limits contributions by political parties and legislative caucuses, and limits the total amount of contributions that a candidate may receive from political action committees (PACs), corporations, and labor unions.

An initiative embodying the suggestions of the California Commission on Campaign Financing (Proposition 68) received a majority of votes in the June 1988 election. However, another campaign finance initiative on the same ballot (Proposition 73) received more votes; therefore under Article 2, Section 10 of the state Constitution, provisions of the initiative receiving more votes (Proposition 73) went into effect. However, Proposition 73 was later ruled unconstitutional by the federal courts!

Even if Propositions 68 and 73 had survived court challenge, they are not cure-all measures. Each plan covers only money contributions. What about in-kind contributions of manpower or equipment that can be used for election-day phone banks or get-out-the-vote drives? If political contributions are a form of political expression, are contribution limits a violation of the First Amendment of the U.S. Constitution? Moreover, for those persons who have little free time, campaign contributions may be their only chance for political activity other than voting.

The California Commission on Campaign Financing suggested expenditure ceilings, but expenditure floors may be more important. (One construction analogy is as good as another.) Publicly financed expenditure floors ensure a minimum level of access to the electorate by the challenger. The challenger's expenditures, rather than the incumbent's expenditures, may have a greater effect on the outcome of the election. The incumbent is already known, but "a challenger must depend on the campaign to make himself [or herself] known, and this task requires money. . . . [E]fforts to increase competition for legislative seats through campaign finance reform should focus on methods of providing challengers with more money."[13]

Finally, there is the issue of whether these reforms treat only symptoms and not causes. The heart of the problem is that the taxing, spending, and regulatory policies of government have vast economic and social consequences. As long as Californians want large-scale government, the affected groups (business, labor, farmers, doctors, lawyers, teachers, state employees, utilities, gun owners, and countless others) will find some way to influence the process and to protect their interests.

In conclusion, campaign spending needs to be put in perspective. Because of the state characteristics noted earlier, campaign spending in California calculated on a cost-per-vote basis has to be higher than in other states. The size and diversity of this state (see Chapter 1), antipartyism, weak political parties, low party loyalty among voters, personalized appeals by candidates using media and direct mail, campaign-

---

13. Stanton Glantz et al., "Election Outcomes: Whose Money Matters?" *Journal of Politics,* 38 (November 1976): 1038.

management firms—all of these drive up campaign costs. Also, the availability of money means that more money will be spent: Interest groups and wealthy individuals are able to contribute money and are inclined to do so. On the other hand, Sears, Roebuck and Company or General Motors or Procter & Gamble may annually spend more money for product advertising in California than it costs to elect a legislature and statewide officers.

POLITICAL REFORM

As noted earlier, reform has been a tradition in this state since the early 1900s. In 1974 California voters, spurred by Watergate revelations, approved an initiative (Proposition 9, the Political Reform Act) with far-reaching consequences. The act, as amended, applies to both state and local candidates. Its election provisions include the following:

1. Public reports: A candidate must report the names of contributors of more than $100 in money, goods, or services, along with the amount contributed and other details. Anonymous contributions above $100 are illegal. Reports of all amounts received and all expenditures above $100 must be filed both before and after an election. No contributions or expenditures above $100 may be made in cash.

2. Conflict of interest: Any financial holdings that might bias an official's judgment must be reported; for example, these could include income, real estate, or investments. The official may not participate in the making of a government policy in which he or she has a financial interest.

3. Ballot pamphlets: Citizens are given the opportunity to challenge in court any information in ballot pamphlets that they believe is false or misleading. This challenge may be made before the pamphlets are printed and mailed to the voters.

4. Fair Political Practices Commission (FPPC): A five-member commission was established to enforce the act. No more than three members of this commission can be of the same political party. The governor may appoint two members; the attorney general, the secretary of state, and the controller each appoint another.

Clearly the Political Reform Act has not decreased overall spending or contributions, although the act has opened up the election process by compelling disclosure of who is contributing how much to whom.

A CHANGED ENVIRONMENT FOR THE PARTIES

In the three decades from the mid-1960s to the mid-1990s, California has undergone truly dramatic demographic change. Early in the next century, California will become a "minority-majority" state in which whites are a minority of the population. "California's most recent population increases have come almost solely from foreign immigration, both legal and illegal, accompanied by an in-state baby boom, largely of immigrant origin."[14] Despite wholesale changes in the demographic composition of the state as a whole in the last thirty years, the composition of the people who vote has been virtually unchanged. Voters are older, better educated, have higher incomes, and tend to be homeowners rather than renters. Latinos and Asians are much less likely to be voters than are whites or blacks for the following reasons: The ethnic and racial minorities are younger, they are less likely to be registered to vote, and if they are registered to vote, they are less likely to turn out on election day. These trends are reflected in Table 3.5.

The general assumption has been that, as Latinos and Asians become voters, the Democratic Party will be the beneficiary. However, Republicans have done quite well in presidential elections among middle-class culturally conservative Latinos and among Vietnamese.[15]

In the midst of all the racial, ethnic, and class undercurrents of party politics in California, another potentially destabilizing force is a ballot proposition that is likely to appear in 1996. Known as the California Civil Rights Initiative (CCRI), it provides that race, ethnicity, or sex cannot be used as the basis for "discriminating against, or granting preferential treatment to, any individual or group." Like Proposition 187 of 1994, this measure originated with Republican-leaning activists, and it has the same potential to devastate the Democratic Party by driving middle-class swing voters to the Republicans. President Bill Clinton cannot be re-elected without winning California's electoral college votes: He and other Democrats running for U.S. House and state legislative seats in California will face a hostile electorate when one considers the reality posed by Table 3.5. In addition to the political party dynamics involved, CCRI raises absolutely fundamental issues of equality and justice that American culture has never resolved. The proponents of the measure see themselves as trying to achieve the purposes of the federal Civil Rights Act of 1964, because the words of that landmark law are almost identical to the CCRI. The leading advocate for the 1964 Civil Rights Act was Senator Hubert Humphrey, one of the greatest liberals of American history, who said that he would "start eating the pages" of the 1964 act if anyone could find a clause in it that calls for racial preferences or racial balance in education or hiring. The purpose of the 1964 act was to end discrimination, which the act defines as making a "distinction," either for or against an individual or group, on the basis of race, national origin, or sex. Proponents of CCRI assert that if a preference is given to individual A or group A, then individual B or group B is dispreferred or discriminated against. Proponents also argue that preferences divide races and genders rather than unite them.

---

14. Field Institute, "California Opinion Index: Political Demography" (November 1992): 1.

15. Richard Santillan and Federico Subervi-Velez, "Latino Participation in Republican Party Politics in California," in *Racial and Ethnic Politics in California,* ed. by Bryan Jackson and Michael Preston (Berkeley: Institute of Governmental Studies, 1991), pp. 285–318.

Table 3.5 Racial Differences Between Voters and Nonvoters, 1994

| | PERCENTAGE OF | | | |
	POPULATION	CITIZENS ELIGIBLE TO VOTE	REGISTERED VOTERS	VOTER TURNOUT
WHITES	57	71	83	81
BLACKS, LATINOS, ASIANS, AND OTHER MINORITIES	43	29	17	19

Opponents of CCRI, who are almost always Democrats, reject the assumptions, the conclusions, and the motives of CCRI supporters. Opponents point to statistics showing racial and gender discrepancies in earnings, occupational entry, and educational levels that they assert prove that discrimination and racism still exist in the United States and in California. Indeed, Table 3.5 itself shows dramatic social and racial stratification. Opponents say that CCRI is racist in intent and encourages racial polarization. Opponents counterattack by saying that justice requires compensation for hundreds of years of past injuries based on race and gender. They point to the words of the concurring opinion of U.S. Supreme Court Justice Harry Blackmun in *Regents of the University of California v. Bakke,* 438 U.S. 265 (1978): "In order to get beyond racism, we must first take account of race. There is no other way. And in order to treat some persons equally, we must treat them differently." Finally, opponents question the motives of CCRI supporters, saying the measure was put on the ballot not to promote fairness, but rather to win an election.

Should CCRI be approved, the fundamental issue of racial discrimination and racial preferences will hardly be settled. Like its predecessor, Proposition 187, CCRI will lead to a lengthy legal battle in the courts. However the legal ramifications are later determined, the underlying philosophical dispute may never be settled.

Another development that could have important political ramifications is the rise of the Green Party. The Greens have a strongly liberal or left-wing platform that covers a wide variety of issues including a complete ban on pesticides and offshore oil drilling, universal health care, unrestricted abortion, legalization of homosexual marriages, abolition of the death penalty, a 75 percent reduction of defense spending, and publicly financed elections. Although the Greens are still a tiny political party, the reception given them by the Republican Party and the Democratic Party has been decidedly unwelcome. The Republicans completely reject the liberal and left-wing principles of the Greens, saying "The Green Party has red roots." The Democrats, on the other hand, do not necessarily reject the principles of the Greens, but the Democrats are afraid that every vote cast for the Greens is a vote taken away from the

Democratic Party. The Democrats have tried unsuccessfully to prevent the Greens from appearing on the ballot.

Finally, two largely unnoticed, simultaneous trends are at work in California. First, there has been a steady increase since 1968 of voters registered with a minor party and especially those registered as "decline to state." The percentage of registered voters who have not signed up with either the Democrats or the Republicans has gone from 4.5 percent to approximately 14 percent. Second, a much larger group of people *consider* themselves as not part of either party, even if they are registered as Democrats or Republicans. This group has gone from 4.4 percent to 33.7 percent.[16] These data suggest a rather volatile electorate for statewide races—and a very unstable environment for candidates, campaign managers, and campaign watchers.

SUMMARY

In this chapter, we have discussed antipartyism, the Progressive heritage, campaigns and media appeals, voter registration and absentee voting, types of elections, election turnout, campaign-spending issues, political reform, and the parties' changed environment. Antipartyism has many manifestations in California, but it can be seen principally in ticket splitting on the part of voters, weak organizational structures on the part of political parties, and independent campaigns and personalized appeals on the part of candidates. Manifestations of antipartyism are quite striking in races conducted in the competitive statewide arena, but these manifestations also are present in local legislative races. For example, incumbents with strong name identification have an advantage in district races, regardless of party. Furthermore, we can find evidence of antipartyism in any type of election, whether primary, general, or special. Antipartyism is a statewide phenomenon, but some political regions will abandon it for an attractive candidate. Antipartyism, a product of early twentieth-century political reform, has in turn spurred contemporary reform, especially in the area of the corrupting influences of money in politics.

Political parties in California have frequently been said to be electoral mechanisms and not policy mechanisms; that is, they are more effective in winning elections than in formulating public policies. Some cynics even contend that public policy is a means of furthering politics and is not a product of politics; they also argue that public policy is really made by interest groups and not political parties. In any event, we turn to interest groups in Chapter 4.

---

16. Chris Collet, "Independent Voters," *California Journal* (November 1993): 34.

DISCUSSION QUESTIONS

1. Pretend that you are a candidate for the California legislature. Bearing in mind what this chapter has said about antipartyism, how would you conduct your campaign?

2. Whether or not reform is motivated by the best of intentions, it sometimes goes awry. Why is the absentee voting law a "time bomb waiting to explode"? Would you change how nonvoters are purged from the voting lists?

3. Describe a recent example of intraparty factionalism.

4. Is it a contradiction that incumbents in districts with a high registration for their party have an insatiable demand for campaign funds? Why are off-year fund-raising and out-of-district contributions a problem?

5. The Political Reform Act of 1974 reflects the California reform tradition. Name some of its provisions.

6. How can television or radio campaign commercials or direct mail pieces be targeted to a specific audience?

7. How does the demographic composition of the state as a whole differ from the demographic composition of the people who vote?

8. What are the four types of nonvoters?

Chapter 4

Interest Groups

C alifornia is a diverse state. Californians have an amazing number of interests, ideas, and aims that they would like to see reflected in public policy. Therefore, people organize—they form interest groups. Most interest groups exist to protect the economic self-interest of their members, but some groups have formed because they want to move California in the direction of their notion of a good society. Consider the variety of interests represented by the following interest groups:

1. Business
   California Chamber of Commerce
   California Manufacturers Association
   Association of California Insurance Companies
   California Bankers Association
   Mobil Oil
2. Labor
   California Labor Federation
   American Federation of Labor–Congress of Industrial Organizations
     (AFL–CIO)
   California State Employees Association
   California Teamsters Public Affairs Council
   United Farm Workers
3. Agriculture
   California Farm Bureau Federation
   Agricultural Council of California
   California State Grange
4. Professional associations
   California Medical Association
   State Bar of California

5. Education
   Association of California School Administrators
   California School Boards Association
   Alhambra School District
6. Government officials and local governments
   County Supervisors Association
   League of California Cities
   Association of California Water Agencies
   City of San Jose
7. Public utilities
   Pacific Gas and Electric Company
   General Telephone Company
8. Ideological organizations
   American Civil Liberties Union (ACLU)
9. Racial, ethnic, demographic, and religious organizations
   National Association for the Advancement of Colored People (NAACP)
   Mexican American Political Association (MAPA)
   American Association of Retired Persons
   National Organization for Women
   California Catholic Conference
10. Miscellaneous
    California Taxpayers Association
    Sierra Club
    Los Angeles Dodgers
    Girl Scouts
    Ringling Bros. and Barnum & Bailey

Although many interest groups have people who speak for them in Sacramento, not everyone speaks with an equally loud voice, and not all voices fall on equally receptive ears. Spokespeople for local governments, school districts, and government officials are the most numerous, although private business organizations (corporations) are probably the most influential. Groups are usually not concerned with all public questions, only with those affecting their own interests. Many governmental actions "do not concern many people directly . . . [but] they do concern a few vitally."[1] Interest groups can exert maximum influence on issues that do not significantly touch the interests of a large number of people and that do not receive extensive media coverage. Industries that are under fairly close state regulation, such as the liquor industry, railroads, and trucking, must *lobby*—attempt to influence public officials—rather heavily. Groups whose welfare depends on state aid and state legislation must also make their influence felt; for example, many observers rate the California

---

1. Charles R. Adrian, *State and Local Governments,* 4th ed. (New York: McGraw-Hill, 1976), p. 289.

Teachers Association (CTA) as extremely powerful. Interest groups can be considered as a kind of representation, but it is self-interested representation to be sure.

LOBBYISTS

Men and women who speak for interest groups in Sacramento are known as **lobbyists,** or **legislative advocates.** Currently some 950 lobbyists are officially registered, although many lobby part-time or only occasionally. Approximately 1,700 clients are represented.

Lobbying is still primarily a male occupation, but approximately one-fifth of the lobbyists are women. The public's rating of lobbyists is quite low, "somewhere between a used car salesman and a piano player in a house of ill repute."[2] The 950 legislative advocates can be identified by five broad categories:

1. *Private-interest lobbyists* work for a single corporation, industry, or labor union.

2. *Contract lobbyists* are engaged to represent clients in various fields. A famous multiclient lobbyist was the late James O. Garibaldi, who represented the BKK Corporation, California Association of Highway Patrolmen, Hollywood Turf Club, Signal Companies, Philip Morris, and Wine and Spirits Wholesalers. Conflict of interest sometimes becomes a problem for the multiclient contract lobbyist or lobbying firm. For example, one firm represents both tobacco interests and health care interests that are opposed to smoking.

3. *Lobbyists for governments or public utilities* work for such entities as the Public Utilities Commission, regional governments, or local governments. We could include here lobbyists for state agencies (these people are usually called *legislative liaisons* and need not officially register). The governor also has legislative aides, who have been referred to as the "governor's lobby"; they are very influential. Lobbying of this sort is paid for by taxpayers rather than by interest groups.

4. *"Public-interest" lobbyists* represent consumers, environmentalists, children, and poor people.

5. *"Hobbyists"* are people who like to state their opinions before legislative committees.

TECHNIQUES OF INTEREST GROUPS

Interest groups attempt to influence opinion through television, radio, and newspaper advertising. These public-relations efforts can be either short-term (to support or oppose a particular piece of legislation) or long-term (to generate broad support for an organization, industry, or ideology).

---

2. Frank Mesplé and George Cook, "How the Lobbyist Does His Job," in *Capitol, Courthouse, and City Hall,* 6th ed., ed. by Robert Morlan and David Martin (Boston: Houghton Mifflin, 1981), p. 153. Mesplé was a lobbyist for Sacramento County, and Cook was a lobbyist for the California Building Industry Association.

Dennis Renault / The Sacramento Bee

In addition, interest groups attempt to influence legislative opinion. Because thousands of bills are introduced each session, no legislator can be informed about all or even most of them. Therefore, lobbyists provide information for legislators on this myriad of bills. Lobbyists or leaders of interest groups also testify at legislative committee hearings. Participation at such hearings is an important activity because many crucial decisions are made at the committee stage of the legislative process

James Kegley

Lobbyists such as this Sierra Club advocate write bills and advise legislators on strategy, but they exert their greatest influence by making campaign contributions.

(described in Chapter 7). Interest groups can inform legislators concerning the actual effects of a bill under consideration—that is, interest groups can say how the bill will work in practice. When many different groups appear before a legislative committee, it is evident which interest groups are for and which are against the bill. Legislators determine not only the worthiness of the arguments made but also which interest groups might attempt to injure them should they vote against the interests of those groups. The membership of committees with jurisdiction over a group's interests is of vital concern to lobbyists. Interest groups want "friends" assigned to these committees, and they want to keep hostile legislators off them. These groups frequently draft bills and ask friendly legislators to introduce these bills.

Lobbyists also meet informally with legislators on the so-called wine-and-dine circuit. By entertaining legislators, lobbyists hope to establish favorable social relationships with them. The lobbyists' aim, of course, is to increase their access to, and influence over, decision makers. The wine-and-dine technique has been somewhat curtailed in California under the restrictions of the Political Reform Act, which is described at the end of this chapter.

A discussion of the entertaining of legislators brings us to the controversial subject of bribery. Do lobbyists bribe legislators? Of course they do, but not so frequently as the American public might be inclined to believe. Two respected political scientists have written realistically about bribery: "Very simply, it is risky business, for legislators as well as lobbyists; it is costly; it is hard to conceal, for to be effective it must involve a number of lawmakers . . . the prevalence of bribery in any form is grossly exaggerated."[3] California is not so scandal-free as Wisconsin or Minnesota—both are usually described as "cleaner than a hound's tooth"—but it has avoided the excesses of Illinois, New York, and many states in the South. This conclusion is appropriate despite evidence uncovered by a recent highly publicized FBI investigation of corruption in the legislature and despite the fact that a minority of legislators engage in the reprehensible actions described in Reading 4.1 (page 106).

An FBI investigation conducted between 1986 and 1994 called "Bribery Special Interest" or "Brispec" resulted in the bribery convictions for extortion, racketeering, and money laundering of four state senators, one member of the Assembly, five legislative staffers, and one prominent lobbyist. Brispec revealed that some members of the legislature had solicited money for votes on pending legislation. In addition, ethical scandals have also tarnished former U.S. Senator Alan Cranston, former Superintendent of Public Instruction Bill Honig, and former Board of Equalization member Bill Bennett.

Campaign Contributions

Interest groups also make campaign contributions, which some commentators have considered a form of legal bribery. Campaign contributions go overwhelmingly to incumbents because incumbent candidates are most likely to win; the failure of an interest group to contribute to an incumbent legislator may result in the defeat of legislation favored by the interest group or the passage of legislation opposed by the group. In both the 1988 and 1990 elections, the ten interest groups contributing the most money to legislators gave 92 percent of their contributions to incumbents.

Because campaign contributions are the most effective technique of interest groups, we will examine contributions in some detail. Which interest groups are the biggest givers? The ten largest contributors to state legislative candidates in the 1988, 1990, and 1992 elections are listed in Table 4.1 (page 107). Note that many of the same contributors appear every year.

3. William Keefe and Morris Ogul, *The American Legislative Process,* 8th ed. (Englewood Cliffs, NJ: Prentice-Hall, 1993), p. 326.

READING 4.1

A Minority of Legislators Sometimes Misuse Their Positions

- *The massaged bill.* A bill must pass a committee to meet a deadline, but the committee chairman tells the author that there are no votes for it on the panel. That could change with some "massaging," the chairman advises, and heads off a vote on the bill, which dies for lack of a motion. A similar bill is introduced, campaign contributions are made and the second bill becomes law. The key to this maneuver is preventing a vote on the original measure so that switched votes cannot be traced to donations in the interim.

- *The cleanup bill.* This is a common occurrence after passage of a complicated and lengthy bill, such as the reform of the method of taxing assets of multinational corporations, which was enacted a couple of years ago. In each session since, there has been a bill to clean up problems, real

or otherwise, that cropped up with the new law. Wealthy corporations, foreign and domestic, pumped big bucks into the initial legislative battle that ran for years, and now they have to maintain similar interest in follow-up bills to make sure their share of the tax break isn't eroded.

- *The legislator–lobbyist scheme.* A lobbyist who wants to add to his or her client list gets a legislator to introduce a bill that some organization that has no lobbyist would find offensive. He or she notifies the organization of the bill, offers his or her services, and, presto, gets the bill killed. The lobbyist and the legislator share the fee, and the lobbyist has a new client.

SOURCE: Ron Roach, "Scam: 10% of State Legislators May Play Money-for-Influence Game," *San Diego Tribune,* August 31, 1988, p. A8. Reprinted by permission.

Three strategies are used for giving campaign contributions.[4] The first is to give money to incumbents, regardless of party, in order to gain access. Politicians listen much more intently to the groups or individuals who are paying for their re-election campaigns. Needless to say, those who make few or no contributions have greatly reduced access. A second strategy is to give money to candidates of the political party closer to the giver's point of view. Good examples are gun owners (Republicans), Allied Business (Republicans), autoworkers (Democrats), Teamsters (Democrats), AFL–CIO (Democrats), and teachers (Democrats). The third strategy is intended to affect the ideological makeup of the legislature. It attempts to combine the first two strategies and to try to have it both ways: Give to incumbents of either party for access, but also contribute to the candidates of only one party in **open-seat races** when no incumbent is running. Furthermore, larger contributions can be

---

4. California Common Cause, *Twenty Who Gave $16 Million* (Los Angeles: California Common Cause, 1983), pp. 35–37. A word of caution is in order: Money may be *more* important in primaries than in general elections. Because of California's many noncompetitive, gerrymandered districts, the primary is often the real election (see Chapter 7). Those who favor public financing of elections should note this fact.

Table 4.1 The Ten Largest Contributors to State Legislative Candidates, 1987 to 1992

CONTRIBUTORS AND AMOUNTS CONTRIBUTED

RANK	1991-1992		1989-1990		1987-1988	
1	California Medical Association	$1,338,314	California Teachers Association	$1,056,815	California Medical Association	$1,032,562
2	California Correctional Peace Officers Association	1,017,972	California Medical Association	986,573	California Trial Lawyers Association	1,064,079
3	California Teachers Association	992,695	California Trial Lawyers Association	763,639	California Real Estate Association	718,237
4	Allied Business (Evangelical Christians)	917,745	California Real Estate Association	660,051	California Teachers Association	641,450
5	California Trial Lawyers Association	716,722	California Hospitals Association	579,638	California Correctional Peace Officers Association	515,136
6	California Real Estate Association	649,800	AFL-CIO COPE	482,200	California Beer & Wine Wholesalers	467,115
7	Association of California Insurance Companies	604,980	California Dental Association	415,737	Atlantic Richfield Co.	428,180
8	Atlantic Richfield Co.	529,449	California Optometric Association	401,341	California Dental Association	418,286
9	California Dental Association	515,241	Southern California Edison	388,710	California Bankers Association	415,500
10	California Optometric Association	497,271	California Restaurant Association	354,120	IMPAC (Insurance Agents & Brokers)	402,328
Totals		**$7,778,189**		**$6,088,824**		**$6,372,873**

SOURCE: California Common Cause press release, July 1993. Reprinted by permission.

given to candidates of one party. Good examples of the having-it-both-ways givers (with the party getting more) are doctors (Republicans), bankers (Republicans), and state employees (Democrats).

Interest groups are also active at the local level. Important campaign contributors in the city of Los Angeles are real-estate developers, lawyers and bankers, entertainment industry executives, unions for police officers and firefighters, unions for city engineers and architects, Atlantic Richfield and Southern California Gas Company, and a homosexual organization. Similar organizations have "clout" in nearly all cities, as do the Chamber of Commerce, Kiwanis, Lions, Rotary, League of Women Voters, homeowners' groups, renters' groups, construction unions, realtors, antigrowth groups, environmentalists, and historic preservationists.

The impetus for ever-larger campaign contributions does not always come from the donating interest groups. As Reading 4.2 makes clear, the recipients likewise apply pressure. If campaign contributions by interest groups are a form of legal bribery, then what is described in the reading is a form of legal extortion or shakedown.

Other Lobbying Tactics

In addition to making campaign contributions, interest groups also publicly endorse candidates and give them favorable coverage in publications sent to group members. For example, on the eve of elections, union newspapers give extensive coverage to candidates who are considered to be friends of labor.

A different tactic used to influence a legislator through his or her constituency has been called the *rifle* approach—asking people who are influential with an Assembly member or senator to talk to the legislator. Another tactic is the *shotgun* approach, the practice of encouraging **constituents** to write or wire their legislators. In an extreme case, an interest group might threaten to support an opponent in the legislator's next primary or general election. Experienced lobbyists seldom resort to threats because legislators have good memories, and their help may be needed in the future. The words of former Speaker of the Assembly Jesse Unruh are pertinent here: "If I'd slain all my political enemies yesterday, I woudn't have any friends today."[5]

Another legislative strategy is to form coalitions with other interest groups. The purpose of these temporary alliances might be to pass or kill a specific bill. This process may also involve trade-offs or support of other bills. Coalitions of *diverse* interest groups are especially effective because the different elements of the coalition can lobby different legislators; that is, they can piece together a majority composed of different minorities. For example, a coalition of corporations, labor unions, and farm groups would be a force to be reckoned with.

Once a bill has been passed by the legislature, an interest group may urge the governor to sign or veto it. If the bill becomes law, it must be administered; therefore, interest groups also attempt to influence administrators. Although the subject matter

---

5. California Journal, *Political Action Handbook,* 4th ed. (Sacramento: California Journal Press, 1992), p. 16.

READING 4.2

Lobbyists Get Word: "Give"

The leadership of the Senate has given some of Sacramento's top lobbyists a not-so-subtle hint to make larger campaign contributions to upper house Democrats or face a less hospitable reception in the Senate.

No one has been harder hit by the toughened stance than California savings and loan associations. Their lead lobbyist, Larry D. Kurmel, was called into the office of Senate Democratic Caucus Chairman Paul D. Carpenter, D-Cypress, Tuesday night and told that in the last election far more money was given to Assembly members.

The meeting came hours after a controversial bill to allow state-chartered financial institutions to make variable rate loans was temporarily derailed by Senate President Pro Tempore David Roberti. Roberti ruled the measure would have to be sent to the Senate Finance Committee, thus delaying possible passage until August.

The bill, which would allow home mortgages to rise or fall with prevailing interest rates, had been awaiting a Senate floor vote.

Both Carpenter and Roberti denied the meeting with Kurmel had anything to do with delay of the measure.

Carpenter said he had been holding discussions with lending industry lobbyists for "more than a month" about increasing financial contributions.

Nonetheless, the meeting with Kurmel was the latest in a series Carpenter has held with lobbyists. And, Carpenter said in an interview, there will be more with other lobbyists in the future.

"Senate Democrats were receiving a disparate amount," Carpenter said. "People who make contributions apparently feel it doesn't cost any money to be re-elected in the Senate. I don't think it's fair."

The first public indication Senate Democrats were unhappy with the level of contributions came about 10 days ago at a Sutter Club $500-a-plate dinner to benefit the Democratic Caucus. During the dinner, with Roberti and other Senate leaders present, Carpenter told lobbyists he realized large contributions went to Assembly members last year because of a battle over the speakership, according to two lobbyists who attended.

But, he said, Senate Democrats need money too. And he was serving notice they would ask for more.

In the Tuesday meeting, Carpenter said he worked from a black three-ring binder filled with an analysis of savings and loan and lobbyist-controlled political contributions in Sacramento for the last two years.

"I felt they ought to know I had that kind of data," Carpenter said. He added he did not know whether Roberti had the information.

Kurmel refused all comment. "I don't know nothing," he said. "I don't recall any meeting with Sen. Carpenter."

But several other lobbyists say Kurmel has complained of what he called extortion by the Senate leadership.

SOURCE: From "Lobbyists Get Word: 'Give'," *Sacramento Bee,* July 3, 1981, p. A1. Copyright, Sacramento Bee, 1981. Reprinted by permission.

of many laws may be quite complex, laws are typically somewhat ambiguous because legislators want to give administrators flexibility to deal with unforeseen problems and because the interest groups that favored or opposed the bill during the legislative process were unable to work out a satisfactory compromise. Legislators therefore grant substantial authority to administrators to issue rules and regulations necessary to carry out a law. Interest groups want a law carried out in a manner favorable to them. To this end, interest groups often have been instrumental in establishing a new agency or department. Likewise, the interest group may have persuaded the governor to appoint sympathetic department heads or commissioners. Sometimes the interest group *is* the agency, as in the case of state boards that license chiropractors and barbers. The legislature has attempted to correct this problem by requiring the appointment to boards and commissions of more members who are not linked to established interest groups, so-called public members.

Although economic interest groups often loudly oppose government regulation of their activities, they also frequently seek regulation. When the state government licenses such diverse professionals as court reporters, geologists, dry cleaners, architects, cosmetologists, and income-tax preparers, in effect it is limiting access to these professions, thus benefiting those already licensed. Moreover, the state cannot always guarantee that the licensed person is competent. In 1986 the legislature finally abolished the Board of Fabric Care, which was supposed to regulate dry cleaners. Legislators had tried four previous times over two decades but had been unsuccessful. Although created to eliminate incompetent practitioners, the board had canceled only one dry cleaner's license in the previous decade. In fact, it set artificially high licensing standards that had no plausible relationship to quality. In the words of a *Sacramento Bee* editorial, all of the board's actions were intended to "keep competition down and prices up" and the board was "taking the public to the cleaners."[6]

Many people wonder why laws seem to be weakly enforced after they are passed. This problem occurs because the administrative process is an extension of the legislative process and because the struggle for power and influence among interest groups has now shifted from the legislative to the administrative arena:

> Once the legislation is enacted, the supporting coalition tends to lose interest in the matter, assuming that with the enactment of legislation the problem is adequately cared for. The groups that opposed the law and perceive themselves as bearing the brunt of it remain concerned and active. . . . Much more is heard from them by the enforcing agencies and the legislature concerning the undesirable effects of the legislation. The result may be administrative action and legislative changes tempering the original legislation. Conversely, it may become very difficult for supporters of the original legislation to get together again to secure amendments to strengthen the law.[7]

---

6. "Taking the Public to the Cleaners," *Sacramento Bee,* January 21, 1985, p. B6.
7. James E. Anderson, *Public Policy-Making,* 3d ed. (New York: Holt, Rinehart & Winston, 1984), p. 157.

Table 4.2 The Five Interest Groups Spending the Most on Lobbying in 1993–1994

RANK		AMOUNT SPENT
1	Pacific Telesis	$4,826,670
2	California Medical Association	4,109,661
3	California Teachers Association	3,843,928
4	Association of California Insurance Companies	3,512,037
5	Western States Petroleum Association	3,309,923

The intermeshing of public agencies and private groups has long been decried by reformers. The close ties between the Public Utilities Commission and telephone and power companies, between the Department of Education and the California Teachers Association, between the Department of Food and Agriculture and agricultural interest groups have led many observers to compare this nexus of groups and government to the much-discussed military-industrial complex at the federal level.

Interest groups spend a great deal of money lobbying the administrative branch of government and the legislature. The five interest groups that spent the most money in 1993–94 on lobbying are listed in Table 4.2.

Note that many of the groups in Table 4.2 that spend the most on lobbying also spend the most on campaign contributions (see Table 4.1).

After trying to sway legislators, the governor, and administrators, interest groups will seek to influence judges. However, it must be understood that approaching judges necessitates a specific kind of interaction. The medium of interaction is the court case. Groups that have not been influential with the institutions we have mentioned might seek to have a court declare a law unconstitutional by means of the court's power of **judicial review.**

And litigation (bringing suit) is not the final stage. Interest groups also circulate and campaign for initiative laws and constitutional amendments (see Chapter 5). As a last resort, groups may engage in marches or protest demonstrations to dramatize their grievances.

REGULATION OF LOBBYING

In Chapter 3 we mentioned that California voters passed the Political Reform Act (Proposition 9) that contained many provisions, some of which relate to lobbying. Passed in 1974, the act, which has since been amended more than 150 times, requires that every lobbyist—a "person employed or retained . . . to influence legislative or administrative action"—register with the secretary of state and keep detailed records of lobbying expenses. Employers of lobbyists and any person spending more than

Wide World Photos

Former state Senator Paul Carpenter was sent to federal prison as a result of the FBI's "Brispec" bribery investigation.

$5,000 per quarter must also report payments made in support of his or her lobbying efforts. Furthermore, lobbyists may not make gifts of more than $10 to a state officer in any one-month period. The provisions of the Political Reform Act also apply to lobbyists at the city and county levels and to local candidates. A major weakness of the Political Reform Act is that it did not establish an independent prosecutor to bring to trial those who violate the act.

Despite its apparently stringent provisions, the Political Reform Act has not significantly altered lobbyist activity in Sacramento, although wining and dining has been somewhat curtailed. However, entertainment is not so important in the influencing of public officials as are campaign contributions, and limiting these is beyond the scope of the Political Reform Act.

The Political Reform Act has produced a great deal of openness: It is now a matter of public record for anyone to see how much lobbyists spend on their activities, how much money lobbyists contribute and to which candidate they contribute, how much

READING 4.3

How California Podiatrists Won "Battle of the Ankle"

SACRAMENTO—The fight over the bill could properly be called "the battle of the ankle."

Medical doctors and podiatrists fought one another with intensive lobbying and sizeable campaign contributions over legislation that gave podiatrists, who are trained to care for the foot and do not have medical degrees, the legal authority to perform surgery on the ankle.

The California Orthopedic Assn., representing the state's orthopedic surgeons, fears that the medical turf war is not over and that podiatrists will in future sessions try to advance on up the leg.

The podiatry bill was singled out earlier this month by the state Fair Political Practices Commission as the most clear-cut example this year of the effect of big spending in influencing the Legislature.

For seven years, the California Podiatry Assn., representing about half the state's 1,600 podiatrists, had unsuccessfully labored to include the ankle in the legally defined scope of practice of its members—an issue with powerful economic consequences.

This year, after pouring $90,000 into the campaign chests of legislators in less than six months, the podiatrists finally prevailed. The ankle bill, after a close call in the Senate, won legislative approval and became law in July, without the signature of Gov. George Deukmejian.

Deukmejian allowed the bill to pass quietly into law without his endorsement because of "strong opposition from the medical fraternity" on the one hand and no "overwhelming evidence to support a veto" on the other, according to his assistant press secretary, Kevin M. Brett.

Although the podiatrists won the contest that pitted them against the affluent and powerful California Medical Assn., representing about 30,000 medical doctors, and the California Orthopedic Assn., representing half the state's 1,500 orthopedic surgeons, the fight is not over.

The podiatrists' political action committee still had $146,000 on hand after the ankle bill was enacted and have other bills before the Legislature that would give them "parity" with medical doctors in prepaid health plans and on hospital staff committees.

Representatives of both sides deny publicly that money was the deciding factor with this year's bill. Legislators cannot be bought, they say, a point insisted on by several of the legislators themselves.

But at least one orthopedic surgeon said privately: "I think they (the podiatrists) bought the bill, but you can't prove that."

And the chairman of the state Fair Political Practices Commission, Don Stanford, pointed out that the podiatrists, who were pushing for similar legislation in past years, won only when they began making heavy political contributions.

SOURCE: "How California Podiatrists Won 'Battle of the Ankle'," by P. Jacobs, *Los Angeles Times*, September 9, 1983, pt. 1, p. 1. Copyright 1983, Los Angeles Times. Reprinted by permission.

candidates spend on media, direct mail, and so on. But this openness has had a kind of perverse effect. Because everyone knows who is contributing what to whom, politicians can pressure lobbyists for larger contributions by saying, "You gave $25,000 to Senator Jones; why are you only giving $5,000 to me?" The activities described in Reading 4.2, "Lobbyists Get Word: 'Give'," were made possible by the openness mandated by the Political Reform Act. Senator Carpenter, who is mentioned in the reading, has since been sentenced to federal prison as part of the FBI's Brispec investigation.

ATTRIBUTES OF EFFECTIVE INTEREST GROUPS

Some combination of the following factors makes an interest group effective: size (number of members), money, unity (an interest group divided against itself will not be effective), members who are willing to devote time to achieve the group's goals, prestige (the group must be accepted as legitimate by public officials), good leadership and good organization, and a skillful and experienced lobbyist. Interest groups are also helped by weak opponents. Reading 4.3 (page 113) not only describes a clash between three powerful groups but also shows that the legislative process can be distorted by the inordinate amount of time that is spent on bills that have the potential for campaign contributions. The substance of these bills may not be important for society, but if large campaign contributions are at stake, such bills can rivet the legislature's attention.

In recent years, California state and local governments have seen the rise of interest groups with fairly small memberships but with influence far out of proportion to their numbers. Legislators cast thousands of votes each session; however, these groups focus on only single issues such as gun ownership, abortion (either for or against), some environmental matters, and other issues. By the use of direct mail, these single-issue groups can target a particularly motivated audience to raise money, which they then can use to attempt to defeat a legislator who has voted incorrectly from the group's perspective. The weakness of California political parties contributes to the effectiveness of single-issue groups. The actions of these groups reduce political compromise and the building of political consensus, and make coherent policy making much more difficult.

SUMMARY

Interest groups come in all shapes and sizes. In this chapter, we have described their diversity. The range of techniques or strategies used by interest groups is also quite broad. A fear of improper techniques prompted Californians to pass the 1974 Political Reform Act (Proposition 9), which was aimed especially at the activities of interest group spokespersons, called *lobbyists* or *legislative advocates*. Interest groups and their lobbyists are especially strong in a state such as California, which has weak political parties. An important means that interest groups use to achieve their ends is seeking the passage of ballot measures. In Chapter 5 we turn to direct democracy.

DISCUSSION QUESTIONS

1. What kinds of interest groups have lobbyists in Sacramento?
2. Can you name some of the techniques or strategies employed by interest groups? Which of these activities were affected by the 1974 Political Reform Act? Which key activity is not significantly regulated by the act?
3. It is true that interest groups spend much of their time with legislators, but which of their activities are directed toward members of the executive and judicial branches and toward the general public?
4. What factors make an interest group effective? If a special interest had only money, would it still be effective?

Chapter 5
Direct Democracy

The **initiative, referendum,** and **recall** are forms of **direct democracy.** By means of these three processes, average citizens decide public issues directly rather than through representatives. (American government is generally thought of as representative democracy, with citizens electing representatives to decide public issues.) The initiative involves voters making laws; the referendum means voters repealing laws; and the recall involves voters removing public officials before the end of their terms. Not all states have these processes, and the national government does not—having these processes is a matter of state discretion.

States that have the direct democracy devices are generally states in which the Progressives were strong early in this century. As we saw in Chapter 3, the Progressives believed in the wisdom, virtue, and public-spiritedness of the common person. Note that these direct democracy processes were intended to be means by which a wise and virtuous public might promote the public interest and control special interests. Whether the California Progressives built better than they knew or whether they were well-meaning but naive reformers is something for the reader to decide from the information presented in this chapter.

INITIATIVE

The initiative is a means by which voters can enact laws and add amendments to the state constitution. Some initiatives appear in Figure 5.1 as Propositions 5 through 8. The initiative procedure begins with a petition that goes to the attorney general for approval of the initiative's official title and for a short summary that must appear at the head of each petition to be circulated. Those who circulate the petition have 150 days to get the required number of signatures. For an initiative constitutional amendment, the required number of signatures is 8 percent of the number of votes cast for all gubernatorial candidates in the previous election (692,711 valid signatures

MEASURES SUBMITTED TO VOTE OF VOTERS
STATE

1 FOR NEW PRISON CONSTRUCTION BOND ACT. Provides $495,000,000 bond issue to be used for the construction of the state prisons. | + |

AGAINST NEW PRISON CONSTRUCTION BOND ACT. Provides $495,000,000 bond issue to be used for the construction of the state prisons. | + |

2 PRESIDENT OF SENATE. Repeals Constitutional provision that Lieutenant Governor is President of Senate. Fiscal impact: No direct state or local impact. | YES + / NO + |

3 TAXATION. REAL PROPERTY VALUATION. Amends "change in ownership" definition to exclude replacement of property taken by eminent domain type proceedings. Fiscal impact: Significant loss of property tax revenues and increase in administrative costs to local governments. Increased state costs to provide offsetting aid to local school and community college districts. Increase in state income tax revenues due to lower property tax deductions. | YES + / NO + |

4 BAIL. Prohibits release on bail where court makes findings regarding likelihood of released person causing great bodily harm to others. Fiscal impact: Increase jail and bail hearing costs of local governments. Could be offsetting savings if person later sentenced to jail or prison. | YES + / NO + |

5 GIFT AND INHERITANCE TAXES (Proponent Miller). Repeals existing taxes. Reenacts state "pickup" estate tax equal to specified federal tax credit. Fiscal impact: Reduce state revenues by about $130 million in 1982-83, $365 million in 1983-84, and higher amounts thereafter. Save state about $6 million annually in administrative costs. State revenue reductions would result in corresponding reductions in state payments to local governments and schools. | YES + / NO + |

6 GIFT AND INHERITANCE TAXES (Proponent Rogers). Repeals existing taxes. Reenacts state "pickup" estate tax equal to federal tax credit. Fiscal impact: Reduce state revenues by about $130 million in 1982-83, $365 million in 1983-84, and higher amounts thereafter. Save state about $6 million annually in administrative costs. State revenue reductions would result in corresponding reductions in state payments to local governments and schools. | YES + / NO + |

7 INCOME TAX INDEXING. INITIATIVE STATUTE. Provides continuing personal income tax brackets adjustments by using full Consumer Price Index percentage changes. Fiscal impact: Reduce state revenues by about $230 million in 1982-83, $445 million in 1983-84, and increasing amounts thereafter. State revenue reductions would result in corresponding reductions in state payments to local governments and schools. | YES + / NO + |

8 CRIMINAL JUSTICE. Amends Constitution and enacts statutes concerning procedures, sentencing, and release of accused and convicted persons and regarding victims. Fiscal impact: Major state and local costs which cannot be predicted with any degree of certainty. | YES + / NO + |

9 WATER FACILITIES INCLUDING PERIPHERAL CANAL. "Yes" vote approves, "No" vote rejects, a law designating additional Central Valley Project water facilities. Fiscal impact: Under present policies, no increase in state taxes or reduction in funds for other state programs required. Potential construction costs at 1981 prices are in excess of $3.1 billion plus unknown additional costs to be financed by increased user charges. | YES + / NO + |

10 REAPPORTIONMENT. CONGRESSIONAL DISTRICTS. "Yes" vote approves, "No" vote rejects, statute enacted by 1981 Legislature adopting boundaries for 45 Congressional districts. Fiscal impact: If approved, no state or local costs. If rejected, state costs of $250,000 and county costs of $350,000. | YES + / NO + |

11 REAPPORTIONMENT. SENATE DISTRICTS. "Yes" vote approves, "No" vote rejects, statute enacted by 1981 Legislature revising boundaries of 40 Senate districts. Fiscal impact: If approved, no state or local costs. If rejected, state costs of $370,000 and county costs of $500,000. | YES + / NO + |

12 REAPPORTIONMENT. ASSEMBLY DISTRICTS. "Yes" vote approves, "No" vote rejects, statute enacted by 1981 Legislature revising boundaries of 80 Assembly districts. Fiscal impact: If approved, no state or local costs. If rejected, state costs of $400,000 and county costs of $650,000. | YES + / NO + |

Figure 5.1 The June 1982 state ballot included several significant measures. Propositions 5 and 6 both passed, but Proposition 6 received the higher number of votes, so it became law. Proposition 7 is discussed in Chapter 10, and Proposition 8, the "Victims' Bill of Rights," is examined closely in Chapter 8. Propositions 9 to 12 (Chapter 5) are the only referenda to appear on a statewide ballot since 1952.

are required through November 1998). To get 692,711 *valid* signatures, more than that number of signatures must be collected. The secretary of state must reject many signatures because the signers do not live in California, are not registered to vote, or have moved since registering to vote. Many Californians will sign nearly anything if it sounds impressive or if they want to escape the petition circulator. For an initiative statute (law), the required number of signatures is 5 percent of the number of votes cast for all gubernatorial candidates in the previous election (432,945 valid signatures). If the required number of signatures has been obtained within the 150-day period, then the petitions go to the secretary of state for signature verification. The initiative constitutional amendment or initiative statute then goes on the ballot at the next statewide election. How have the initiatives fared? Since 1912 voters have approved approximately 32 percent of the initiative constitutional amendments and initiative statutes on the ballot.

Examples of recent initiatives include:

- the Political Reform Act of 1974 (Proposition 9)
- the nuclear power safety initiative of 1976
- Proposition 13 in 1978
- the 1978 initiative prohibiting school employees from advocating homosexuality
- the "tax-big-oil" initiative of 1980
- handgun control and deposits on bottles and cans in 1982
- the 1984 welfare and reapportionment initiatives
- "deep pockets" (tort liability) and acquired immune deficiency syndrome (AIDS) in 1986
- campaign finance and insurance rate reduction in 1988
- term limits, "Big Green," the gas tax, and criminal procedure in 1990
- physician-assisted suicide, reduced welfare spending, and increased business taxes in 1992
- school vouchers in 1993
- immigration, "three-strikes-and-you're-out," and medical care in 1994.

Clearly, many of the most controversial issues in state government have been thrashed out in the form of initiatives. Sponsors of initiatives (usually interest groups) prefer constitutional amendments to statutes because once legislation has been written into the state constitution, a two-thirds vote of the legislature and another vote by the people (or a completely new initiative amendment) are required to change what has been done. On the other hand, initiative statutes may be revised or repealed by a majority vote of the legislature and can be declared unconstitutional by either state or federal courts.[1] In the event that two conflicting initiatives are approved by the voters, the one receiving the higher vote becomes law. For example, Propositions 5 and 6 (in Figure 5.1) both passed in June 1982. Because Proposition 6 received the higher number of votes, it became law. Initiatives can take effect the day after the election.

---

1. Changes made by the legislature in an initiative statute must be approved by the voters unless the initiative permits such changes without voter approval. Furthermore, initiative constitutional amendments may be declared in violation of the U.S. Constitution.

California citizens who feel strongly about an issue may be able to gather enough signatures to place an initiative on the ballot.

REFERENDUM

The referendum (or *petition referendum,* as it is sometimes called) is the electorate's means of stopping a recently enacted law from going into effect. Except for **urgency laws,** state laws do not take effect for at least ninety days after passage. During this ninety-day period, opponents of a recently enacted statute circulate referendum petitions in an effort to obtain the required number of signatures—5 percent of the votes cast for all candidates for governor in the previous gubernatorial election, the same number required for initiative statutes. If enough signatures are gathered, the law is suspended until the next statewide election, when voters may approve or reject the law. Certain laws are exempt from the referendum procedure, however:

1. urgency statutes, which are passed by a two-thirds vote of each house and take effect immediately

2. statutes providing for taxes

3. laws for appropriating money

4. laws calling for special elections.

In 1982 a referendum to prevent construction of the Peripheral Canal and three referenda to invalidate legislative reapportionment plans appeared on the ballot. (See Proposition 9 and Propositions 10, 11, and 12 in Figure 5.1.) These were the first referenda presented to Californians since 1952.[2] The petition referendum is used more frequently at the local level.

Another kind of referendum—the *compulsory referendum*—is seen frequently at all levels of government. When the state legislature has passed an amendment to the state Constitution or has issued a bond for more than $300,000 (that is, it has proposed that the state go into debt for more than $300,000), the electorate must approve each of these actions by majority vote. However, local bond issues—in cities, counties, and school districts—must receive a two-thirds vote. This requirement means that local bond issues are frequently defeated, although they have received a majority vote. As noted in Chapter 1, the two-thirds vote requirement has serious implications for school district bond issues. Referenda take effect the day after the election. The state legislature may amend or repeal referenda.

PRO AND CON ISSUES

When we discuss the arguments for and against the initiative and referendum, we do not imply that Californians are considering abandoning these devices. Rather, by noting that initiatives and referenda have both virtues and vices, we can better understand them.

Arguments in Favor

Strengthen Popular Control Over Government If American government is government by the people, then initiative and referendum processes allow average citizens to express their will, especially if representative institutions are not reflecting public opinion. Theodore Roosevelt said that "the movements in favor of [initiative and referendum] were largely due to the failure of the representative bodies really to represent the people."[3] Contemporary proponents of direct democracy argue that "the very essence of democracy [is] the right to decide issues."[4] California received

---

2. A group that does not move quickly enough to qualify a referendum during the ninety-day period before a law goes into effect can try to overrule the law by means of an initiative. Proposition 14 in 1964 repealed the Rumford Fair Housing Act of 1963.

3. Quoted in Winston W. Crouch, *The Initiative and Referendum in California* (Los Angeles: Haynes Foundation, n.d.), p. 3.

4. Laura Tallian, *Direct Democracy* (Los Angeles: People's Lobby Press, 1977), p. 2.

such worthwhile improvements as the merit system of state employment and the executive budget by means of the initiative. Without this device, the legislature might have held up these reforms for many years. Whether or not one favors term limits, they could only have been adopted by the initiative process. The only fair and impartial form of publicly financed elections probably will be achieved by the initiative. The political theory of direct democracy was summarized by John Dewey: "The cure for the ailments of democracy is more democracy."[5]

In recent years, the number of initiatives being circulated has increased dramatically. As public confidence in political leaders and governmental institutions goes down, initiative use goes up.

Control Special Interests If moneyed interests have excessive influence in the legislature (as happened in California during the Artie Samish era of the 1940s), direct democracy allows citizens to regain control over their own government. Indeed, direct democracy was first introduced to break the pervasive control of the Southern Pacific Railroad over California politics in the early twentieth century.

Make Legislature Responsive The initiative spurs a lethargic legislature to action, and the referendum serves as a check on unpopular legislation. Moreover, if elected officials are evading or sidestepping vital public issues, these issues can be *publicly* resolved by the initiative process.

Resolve Emerging Issues Because of the weakness of political parties and the public's lack of confidence in elected officials, the initiative and referendum are the best way to resolve emerging or nontraditional issues in such areas as the environment, energy, health, and lifestyle values, among others.

Aid Civic Education As vital questions receive a public airing, Californians' understanding of the issues of the day is furthered: "In the discussion and controversy over popular issues may be found the vitality of California government."[6] Furthermore, as citizens rule themselves directly through these processes, election turnout will be increased and public apathy decreased.

Arguments Against

Impair Representative Government The crucial decisions of American government are supposed to be made by representatives elected by the people. Devices such as initiative and referendum were precisely what the founders of this nation wished to avoid.[7] Furthermore, the existence of the initiative allows the legislature to turn

---

5. John Dewey, *The Public and Its Problems* (Chicago: Gateway Books, 1946), p. 146.

6. Crouch, *The Initiative and Referendum in California*, pp. 10–11.

7. See James Madison, Alexander Hamilton, and John Jay, *The Federalist Papers* (New York: Mentor Books, 1961), and Herbert Croly, *The Promise of American Life* (New York: Macmillan, 1914), p. 320.

over controversial issues to the voters and to abdicate responsibility. Legislators and the governor are elected (and paid) to make decisions, and they should make them.

Lengthen the Ballot Californians already elect a bewilderingly large number of officials at the state, county, city, and special-district levels. Added to this total are numerous ballot propositions. How many citizens can adequately inform themselves on all of these matters?

Aid Special Interests The intent of the California Progressives was to control special interests, but initiatives and referenda have become the *tools of* special interests. In 1912, 85,000 signatures were needed to put a constitutional amendment on the ballot; now, more than two-thirds of a million signatures are needed. Only a wealthy group can get that many signatures. A special-interest group does not need a large membership (although that helps) but, rather, money. It can hire a petition-circulating firm to gather the signatures (at roughly $1.50 per valid signature). Money is not only necessary to get an initiative on the ballot but also even more needed to hire a campaign-management firm to run the initiative campaign and to buy the television and radio time for advertising. In Table 5.1, the ten most expensive initiative campaigns through the 1990 election, note especially the recent astronomical increases in expenditures by interest groups and the frequent large imbalances in spending between contending groups.

A note of caution: The side that spends the greater amount of money in an initiative campaign is not guaranteed success. Lavish spending is probably more effective in defeating a measure than in promoting it. Opponents can hammer away at weak points or inconsistent parts of an initiative. Californians seem to be guided in initiative voting by the premise "When in doubt, vote 'No.'" The inclination to vote negatively is strongest when ballot measures are complicated or confusing. Well-financed initiative opponents can play on this disposition. All of these factors taken together may help to explain why two of every three initiative campaigns fail.

Allow Poorly Drafted Legislation Because an initiative is drawn up by an interest group to further its own goals, the measure may be more the product of ideological zeal than of careful legal drafting. (This is not to say that statutes passed by the California legislature are without fault, but laws passed by the legislature have been drafted by the legislative **counsel** and have survived the give-and-take compromises of the legislative process.) Whatever their merits or defects may be, all initiative and referendum proposals must be accepted or rejected in their entirety. Many initiatives are ruled unconstitutional by the courts.

Contribute to Civic Miseducation Groups do not enter the direct democracy arena because they want to educate the public in a great political science seminar. They usually have financial ends in mind. Misleading claims and emotional propaganda may be more effective than the truth in furthering the aims of these groups. A favorite

Table 5.1 The Ten Most Expensive Initiatives Through the 1990 Election[*]

1. No-Fault Auto Insurance (1988) $37,500,00: Proposition 104 was the most expensive ballot campaign in the nation's history.

2. Tax on Alcohol (1990) $24,208,000: Beer and liquor interests went all out to defeat a tax on their products.

3. Tax on Cigarettes (1988) $23,078,000: Tobacco companies spent eleven times as much as their opponents spent but still could not defeat a tax increase.

4. Oil Conservation (1956) $22,697,000: Various oil companies squared off in a costly turf war.

5. Auto Insurance (1988) $22,487,000: Personal injury attorneys outspent insurance companies on Proposition 100.

6. Big Green (1990) $17,738,000: A hotly debated environmental proposal was defeated by nearly two to one.

7. Right-to-Work (1958) $13,921,000: Labor unions and employers clashed over compulsory union membership.

8. Regulation of Indoor Smoking (1978) $13,462,000: Tobacco companies outspent their opponents ten to one.

9. Handgun Control (1982) $12,398,000: More money was spent on this ballot proposition than was spent by either candidate running for governor in the same year.

10. Tort Liability (1986) $12,273,000: Personal injury attorneys and insurance companies again, this time over personal injury liability.

[*]Propositions have been ranked from most expensive to least expensive in 1988 dollars.

SOURCE: California Commission on Campaign Financing, *Democracy by Initiative* (Los Angeles: Center for Responsive Government, 1992), p. 379.

tactic is to stress slogans that the groups know are false but which they believe will be effective. For example, opponents of the 1972 coastal conservation initiative advertised, "Don't let them lock up our coast," although the initiative was designed to prevent just that. In 1976 opponents of the farm-labor initiative declared that the proposition's access rule violated private property rights, despite the fact that the state Supreme Court, with the silent concurrence of the U.S. Supreme Court, had ruled that private property rights were not violated. In 1980 realtors and apartment owners placed on the ballot an initiative to restrict rent control, but they advertised their measure as furthering rent control. In 1988 the tobacco industry stated that an increase in the cigarette tax would lead to an explosion of crime. In 1990 Speaker of the Assembly Willie Brown waged an expensive media campaign against an initiative to establish a reapportionment commission, labeling it a power grab by large corporations. However, Brown's television campaign was financed by these same oil and chemical companies, banks and insurance companies, and real estate and development interests. Reading 5.1 describes trickery on both sides of an issue.

The essence of the problem is twofold. Voters are asked "to make policy decisions on questions that are often complex, technical, and minutely detailed."[8] For example, the "Big Green" environmental initiative of 1990 was thirty-nine single-spaced pages long. At the same time, "voters seldom have clearly defined opinions about most measures even on the eve of voting. . . . Opinions of this type are often subject to quick change under the pressure of massive propaganda and emotional appeals."[9] The situation favors highly skilled public relations firms that can severely simplify complex issues.

A remarkable tendency in some recent elections has seen voters begin the election year strongly in favor of a particular measure but, after an intensive and expensive media barrage by opponents, defeat the initiative overwhelmingly on election day. The 1978 measure to regulate indoor smoking and the 1982 propositions on handgun control and mandatory deposits on bottles and cans are good examples. Victory usually goes to the side that can define the issues. Opponents often train their media weapons only on a small part of a ballot proposition and then hammer away on that point. For example, opponents of the 1978 clean-indoor-air initiative succeeded in confining the debate to a discussion of intrusion by "big brother government," rather than of research on the harmful effects of secondhand smoke and nonsmokers' rights. (The fact that they could outspend their opponents ten to one was also a key factor here, too.) Had the debate revolved around the latter issue, the result might have been different. Assembly Speaker Willie Brown was the principal force behind the successful 1984 campaign against a reapportionment initiative; after the election was safely over, Brown described the media campaign as "the most extensive collection of con jobs I've ever seen."[10] He also went on to say, "I firmly think the initiative process in California is the single greatest threat to democracy in California."

THE DISTORTION OF THE PROCESS

The initiative is undergoing a gradual but significant transformation in California. It was originally thought of as a gun behind the door to be used only in extraordinary circumstances, but now it has become a *regular* part of the political process. In fact, a member of the state legislature may imply, when introducing a piece of legislation, that if it is not passed he or she will immediately start circulating initiative petitions.

---

8. Charles Adrian, *State and Local Governments,* 4th ed. (New York: McGraw-Hill, 1976), p. 137.

9. "Initiatives: A Question of Control," *Los Angeles Times,* March 26, 1982, pt. I, p. 20. The quotation is from Mervin Field, who operates the respected California Poll, or Field Poll.

10. "Brown Labels Anti-Proposition 39 Ads 'Con Jobs,'" *Los Angeles Times,* November 22, 1984, pt. 1, p. 3. See also David Magleby, *Direct Legislation* (Baltimore: Johns Hopkins University Press, 1984), pp. 59–60, 168.

Proposition 37 Has That Layered Look

Remember that oath that witnesses in court are required to take, the one where they promise to tell the "truth, the whole truth and nothing but the truth?" It doesn't apply to politics.

Take, for example, the campaign for and against the state lottery (Proposition 37) on the Nov. 6 ballot. This is a measure with the layered look.

Ostensibly, a group of Californians worried about the fate of the schools—calling themselves, of course, Californians for Better Education—gathered their collective energies and in the true spirit of volunteerism sponsored a measure to provide more money for education.

Their solution to the perennial needs of the schools would be a lottery that, they said, would provide a half-billion dollars a year.

By and by, it became known that Californians for Better Education was just a front for a corporation called Scientific Games, which is a major supplier of materials for state lotteries and which put up a million bucks for the campaign that put Proposition 37 on the ballot. That was one layer peeled back.

Those who analyzed Proposition 37 carefully concluded that its provisions meant that it would be difficult for anyone other than Scientific Games to obtain the very lucrative contracts to supply materials for what could be a multi-billion-dollar lottery in the nation's largest state.

And then it was revealed that Scientific Games is a subsidiary of the Bally Manufacturing Corp., which is into gambling in several ways, including its domination of the slot machine-making market. Another layer.

Californians for Better Education ran around lining up school board members and others who would place their names on the measure as supporters, trying to provide some legitimacy to the contention that it was all for the kids.

Why education? Because Californians support the public schools. In reality, it would be difficult to guarantee that the proceeds from the lottery would go to education because there is nothing to prevent the governor and the Legislature from "backing out" the money they otherwise would have spent on increases in school aid in the future. That, in effect, would allow the lottery proceeds to go for other state programs. But, as one can readily see, a lottery promoted under the name of "Californians for Higher Welfare Payments" wouldn't go very far. Education is simply a marketing tool to sell California voters on a lottery. It's just another layer.

(continued)

When Howard Jarvis qualified his income-tax-cutting initiative for the 1980 ballot, he did not rely on volunteers to circulate his petition. Instead, Jarvis replaced volunteers with a carefully worded computer-printed letter that contained not only an initiative petition but also a stamped envelope for financial contributions. The experiment was a stunning success. Of the 6 million mailers sent out, 400,000 came

The opposition to Proposition 37 has some layers of its own. Out front, the opponents are political leaders such as Gov. Deukmejian and Attorney General John Van de Kamp, who worry about the impact of expansion of gambling, and the traditionally antigambling churches.

Organizationally, however, the chief opposition is something called Californians Against the Eastern Lottery Fraud, which is conducting a sophisticated media campaign against Proposition 37.

The campaign makes much of the fact that Scientific Games and Bally are bankrolling the pro-lottery campaign.

One TV spot uses two shady-looking characters who chortle over their use of Californians for Better Education as a front to hide that "we had organized crime connections. . . ." That is a reference to a never-proven-in-court allegation that Bally's executives had some dealings with organized crime figures.

That's hardball politics, perhaps, but within the parameters of legitimacy.

It turns out, however, that Californians Against the Eastern Lottery Fraud is not exactly a grassroots citizens group either.

Campaign finance statements reveal that virtually all of the money for the slick anti-Proposition 37 campaign comes from the state's horse racing tracks. Another layer.

Now why would the horse racing people care whether there is a state lottery?

One theory is that there's only so much gambling action available and at least some of the money that would be spent on lottery tickets would be money that otherwise would go for $2 bets on horse races.

But it's also interesting to note that the horse racing executives who are putting up cash for Californians Against the Eastern Lottery Fraud had a lottery proposal of their own in the Legislature. Called a "special sweepstakes," the horse racing lottery would have provided daily payoffs based on results of specified races—with much of the money going to the tracks and the breeders.

If Proposition 37 is passed, the horse people can kiss their "special sweepstakes" goodbye.

Another layer.

SOURCE: From "Prop. 37 Has Layered Look," by Dan Walters, *Sacramento Bee,* October 17, 1984, p. A3. Copyright, Sacramento Bee, 1984. Reprinted by permission.

back with 820,000 signatures, far more than needed to qualify the measure. Half of the returned envelopes contained contributions; they totaled $1.8 million. The whole effort paid for itself.

Direct mail firms advertise that computer-assisted mailing is cheaper than paid petition circulators. A company will rent to clients a list of people who have contributed to initiative campaigns. This list can be used repeatedly and refined, paving the way for successive campaigns by groups or wealthy individuals with an interest or cause to promote. Hiram Johnson and the California Progressives would have a difficult time recognizing their brainchild; nowadays the initiative is viewed not as an extraordinary remedy for political abuses but as a regular method for accomplishing political aims. Moreover, instead of concerned citizens asking other citizens face-to-face to support an initiative that will shatter special-interest influence, a computer cranks out clever letters for those who can pay the price.

The direct mail firm is an integral part of what has come to be known as the "initiative industry." This industry consists of profit-making firms that are in the long-term business of promoting initiatives. Such firms can draw up the initiative, using staff lawyers aided by campaign consultants who will word the proposition for maximum political appeal. The firm can then gather the required signatures, manage the subsequent media campaign, and later use its attorneys to fend off any legal challenges to the successful initiative. The initiative industry is a peculiarly California brand of "one-stop shopping." Because these firms plan to stay in business for a long time, they are always looking for creditworthy customers with an idea to promote. It is also not inconceivable that firms in the industry might think up a winning idea and then search out a group with seed money to fund the campaign. The basis is laid for nonstop initiative campaigns in a kind of political perpetual-motion machine. According to one longtime observer of California politics, the initiative process "is becoming a self-perpetuating system in which the major winners are campaign consultants, lawyers, pollsters, signature-gatherers, computer mail specialists, electronic media, and billboard companies."[11]

The ways in which use of the initiative has become distorted is probably most graphically demonstrated by the November 1988 election, in which the voters faced five initiatives dealing with insurance-rate regulation. Insurance companies and personal injury attorneys spent an amazing $1.64 billion (an amount equivalent to the entire state government budget in the mid-1950s) in an attempt to further their special interests. Issues such as whether no-fault insurance should be adopted or to what extent the insurance industry should be regulated are essentially legislative questions, but the legislature had failed in its role as policy maker. Both groups had made extensive campaign contributions to legislators: Republicans were indebted to the insurance companies, and Democrats were beholden to the personal injury attorneys. The result was a stalemated legislature that could not take action in the face of rapidly rising auto insurance rates. The fault for escalating insurance rates rests with both the insurance companies and with the lawyers who sue insurance companies—and the fault also lies with them for a deadlocked legislature on this issue. The legislature should have been a neutral decision maker, sifting through the competing

---

11. Richard P. Simpson, quoted in Robert T. Monagan, *The Disappearance of Representative Government: A California Solution* (Grass Valley, CA: Comstock Bonanza Press, 1990), p. 78.

claims of insurers and lawyers as it protected the public interest of all Californians. Instead, the legislature was fearful of offending either powerful group—or each political party in the legislature had made a Faustian bargain and was unable to act—so it did nothing. The legislature was waiting for the two interest groups to "cut their own deal," which the legislature could later ratify by a statute. But the insurers and lawyers have been bitter enemies for years, thus no "deal" was forthcoming. With frequent use of the initiative for selfish purposes an accepted part of the state's political environment, an alternative was readily available. The result was a garish billion-dollar campaign in which the only measure to pass was one pushed by a third party (the Ralph Nader Proposition 103 group) that did not stand to gain financially from its effort.

Recent elections have also provided three further distortions of the initiative process: the counterinitiative, the candidate's initiative, and the diversionary initiative. The *counterinitiative* is a weapon used by business and agriculture in their long-running struggle with environmental groups and liberal politicians. If the latter groups qualify an initiative for the ballot that is stringent or even extreme, business and agriculture qualify a counterinitiative that will accomplish many of the same goals but which is much less far-reaching. The idea is that simply spending money against an initiative that you oppose is not effective; it is better to propose your own alternative, which may appear more moderate. Should the industry–agriculture initiative actually get more votes, its provisions will go into effect. On the other hand, two (or more) initiatives on the same subject may so confuse voters that all of the measures will be rejected. In any event, the proponents of the counterinitiative have achieved their objective. The *candidate's initiative* allows a person running for office to generate favorable media publicity by sponsoring an initiative on a popular issue. In 1990 Pete Wilson sponsored one initiative and John Van de Kamp sponsored three as part of their campaigns for governor. The *diversionary initiative* is an initiative placed on the ballot not because its proponents expect it to pass, but because they want their enemies to divert (and waste) money to defeat it. Proposition 167 (described in Chapter 10) may have been a diversionary initiative intended to draw corporate money away from another initiative and also away from Republican candidates.

As initiative use has increased since the 1980s, so have proposals for reforming the initiative. Many of the reform proposals are really intended to thwart the initiative. However, Philip Dubois and Floyd Feeney have suggested five useful changes:[12]

1. Initiative propositions should be worded so that an affirmative vote is a vote to adopt the proposal, and a negative vote is a vote to defeat the proposal.
2. The ballot itself should contain a brief statement explaining the effect of a "yes" vote and the effect of a "no" vote.

---

12. Philip Dubois and Floyd Feeney, "Improving the California Initiative Process," *California Policy Seminar Brief,* 3 (November 1991): 4.

3. Initiatives currently appear on the ballot after bonds and constitutional amendments referred by the legislature. To minimize voter confusion, initiatives should appear first on the ballot (and also first in the ballot pamphlet).

4. Every print or electronic advertisement for or against an initiative should identify the advertisement's largest funding source. The source could be an industry, group, company, labor union, or individual; it is the largest source of funding if it has contributed at least $50,000 to the campaign and if no other funding source has contributed more.

5. The state legislature should pass a law requiring political action committees (PACs) to use names that clearly identify the committee's economic interest or the common employer of the majority of its contributors.

The Dubois–Feeney reforms are intended to increase useful information for voters so that they might make more informed choices. Another reform in this vein is to require tax-reduction initiatives to specify where spending must be cut or to require new- or increased-spending initiatives to specify how they will be financed.

We wish to end this discussion of initiative use at the state level on a positive note. Please see Reading 5.2 (page 130).

RECALL

The recall is a means by which state or local elected officials—from the governor to local school board members—can be removed from office before the end of their terms. (Members of the U.S. House of Representatives and U.S. Senate, because they are federal officials, cannot be recalled.) The recall, like other direct democracy devices, begins with a petition.

To initiate the recall of an officer elected statewide, a group must obtain valid signatures equal to 12 percent of the votes cast for that office in the previous election, and signatures must come from at least five counties (to prevent a single large county such as Los Angeles from recalling state officials). The number of signatures in each of these five counties must equal at least 1 percent of the votes most recently cast for the office in that county.

The recall of other state officials—such as judges, members of the legislature, and members of the Board of Equalization—requires signatures equal to 20 percent of the most recent vote cast for the office. The petition must state the grounds for removal, but this statement typically is couched in vague terms. Officials need not do something illegal to be recalled; the grounds for recall may amount to no more than personal animosity.

Recall supporters must file their petitions with the California secretary of state within 160 days after they begin circulating them. If the required number of signatures has been secured, then the governor must call a recall election within 60 to 80 days after the petitions have been certified by the secretary of state. The ballot

---

READING 5.2

Proposition 161:
For Once, the Process Worked Pretty Well

In 1992, California voters had to decide the most dramatic and compelling of all public policy issues: the taking of human life. Proposition 161 would have established in California a right to physician-assisted suicide. Fortunately for Californians, the initiative process worked pretty much as its founders hoped that it would: the electorate was presented with a sophisticated debate remarkably free of the media hype and misleading arguments that characterize most ballot campaigns. Proponents of the measure, which included the American Civil Liberties Union (ACLU) and the Hemlock Society, argued that the measure would reduce unnecessary pain and suffering. Proposition 161 was said to be the only way a terminally ill person could die with dignity by allowing the person to request that a doctor kill him or her gently and humanely. Responding to the argument of opponents that the measure lacked sufficient safeguards, proponents noted that the request for euthanasia could be terminated at any time and that euthanasia is a medical procedure covered by California's strict "informed consent" laws. Under the informed consent process, doctors are legally required to discuss with patients alternatives to a medical procedure before performing that procedure. Finally, proponents made a personal autonomy or individual rights argument: "It's my body, I ought to have the right to do what I want with it."

In many striking ways, the debate over physician-assisted suicide echoed the intense debate over abortion. Opponents were led by religious conservatives, especially the Catholic Church, who argued that no one should have the right to take innocent human life. They argued that those most likely to die by physician-assisted suicide are the elderly, the poor, the weak, the powerless, the uneducated, the crippled, and the retarded. As Chapter 1 indicated, California faces increased competition between the older generation and the younger generation for scarcer and more costly medical care. Euthanasia might come to be viewed as the cheapest way out of this serious situation. Opponents of Proposition 161 argued that California should not abandon its duty to care for the elderly and the incurably ill. Opponents argued that, if the measure were approved, the elderly, the disabled, or the terminally ill would be subjected to overt or covert pressure to kill themselves so as not to be a financial burden on their families. Finally, opponents stressed the argument that Proposition 161 lacked sufficient safeguards: because there was no minimum waiting period between the request for physician-assisted suicide and the carrying out of the procedure, there was said to be insufficient time for a depressed person to reflect on what was happening.

Proposition 161 was rejected by the voters 54 percent to 46 percent. For this one instance, one in which significant issues of individual rights and the value of human life were seriously debated, the initiative process rose above the hype and the invective that typify the usual debates over crass economic self-interest.

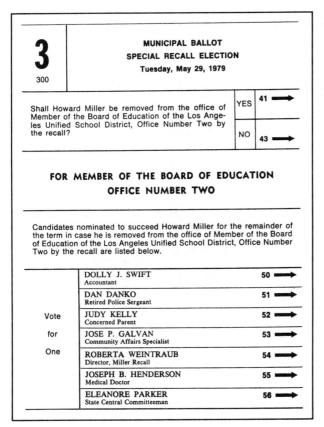

Figure 5.2 Sample ballot, May 29, 1979

in this election requires two distinct choices. First, the voters decide a question similar to the following: "Shall Joe Zilch be recalled from the office of ——————? Vote yes or no." A majority of "yes" votes is needed to recall the incumbent. Next follows a list of candidates, excluding the incumbent, who would like to serve the rest of the unexpired term. Only a plurality vote is needed for victory in the second step of the process. If a majority of votes is negative in the first step on the ballot, then all votes for candidates in the second step are disregarded. Figure 5.2 shows the ballot used in the successful 1979 recall of the chairperson of the Los Angeles School Board.

Although it thrives at the local level, recall has never been a realistic threat at the statewide level in California. From time to time, the opponents of a governor or state supreme court justice will circulate recall petitions, but this gesture is not a serious attempt: It is more a form of harassment, a ploy to embarrass the governor or justice. If an official's opponents get the required number of signatures (an unlikely event, considering the 12 percent requirement) but the recall attempt fails, then the state

Bettmann

Voter turnout in California is too low, but fortunately it is a problem that you can help solve.

will reimburse the official for all expenses incurred in defeating the recall. Therefore, he or she is encouraged to make every effort because as far as spending is concerned, the sky is the limit. But, of course, the official had better beat the recall attempt.

As noted in Chapter 7, angry Republicans in 1995 recalled Assembly member Paul Horcher of Diamond Bar. Horcher had been elected in 1994 as a Republican, but his first official act after election was to change party affiliation to Independent and vote for Democrat Willie Brown as Speaker of the Assembly. Horcher's action prevented the Republicans from gaining a majority in the Assembly for the first time in a quarter of a century. This was the first successful recall of a member of the state legislature in more than eighty years.

In closing our discussion of recall at the state level, we give one word of caution: recall should not be confused with impeachment. Recall is done by *the voters,* but impeachment is done by the *legislature.* Impeachment requires allegations of serious lawbreaking; recall does not.

DIRECT DEMOCRACY AT THE LOCAL LEVEL

Referendum and recall are rare at the state level but frequent at the local level. The initiative occurs frequently at both levels. Recalls of local officers such as mayors, city council members, and especially school board members, occur quite frequently, and

READING 5.3

Voters Angry About Tax Oust Council

. . . The entire Covina City Council was recalled Tuesday because of the city's controversial utility tax. Voters ousted all five council members by wide margins, signaling their displeasure with the 6 percent tax imposed by the Council last year when the city was struggling with a $2.3 million budget deficit.

"This is Proposition 13 revisited," said Earl Purkiser, a leader of the recall movement. "Political leaders throughout the San Gabriel Valley and beyond will see what happened here and conduct themselves with the will of the people in mind. . . . We can put them in and we can take them out.". . .

Covina's tax shows up on gas, electricity, water, and telephone bills. The average household pays about $12.60 a month. Opponents said the tax would not have been needed if the Council had kept a tight rein on finances. Council members say the utility tax was necessary to preserve police, fire, and library services in the wake of a slump in sales tax revenue and the loss of property tax funds to the state. Changing the faces on the Council, they said, will not make the city's financial problems disappear.

City officials said 32 percent of the voters cast ballots, a record for recent municipal elections. A simple majority of votes was needed to recall any Council member.

SOURCE: "Voters Angry Over Tax Oust Board," by Andrew LePage, *Los Angeles Times,* July 14, 1993, p. B1. Copyright 1993, Los Angeles Times. Reprinted by permission.

about half of them are successful. In small communities particularly, recall elections can be terribly bitter and divisive and may lead to recriminations and counterrecalls. In the aftermath of a recall, residents may not cooperate with one another for many years, and divisions within the community may deepen. In some communities, the recall may be used to remove incompetent officials who fail to act or who act wrongly. In other communities, recall might be used to remove competent officials who have pursued unpopular policies too energetically. Reading 5.3 describes a local recall.

As Chapter 9 indicates, growth control became an extremely important issue at the local level throughout the state in the latter half of the 1980s. The initiative and referendum were used in numerous cities to limit "residential building permits, set aside areas for agricultural protection, zone lot sizes on hillsides, and require commercial development proposals to be approved by voters."[13] As we will see later, direct democracy was used at the local level to take over control of the land-use planning process from government officials. On the positive side, many of the antigrowth initiative and referendum proposals struck a responsive chord with the

13. Dan Smith, "Crusade against Growth," *Golden State Report* (January 1988): 28.

public. On the negative side, many were also poorly written and inflexible because they had not gone through the environmental-review and public-hearing process that the planning commission and city council conduct for typical development projects.

SUMMARY

Initiative constitutional amendments, initiative statutes, the referendum, and the recall are instruments of direct democracy intended to serve the public when elected representatives fail to act. For example, California's Proposition 13 was the opening gun of a nationwide tax revolt. Property-tax relief had been a prime legislative and gubernatorial concern for more than a dozen years, but not until Californians reached for the gun behind the door were results obtained.

Beyond the merits or demerits of any specific measure such as Proposition 13, we have considered pro and con arguments about the wisdom of direct democracy itself. However one evaluates direct democracy—and sensible men and women can be found on either side—the process reflects something of the self-confident spirit of California itself. Initiative use is on the rise, partly as a result of the efforts of the initiative industry and partly as a result of a public policy gridlock in state government, especially in the state legislature, in which powerful interest groups seem to have checkmated one another. Another source of public policy gridlock in the legislature is that legislators elected as Democrats tend to be ultraliberal, and those elected as Republicans are ultraconservative. Compromise is in short supply, so the legislature finds it difficult to legislate on important issues. If gerrymandered districts have produced insulated and unresponsive legislators, one alternative for dissatisfied individuals and groups is to "go the initiative route."

DISCUSSION QUESTIONS

1. *Resolved:* Direct democracy has worked about as well as the Progressives believed that it would work. Argue one side of this issue, then argue the other side. In this exercise, you need not become like the ancient Greek Sophists, who would argue any side of any question because they did not believe in the possibility of truth. Rather, by knowing the strongest and weakest elements of an argument, you can better understand the issues involved.

2. Neal Pierce, a writer on state government, suggests that California return to the indirect initiative. Under an indirect initiative process, a minimum number of signatures can force the legislature, not the general public, to vote on a measure. The legislature may pass the measure, amend it, or reject it. If the legislature chooses either of the latter two, the measure's sponsors can require that the original measure go on the ballot. Evaluate this proposal.

3. As you answer the following questions, consider what your answers reveal about the theory and practice of direct democracy. Why are more signatures required on a petition for an initiative constitutional amendment than on a petition for an initiative statute? Have most initiatives been approved by the voters? Why are some laws exempt from the petition referendum? Do you favor extending the petition referendum to laws that levy taxes and spend public money? Are the signature requirements for recall of state officials too high? If state officials could be forced into a recall election with fewer signatures, how would the conduct of state government be changed?

Part Three
MAJOR INSTITUTIONS

*T*he major institutions of government in California are the executive branch, the state legislature, and the state court system. These institutions of government determine and resolve questions of policy.

In Chapter 6, we will study the office of governor and other executive offices such as those of the attorney general and the state controller. Various boards, commissions, and agencies are also part of the executive branch, but the towering figure in the executive branch and in all of state government is the governor, the person who provides the leadership for California government. The governor's position is preeminently a policy position. The one policy maker most likely to have a significant effect on the issues we mentioned earlier—in the areas of energy, jobs, education, and so forth—is the governor.

We will consider the California legislature in Chapter 7. In the legislature, most of the great issues of state government are debated and voted upon, and the state budget is passed. Academic observers once rated California's as one of the best state legislatures in the country. It can be a formidable adversary for the governor.

The state court system is the topic of Chapter 8. A wise political philosopher once wrote, "Scarcely any political question arises in the United States that is not resolved, sooner or later, into a judicial question."[1] Controversial issues such as environmental protection, school finance, the death penalty, water rights, and integration have all been ruled upon by the state courts.

---

1. Alexis de Tocqueville, *Democracy in America*, ed. Phillips Bradley (New York: Vintage Books, 1945), 1:290.

Chapter 6
Executive Branch

*I*n this chapter, we consider the executive branch of state government, which consists of the governor, the governor's cabinet, other state constitutional officers, a wide array of agencies and departments, and various boards and commissions.

The public expects the governor to be chief executive, or head of the executive branch, and holds the governor accountable for the performance of the executive branch. However, for reasons we will examine, the state Constitution really invites the governor to strive to be the chief of the executive branch. Some governors are more successful than others.

Despite the office's limitations, the governor of California is the most important person in state politics and one of the most important people in national politics as well. California's governors have often been individuals of great stature or personal magnetism who have left indelible marks on the state's history and have also influenced national events. A sketch of gubernatorial powers follows. Bear in mind that whether a governor uses these powers creatively or perfunctorily is largely determined by the individual governor's conception of the office.

POWERS OF THE GOVERNOR

Each year, the governor delivers the State of the State message, a report to the legislature about the condition of the state. This message typically is rather general, but it is soon followed by a package of specific bills—the governor's legislative program—that may constitute the legislature's agenda for much of the upcoming session. The aphorism "the executive proposes and the legislature disposes" is simplistic but accurate: The person who most influences what the legislature produces does not even belong to the legislative body. The extent of the governor's legislative success depends on many factors: public popularity, especially as gauged by respected public opinion polls such as the Field Poll; how many seats his or her party has in each chamber of the legislature; the loyalty of members of the governor's party; the governor's ability to work with the legislative leadership; and the issues on which the governor chooses to take a stand.

In any case, we have noted that one of the ways the governor can exercise power is by vetoing bills passed by the legislature. Although recent governors have vetoed 12 percent of all bills passed, the threat of a veto is nearly as important as the act itself. By using this threat, the governor can prevent laws or parts of laws from passing the legislature in the first place. The veto can also crucially affect the many bills, often the key ones of the session, that are passed at the end of the session.

The legislature can override a governor's veto by a two-thirds vote in each house, but the chances of this happening are slim indeed. Since 1946, there have been only seven successful overrides of a governor's veto. The unfortunate governors were Earl Warren (once), Ronald Reagan (once), and Jerry Brown (five times). In July 1979, after relations between Brown and the legislature had seriously deteriorated, he was overridden three times in a single month! (Two bills would have allowed retroactive pay increases for state employees; the third prohibited banks from selling automobile, homeowner, and casualty insurance.)

The governor's most significant duty is to submit the state budget to the legislature in the first ten days of each year. The governor recommends expenditures, estimates revenues, and sometimes proposes new sources of revenue. The financial problems that California has faced since 1990 make the crafting of a budget the governor's number one responsibility and a major drain on his or her time and energy. Chapter 10 describes how Governor Pete Wilson has approached California's fiscal crises.

When the legislature has modified and returned the budget bill, the governor may exercise an **item veto.** This weapon allows the governor to reduce or eliminate, but not raise, any item in an appropriations bill. The item veto is a powerful tool because it prevents the legislature from presenting the governor with take-it-or-leave-it spending bills. Rather, the governor can use the threat of an item veto to pressure the legislature. (In 1995, Congress passed a statute giving the president of the United States an item veto.) The potency of the item veto in the hands of a conservative Republican governor was clearly demonstrated by Governor George Deukmejian. The "Iron Duke," as he was called by his opponents, would send the budget to the Democratic legislature in January. The latter would then debate the budget for the next six months and amend it extensively by increasing appropriations. When Deukmejian received back his heavily amended budget in June, he would use his item veto to return the budget to nearly the identical form in which he had sent it to the legislature earlier. Backed by the members of his own party in the legislature who would prevent a veto override, Deukmejian was able to relegate the Democrats who controlled the legislature to almost superfluous participants in the budgetary process.

In addition to the veto power, the governor may call the legislature into special session, during which it must act only on the topics specified in the session's proclamation issued by the governor. By convening a special session, the governor obliges the legislators to settle specific issues they have avoided (or over which they have been deadlocked) or to deal with a current crisis. Recent special sessions have dealt with Orange County's bankruptcy and problems in the workers' compensation system. (Special sessions are also discussed in the next chapter on the state legislature.)

Along somewhat different lines, the governor makes approximately 3,000 appointments, but as indicated earlier, California is not a high-patronage state. For example, the governor appoints agency secretaries and department heads, such as the secretary of resources and the director of the Department of Motor Vehicles, and makes appointments to boards and commissions, such as the Public Utilities Commission, the Trustees of the California State University System, and the Board of Governors of the state's community colleges. In addition, should any of the following die or resign, the governor may name a successor: U.S. senator, state constitutional officer (for example, attorney general or secretary of state), or county supervisor. As we shall see in Chapter 8, the governor also appoints judges. The characteristics of the men and women appointed to these positions are of great interest, because they provide an idea of a governor's basic beliefs. For example, many of former Governor Jerry Brown's appointees viewed themselves as agents of change, people dissatisfied with traditional practices and interested in trying avant-garde or even radical approaches in state and local government.

Some of the governor's nominations require approval by the Senate or by both chambers of the state legislature. Governors Deukmejian and Wilson each suffered rejections of important nominees by legislatures controlled by the opposing party. If the power to veto legislation gives the governor the upper hand in the legislative process, the roles can be reversed when it comes to filling high-level executive positions.

Gary G. Hamilton and Nicole Woolsey Biggart have described the governor's relationships with the top nonelected officials in the executive branch and have also evaluated Governors Reagan and Brown as administrators.[1] The governor's personal staff is extremely important because of the many vital issues demanding attention and because the governor's time is limited. These people make many important decisions on behalf of the governor, but they do not exercise authority in their own right—all their authority is derived from the governor. The governor's immediate staff is characterized by personal loyalty to the governor as an individual and by a lack of independence: They tend to be younger people who do not have particularly strong personalities or established nongovernmental careers or even bases of political support outside the governor's office. In other words, they are individuals without competing commitments who have a dependent relationship with the governor. (The staff person's power is measured by his or her amount of access to the governor.)

Typically, the appointed agency secretaries and department heads are older than the governor's personal staff, have considerable experience in a profession, have standing in their community, and are prominent among the clientele served by their

---

1. Gary G. Hamilton and Nicole Woolsey Biggart, *Governor Reagan, Governor Brown* (New York: Columbia University Press, 1984), especially pp. 75–83, 201–213.

agency or department. Although they have been given statutory authority to run important state programs, appointed department heads are characterized by loyalty to the governor's goals and political philosophy.[2]

When Ronald Reagan was governor, he employed a powerful chief of staff (either William Clark or Ed Meese, both of whom also served Reagan when he was president). The chief of staff established formal lines of communication that required all communications to the governor to be routed through him; the duties of other staff people were strictly defined by the chief of staff, who systematized and routinized the governor's office. Reagan's cabinet, consisting of agency secretaries and the governor's top personal aides, met twice a week to discuss the most important matters facing state government and to recommend courses of action, which Reagan usually followed or ratified. Although Reagan always attended these cabinet meetings, he disliked conflict among his top people, and he encouraged them to practice consensus management. Agreement was facilitated by the fact that all of his top appointees believed in Reagan's philosophy.

Governor Jerry Brown's management style contrasted sharply with Reagan's: He encouraged disagreement among his top aides, selected advisors who advocated controversial points of view, did not delegate authority to his top aides in a systematic fashion, and did not meet regularly with his cabinet or use it as a forum for reaching decisions. Moreover, Brown frequently let issues reach a crisis stage before making a decision. His reason for holding office was to use it as a forum for articulating ideas that would foster social change. Hamilton and Biggart note the irony that despite the numerous ideas propounded by Jerry Brown, his ideas often did not become public policy because his top aides and appointees were not concerned with governing and because Brown did not have a coherent philosophy.

The management style of George Deukmejian was similar in many respects to Reagan's. In the person of Steven Merksamer, Deukmejian had a powerful chief of staff who ran a highly structured office. Moreover, like Reagan's, Deukmejian's cabinet met twice a week.

As governor, Pete Wilson's decision-making style is strangely similar to that of Jerry Brown, rather than to the style of Wilson's Republican predecessors. The *Los Angeles Times* describes Wilson's style as "circuitous": "he personally examines a problem from every angle and down to the finest detail before committing himself."[3] And, like Brown's method, Wilson's causes frustrating delays.

As some of the above discussion suggests, the governor is also a policy coordinator. Some federal grant programs designate the governor as the state coordinator and planner, and the money for the program is channeled through the governor's office. California, like more than half of the states, also has a Washington, D.C., office. The office's chief of staff, who is appointed by the governor, is a spokesperson for the state and for the governor.

---

2. Agency secretaries and department heads often feel cross-pressured because they are also loyal to the interest groups that suggested that the governor appoint them to their current posts.

3. "The Trick to Getting Wilson's Ear," *Los Angeles Times,* June 6, 1993, p. A1.

Several features of the legislative process hamper the governor's efforts to coordinate policy. Legislative bills come from many sources, and once these bills are introduced, numerous legislative committees and political factors further shape them. When the bills become laws, different state and local agencies must carry out these laws. The governor is the only official in a position to give a unified direction to this fragmented process:

> Aside from the office and person of the governor, there is no one in a position to provide constant and authoritative review and coordination of policy—the kind of review and coordination needed to minimize program duplication and overlap, . . . to see to it that certain vital problems are not forgotten or ignored, and to make sure that one set of state policies does not counteract others. . . . [The governor] is in a position to maintain some amount of overall perspective on state government activities.[4]

Through the power to appoint agency heads and most members of regulatory commissions, the governor can form vertical coalitions to counteract the horizontal coalitions of middle-level civil servants, their legislative allies, and influential interest groups. To achieve a consistent set of state policies, the governor must master the nexus of groups and government described in Chapter 4. The governor's executive-branch subordinates—the nonappointed civil servants—may be more loyal to their agencies or to outside interest groups than to the governor. Influential legislators approve the budget requests of cooperative administrators and at the same time receive campaign contributions from interest groups regulated by those administrators. State policy making could become dominated by discrete coalitions of administrators, legislators, and interest groups. One of these coalitions might control education policy; another, agricultural policy; another, energy policy; and so on. To prevent this development and to further broader state interests, the governor must use all the appointive and budgetary power available and must also appeal for public support.

Apart from coordinating policy, the state's chief executive also has several specific duties related to the criminal justice system. These include **clemency powers**. The governor may grant a pardon (release from the legal consequences of a crime), a **commutation** (reduction of sentence), or a **reprieve** (postponement in carrying out a sentence). Applying the clemency power in the case of a capital offense can involve a governor in heated and dramatic controversies, as Governor Pat Brown discovered in the famous Caryl Chessman case of 1960.

Chessman, who was known as the "Red-Light Bandit," had been convicted in 1948 of the kidnapping and brutal rape of a teenage girl. By complicated legal maneuvering and repeated stays of execution, Chessman postponed death for twelve years. Governor Brown, who opposed capital punishment, could not commute Chessman's sentence to life imprisonment because of Chessman's prior felony conviction. Accord-

---

4. John A. Straayer, *American State and Local Government* (Columbus, OH: Merrill, 1977), pp. 110–111.

ing to Article V, Section 8 of the state Constitution, the governor may not grant a pardon or commutation to a person twice convicted of a felony unless at least four of the seven state Supreme Court justices grant this permission. The state Supreme Court would not approve commutation of Chessman's sentence. At the last minute, Brown gave Chessman a sixty-day reprieve and called the legislature into special session to consider a bill to abolish the death penalty. The legislature was bitterly divided, and the state was in an uproar. Brown "did not exert himself on the bill's behalf," and the judiciary committee of the state Senate killed the bill.[5] In May 1960, Governor Brown refused Chessman another stay, and the death-row inmate of San Quentin was executed. Because of the many twists and turns of the case, both proponents and opponents of capital punishment were angry with Brown.

Other responsibilities pertain to **extradition.** As mentioned in Chapter 2, when requested to do so by the governor of another state, the governor of California can be required by a federal court to extradite a fugitive to the state from which he or she has fled.

Moreover, the governor is commander-in-chief of the state militia (the National Guard). A military officer directs the troops, should they be called out, but the governor decides when to call them into service. Natural disasters such as earthquakes and civil disturbances such as riots may require use of the National Guard. During the Los Angeles riot of 1992, Governor Wilson ordered into action 12,300 members of the California National Guard and the California Highway Patrol.

On a more positive note, as chief executive, the governor symbolizes the state, so it is not surprising that ceremonial duties also must be performed. Cutting ribbons at dam-opening ceremonies and riding in parades may seem trivial compared to the previously mentioned responsibilities, but the politically astute governor will use ceremonial events as a kind of nonpolitical, interelection campaigning. When representing the state itself before its citizens, the governor has the chance to publicize accomplishments, to garner goodwill, and to influence recalcitrant legislators and other opponents. On the other hand, attending ceremonies can consume a great deal of valuable time.

Usually the governor is also the acknowledged leader of a state political party or at least a faction of it. This recognition assists in negotiations with legislators and other state officers of the same party. It can be an asset, too, on the national political scene. The governor of California has better presidential prospects than governors in other states: Ronald Reagan made one attempt for the White House while he was governor, and Jerry Brown made two attempts. After Pete Wilson's big re-election victory in 1994, he became a 1996 presidential contender. Yet the California governor cannot too openly treat state office as a stepping-stone to the White House. In 1958 William Knowland, then a U.S. senator, gave up his Senate seat to run for the governorship. This maneuver was supposed to enable Knowland to run for the presidency in 1960. As a result, the Republicans lost both the governorship and the Senate seat and Knowland's political career was ruined.

5. Quote from David Lavender, *California* (New York: Norton, 1976), p. 203.

In 1990 the voters passed Proposition 140, which amended the state Constitution to limit the governor to two terms, thus ending the unlimited re-eligibility that earlier governors had enjoyed. In a generally similar fashion, the U.S. Constitution says that no person may be elected president more than twice. (At the same time that they limited the governor's tenure, the voters also limited to two terms the longevity of all other officers elected statewide, as well as members of the Board of Equalization and state legislators.) Although previous governors had no constitutional bar to three or more terms, a political limitation existed. Only the immensely popular Earl Warren was thrice chosen by Californians. When he sought a third term, Pat Brown was overwhelmingly defeated by Ronald Reagan. Heeding this unwritten two-term rule, Reagan left the governor's office after eight years. One important effect of gubernatorial term limits is that the governor may be perceived by some as a lame duck as soon as he or she is sworn in for the second time: This perception can reduce a governor's power, especially in the second half of the second term.

In summary, we can say that the governor is the hub of state politics. The media give this official far more coverage than they do anyone else on the state political scene, and this attention is an important source of power: "Skillfully used, the power of publicity can be more influential than any formal power. Legislators must respect the governor's greater access to the communication media and hence to the minds of their constituents."[6] The key role of the chief executive has led two scholars to call state (and national) political parties "executive-centered coalitions."[7] The governor speaks with one voice, not with the 120 voices of the legislature, and represents the party and its programs in the minds of Californians. When Californians think of the state's Democratic (or Republican) Party, what comes to mind is usually the governor who leads the party. Not surprisingly, the party that does not control the governor's chair must often struggle for identity in the public mind.

PETE WILSON AS GOVERNOR: AN ANALYSIS

Governor Pete Wilson presents two different images to the public: On one hand, there is Pete Wilson running for re-election in 1994 as a hard-liner stressing law and order, crusading against illegal immigration, and bashing his opponent Kathleen Brown for being "soft on the death penalty." On the other hand, there is Pete Wilson, leader of the "moderate" wing of the Republican Party who has had a long-running dispute with his party's right wing. In any event, strong Democrats clearly cannot stand him, and strong Republicans do not trust him. It is not surprising that strong Democrats would dislike Wilson: The main hallmarks of the Wilson governorship are his relentless crusade to cut welfare benefits, his anti–illegal-immigrant posture, his tough law-enforcement program, and his steadfast support of the business

---

6. Thomas R. Dye, "State Legislative Politics," in *Politics in the American States,* 2d ed., ed. Herbert Jacob and Kenneth Vines (Boston: Little, Brown, 1971), p. 205
7. Frank Sorauf and Paul Allen Beck, *Party Politics in America,* 6th ed. (Boston: Little, Brown, 1988), p. 432.

Governor Pete Wilson briefs reporters on details of the state budget.

community. On the other hand, strong Republicans have never trusted Wilson. From Wilson's days as an environmentalist, antigrowth mayor of San Diego, through his opposition to Ronald Reagan in the 1976 presidential primaries, including Wilson's being forced out of the 1982 gubernatorial primary and into the senatorial primary, Republican loyalists have never cared for Pete Wilson. In 1990, they asked him to run for governor because the party had no one else who could win the governor's chair and thus prevent a partisan gerrymander by the Democrats. Since Wilson became governor, his social liberalism has further alienated the party's right wing. Wilson and the staunch conservatives in the Republican Party bitterly part company on issues such as homosexuality, abortion, and government funding of family planning such as providing Norplant contraceptives to teenagers.

Wilson's First Term

The tensions within the Republican Party were played out in the 1991–92 conflict over two bills to outlaw job discrimination against homosexuals: In 1991, Wilson vetoed the first of the bills, but in 1992 he signed a nearly identical one. Wilson vetoed the 1991 bill by a liberal Democratic member of the Assembly, stating that the proposed legislation would have harmed business, especially small firms, and that enough laws already were on the books to protect homosexuals against job discrimi-

Paul Duginski / McClatchy News Service © 1993

nation. Widespread violent demonstrations by gays condemned Wilson for "caving in" to Republican conservatives. When Wilson signed substantially similar legislation a year later, he appeared unprincipled to both sides of the emotional issue. (See Chapter 3 for Wilson's struggles within his own party.)

The 1992 elections were a bitter defeat for Pete Wilson, whose only solace was that at least he was not on the ballot himself. Wilson lost in four ways: (1) He managed President George Bush's re-election effort in California, and Bill Clinton became the first Democratic presidential candidate to carry California since 1964, winning the state by 1.5 million votes; (2) Wilson's handpicked Senate successor (John Seymour) was overwhelmingly rejected by the voters; (3) Wilson's own ballot proposition to cut welfare payments and to expand the governor's budgetary powers (Proposition 165) was defeated; and (4) the Republican Party did poorly in races for the California Assembly and for U.S. House seats from California.

Pete Wilson did win some battles in his first term, namely the 1991–1994 skirmishes with the Democratic leadership of the legislature over the budget. (See Chapter 10 for the issues in each of these struggles.) But a case could be made that Wilson actually lost in the process of winning. Although Wilson usually "won" on the substantive points at issue—for example, keeping tax increases small or protecting California jobs or cutting welfare—he actually lost because the voters were turned off by the bitterness and drawn-out nature of the whole process.

In his first term, Pete Wilson faced several calamities that were not of his making: a serious and prolonged recession, the Los Angeles riots, drought, earthquakes, and fires. Because of factors that he could not control, Wilson never really got to implement his own political agenda, which he called "preventive government." The idea is surprisingly progovernment, which is not typical of most Republicans: Government should direct public resources toward preventing society's ailments and away from remedial action for the afflicted. Wilson believes that social problems can be prevented and that it is cheaper to prevent social problems from happening than mitigating the damage after the problems have already occurred.

By May 1993, Wilson's approval rating in the Field Poll had reached the lowest of any governor in modern times.

Wilson Re-Elected in 1994

Pete Wilson defied conventional wisdom when he came back after being 23 points behind in public opinion polls to defeat Kathleen Brown by 1.2 million votes and 15 percentage points. Wilson beat the political odds by sticking to three consistent themes that struck home with the voters: crime, the death penalty, and support for Proposition 187. Exit polls of voters in 1994 revealed little public affection for Wilson, but voters were still willing to re-elect him overwhelmingly. Kathleen Brown was never able to exploit this potentially fatal chink in Wilson's political armor. (Chapter 3 describes the dynamics of the 1994 election.)

Second-Term Strategies

If we assume that Pete Wilson is not elected president or vice president in 1996, then the state's revenue problems may prevent him from fully implementing his preventive government program. He is likely to emphasize three issues that he has stressed in the past: make substantial reductions in welfare, oppose illegal immigration and accuse the federal government of not paying its "fair share" of dealing with the problem, and maintain an antitax and probusiness program.

Wilson has reduced welfare grants in every budget that he has proposed, saying that by reducing the grants, it might make lower-wage employment more attractive than welfare. He also argues that California's grants are too high compared to those of other states. He has sought other changes in the program such as allowing teenage mothers to be eligible for benefits only if they live at home with a parent and limiting able-bodied adult recipients to two years of benefits.

Pete Wilson will continue to make his argument that the availability of free public services acts as a magnet for illegal immigrants to California, that undocumented persons are draining the state treasury (thus denying public services to legal residents), and that the federal government should pay for services such as education and health services that it requires the state to provide to illegal immigrants. Democrats and minority activists vigorously dispute Wilson's argument, saying that it is jobs, not public services, that draw undocumented workers and that children of illegal immigrants are U.S. citizens with all the rights of citizenship. (Chapter 2 discusses the immigration issue at length.)

Finally, Wilson will say that the solution to the state government's revenue problems is to retain the state's current businesses and to attract new out-of-state employers by a "favorable business climate." He contends that the jobs they provide and the taxes paid by these corporations and their employees are the only avenue out of the state's fiscal problems. He will maintain that the state has a structural deficit (see Chapter 10) and that only spending cuts and not tax increases will solve the problem. Wilson's second-term motto could become his frequent assertion that "Californians are not taxed too little, state government is spending too much."

How can we evaluate Pete Wilson? His supporters point to his tenacity in the face of adversity, his resilience, and his clearness of purpose. His opponents accuse Wilson of being insensitive to the poor because of his welfare cuts, of being a racist who scapegoats illegal immigrants, and of being a demagogue who exploits the crime issue. The irony of Pete Wilson is that he has won statewide races for U.S. senator twice and governor twice, often by large margins, but hardly anyone in California is an enthusiastic fan of Pete Wilson. He has fought the strong conservatives in his own party. He has fought the Democrats in California, and President Clinton in the nation's capitol. California once had a governor who fought everyone in sight and became a legend. Whether Pete Wilson can ever come close to the stature of Hiram Johnson or is remembered as merely combative remains to be seen.

CABINET, AGENCIES, AND DEPARTMENTS

As the person charged with administering the laws, the governor directs the administrative branch of state government. This branch consists of seven state agencies (see Figure 6.1, pages 150–151):

- Business, Transportation, and Housing
- Resources
- Youth and Adult Corrections
- State and Consumer Services
- Health and Human Services
- Child Development and Education
- Environmental Protection Agency.

The secretary of each agency is appointed by the governor. The agencies are subdivided into departments, each with a specific purpose. For example, the Resources Agency contains the Department of Boating and Waterways, the Department of Conservation, the Department of Water Resources, and others.

The secretaries of the seven state agencies, the directors of the departments of Food and Agriculture, Industrial Relations, Veterans Affairs, and Finance, and the governor's executive assistant make up the governor's cabinet, which may be called upon for advice. The director of the Department of Finance is particularly important because this person is the governor's chief fiscal advisor, and his or her department prepares the budget that the governor submits to the legislature. (The budget will be discussed more fully in Chapter 10.) Furthermore, the finance department assesses the financial impact of new legislation and advises the governor on the cost-effectiveness of current state programs. Because spending programs established many years ago may command strong interest group support or because certain appropriations may be required by the state Constitution or by the federal government, 80 percent of all expenditures are beyond the governor's effective control. In reality, then, the chief executive has little flexibility in budget planning, and an ambitious governor will have difficulty in altering the priorities of state spending drastically even in the midst of California's recurrent fiscal crises. According to one politician quoted by the British magazine *The Economist,* "What chief executive would want to run a $50 billion company when he has only 20 percent of the power and 100 percent of the responsibility?"[8]

OTHER STATE CONSTITUTIONAL OFFICERS

The governor is not the only executive officer elected statewide. The following officials are called state constitutional officers because their positions are specified in the state constitution: lieutenant governor, controller, treasurer, secretary of state, attorney general, superintendent of public instruction, insurance commissioner, and members of the Board of Equalization.

Note that the governor cannot have a unified executive administration, and he or she cannot control the other state constitutional officers in the same sense that the president controls their federal counterparts, because the other state constitutional officers may have different political views, be of different political parties, or even be potential opponents of the governor in the next election. Separate election of each of these officials not only discourages cooperation but also encourages one or more of them to try to cut the governor down to size before the next election. Many of these offices, especially those of lieutenant governor and attorney general, are considered to be in the line of advancement to the governorship. All of this competition could be viewed as a kind of checks-and-balances system, although we usually think of checks and balances as operating between branches, not within the same branch, of government.

---

8. "Government in California: Buckling Under the Strain," *The Economist,* February 13, 1993, p. 22.

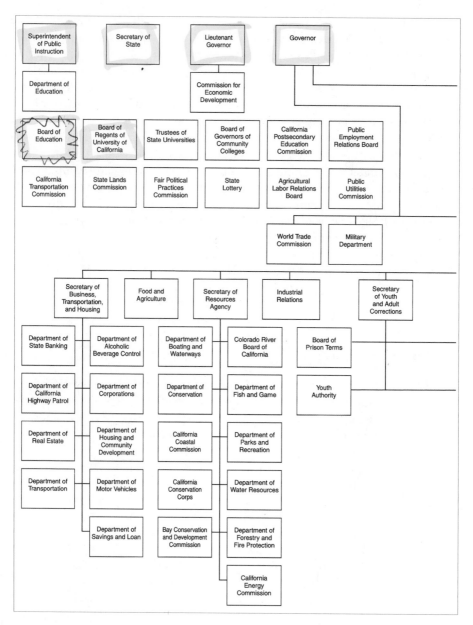

Figure 6.1 The executive branch of California state government

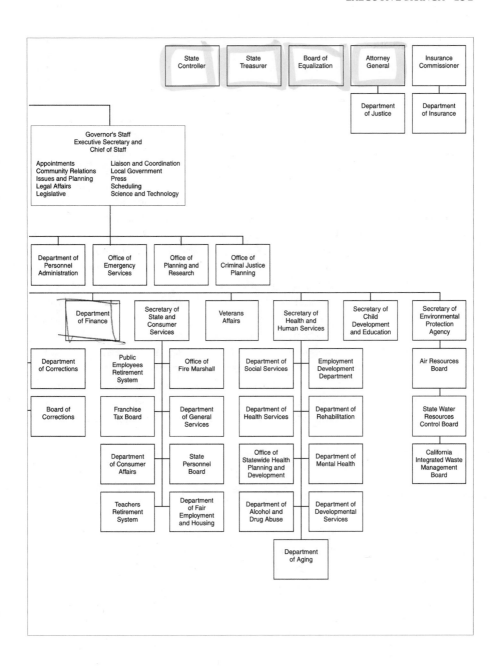

State Controller

State Treasurer

Board of Equalization

Attorney General

Insurance Commissioner

Department of Justice

Department of Insurance

Governor's Staff
Executive Secretary and
Chief of Staff

Appointments
Community Relations
Issues and Planning
Legal Affairs
Legislative

Liaison and Coordination
Local Government
Press
Scheduling
Science and Technology

Department of Personnel Administration

Office of Emergency Services

Office of Planning and Research

Office of Criminal Justice Planning

Department of Finance

Secretary of State and Consumer Services

Veterans Affairs

Secretary of Health and Human Services

Secretary of Child Development and Education

Secretary of Environmental Protection Agency

Department of Corrections

Public Employees Retirement System

Office of Fire Marshall

Department of Social Services

Employment Development Department

Air Resources Board

Board of Corrections

Franchise Tax Board

Department of General Services

Department of Health Services

Department of Rehabilitation

State Water Resources Control Board

Department of Consumer Affairs

State Personnel Board

Office of Statewide Health Planning and Development

Department of Mental Health

California Integrated Waste Management Board

Teachers Retirement System

Department of Fair Employment and Housing

Department of Alcohol and Drug Abuse

Department of Developmental Services

Department of Aging

Lieutenant Governor

Some people think that because the governor is the most important person in state politics, the lieutenant governor is the second-most-important person. This is not true. In fact, the lieutenant governor ordinarily has few significant duties to perform. For instance, he or she presides over the state Senate but is not allowed to vote except in the unlikely event of a tie. "I never go there except to break ties," said a former lieutenant governor. The lieutenant governor also serves **ex officio** on certain boards and commissions, such as the State Lands Commission and the Board of Trustees of the State University System. Serving *ex officio* means that whoever holds the office of lieutenant governor automatically becomes a member of the particular board or commission. The lieutenant governor does not have many other functions, and, in fact, nearly everything that he or she does could just as easily be done by someone else or left undone. This may be why eight states do not have such an official.

On the other hand, in California the lieutenant governor becomes acting governor when the governor leaves the state. The state Supreme Court has ruled that as soon as the chief executive leaves the state's boundaries, the lieutenant governor is free to act on whatever matters may need attention during the governor's absence. For example, in 1980 as Governor Brown sought the Democratic nomination for president in primaries across the country, Republican Lieutenant Governor Mike Curb threatened to make full use of all powers temporarily in his possession. When the governor returns home, the lieutenant governor lapses back into insignificance. The state Constitution could be amended to abolish the lieutenant governorship outright, and an existing constitutional officer, such as the attorney general, could take over when the governor is away.

Why would someone want to be lieutenant governor? Surely not because he or she covets the powers of the office; the position is really just a political holding pattern or a way station to better things. If the lieutenant governor is a talented person, his or her talents are wasted. To say that this person is not gainfully employed would be inaccurate, but the office does need more duties. New tasks could come from the governor, but recent governors have not especially liked or trusted their lieutenant governors. Earl Warren wrote in his memoirs that when he was governor he would lock all bills in a safe-deposit box whenever he left the state in order to prevent the lieutenant governor, Goodwin J. ("Goodie") Knight, from going on a bill-signing binge.[9] Moreover, as we have mentioned earlier, the lieutenant governor could be a political opponent or a member of the opposite party. In fact, in all elections between 1978 and 1994, the voters elected a governor and lieutenant governor from different parties.

Controller

Unlike the lieutenant governor, the state controller has a powerful position. If money talks, then the controller speaks in thunderous tones. He or she accounts for and pays

---

9. Earl Warren, *Memoirs* (Garden City, NY: Doubleday, 1977), pp. 256–265.

out state money and is therefore the most important fiscal officer in the state. Acting as a disbursing and accounting officer, the controller audits state expenditures to make sure they are made in accordance with state law; this practice is known as a *preaudit*. The controller also advises local governments on financial matters and reports on their financial conditions in his or her annual reports to the public. In addition, the controller plays an important role in the "trigger" budget-balancing process noted in Chapter 10.

The controller oversees both money going out and money coming in. He or she chairs the Franchise Tax Board, which collects state income taxes. Any Californian unfortunate enough to owe additional income taxes on April 15 makes out a check to this board. On the other hand, taxpayers due a refund will find their checks signed by the controller. This official also sits on the Board of Equalization, which collects the very important sales tax.[10]

Treasurer

The treasurer has custody over state money, which he or she deposits in various banks, always in search of the highest interest rate. The treasurer also auctions state bonds, but in this case seeks the lowest interest rates that purchasers will allow. In recent years, the treasurer has been given the important duty of deciding which financial underwriters are allowed to resell lucrative tax-exempt revenue bonds to investors. This authority has prompted financial firms to contribute heavily to campaigns for treasurer. Finally, because the treasurer is given the responsibility of investing state money, he or she pools different state accounts into a single higher-yield investment program.

Secretary of State

The secretary of state's functions fall into two categories: record keeping and supervision of elections. The secretary of state keeps the state's official records and maintains the state archives. The secretary of state is also the keeper of the Great Seal of the State of California and affixes it to all documents requiring the governor's signature. In addition, business corporations are granted charters from this office.

In a more important and influential role, the secretary of state is chief election officer for the state. He or she must enforce the state's election laws; print the state ballot pamphlets; certify and publish election results; and check initiative, referendum, and recall petitions for the proper number of signatures. It is somewhat of an anomaly that the person who must enforce the election laws is himself or herself elected. In fact, the election is on a partisan basis. Finally, the secretary of state must also compile a list of potential presidential primary candidates. Early in the presidential election year (1992, 1996, and so on), the secretary of state places on the

---

10. In fact, the controller is a member of more than two dozen boards and commissions. The controller is supposed to attend so many meetings that a deputy is frequently sent in his or her place.

California presidential primary ballot the names of generally recognized contenders. By this means, the secretary of state can smoke out any candidates who would prefer not to contest the California primary. Of course, a candidate can ask the secretary of state to take his or her name off the ballot. The net result is that the secretary of state's actions may prevent a "favorite son" from dominating California's presidential primary and discouraging other candidates from taking part in it.

Attorney General

The attorney general—the state's chief law-enforcement officer and head of the Department of Justice—is one of the most powerful figures in California government.[11] As chief law-enforcement officer, the attorney general has authority over all district attorneys, police chiefs, and sheriffs in the state, but seldom supervises them directly. The attorney general must ensure that state laws are "uniformly and adequately enforced" (Constitution of the State of California, Article V, Section 13). In extreme cases, the Constitution gives the attorney general all the powers of a district attorney if it becomes necessary to enforce state law in a county.

As head of the Department of Justice, the attorney general conducts the legal affairs of the state. Unless an agency or department is allowed to have its own lawyer, it is represented in court by the attorney general's office. The Department of Justice employs many attorneys and is split into several divisions, which deal with various issues such as the environment, consumer matters, and narcotics problems. In addition to enforcing the law, the attorney general must also prepare titles of ballot propositions and summaries of these propositions before they are circulated for signatures.

California voters have shown an interesting tendency to split their ticket between the two most important executive offices in state government, those of governor and attorney general. Table 6.1 shows that in many recent elections, Californians have selected members of different parties for these two offices. Perhaps the voters want an attorney general who will keep an eye on the governor. Table 6.1 also shows that the post of attorney general is an excellent position from which to run for governor. Earl Warren, Pat Brown, and George Deukmejian moved directly from "A.G." to governor. Earl Warren and Stanley Mosk also later became distinguished judges. California has been fortunate in having a long string of exceptionally honest and capable attorneys general. The current incumbent, Dan Lungren, was elected on a law-and-order, "lock-'em-up" platform, but he has won praise for enforcing Proposition 65, the state antitoxics law described in Chapter 1. Lungren has prosecuted plumbing manufacturers who sell kitchen faucets that leach lead, and he has

---

11. The executive branch of government has three elected heads of departments: the attorney general supervises the Department of Justice, the superintendent of public instruction directs the Department of Education, and the insurance commissioner heads the Department of Insurance. None of these important departments is thus under the control of the governor.

Table 6.1 Governors and Attorneys General Since 1939

TERM	GOVERNOR	PARTY
1939–1942	Culbert Olson	Democrat
1943–1946	Earl Warren	Republican
1947–1950	Earl Warren	Republican
1951–1953	Earl Warren	Republican
1953–1954	Goodwin Knight*	Republican
1955–1958	Goodwin Knight	Republican
1959–1962	Edmund G. Brown, Sr.	Democrat
1963–1966	Edmund G. Brown, Sr.	Democrat
1967–1970	Ronald Reagan	Republican
1971–1974	Ronald Reagan	Republican
1975–1978	Edmund G. Brown, Jr.	Democrat
1979–1982	Edmund G. Brown, Jr.	Democrat
1983–1990	George Deukmejian	Republican
1991–1998	Pete Wilson	Republican

TERM	ATTORNEY GENERAL	PARTY
1939–1942	Earl Warren	Republican
1943–1946	Robert Kenny	Democrat
1947–1950	Fred Howser	Republican
1951–1954	Edmund G. Brown, Sr.	Democrat
1955–1958	Edmund G. Brown, Sr.	Democrat
1959–1962	Stanley Mosk	Democrat
1963–1966	Stanley Mosk	Democrat (1963–1964)
	Thomas Lynch*	Democrat (1964–1966)
1967–1970	Thomas Lynch	Democrat
1971–1974	Evelle Younger	Republican
1975–1978	Evelle Younger	Republican
1979–1982	George Deukmejian	Republican
1983–1990	John Van de Kamp	Democrat
1991–1998	Dan Lungren	Republican

*Succeeded or was appointed to the office.

prosecuted dinnerware manufacturers whose plates, bowls, and cups are glazed with lead. Lungren secured a settlement of $2.3 million against various defendants in the lead-pollution cases, including the upscale Wedgewood China Company. This was the largest award in the history of Proposition 65. Lungren also forced the Lucky grocery store chain to pay $5 million to settle a lawsuit that charged it with mislabeling lower grades of meat and reselling them as higher grades.

Superintendent of Public Instruction

The superintendent of public instruction is elected statewide on a nonpartisan basis. Because this office is nonpartisan, all candidates appear on all party ballots in the primary of gubernatorial election years. Should any candidate receive a majority, he or she is elected outright, and no runoff election is held in the November general election.

The superintendent directs the Department of Education, but policies for the department are established by the ten-member State Board of Education appointed by the governor.[12] The courts have ruled that the board is the ultimate governing and policy-making body for the Department of Education. The superintendent is the secretary of the board and is supposed to implement the rules and regulations it adopts. This somewhat curious arrangement of an elected superintendent and an appointed board led to much infighting during the tenure of Bill Honig (1982 to 1993) when there were bitter struggles between Honig and the state board over who had the power to set educational policy. In 1993, Honig was convicted of four felony counts of conflict of interest. Honig, an attorney, was found guilty of knowingly authorizing more than $300,000 in state contracts to an organization run by his wife.

The importance of the superintendent and the state board was enhanced by the passage of Proposition 98, which requires that at least 40 percent of the state budget go to elementary and secondary education. The state Department of Education provides approximately 80 percent of local elementary and secondary school districts' budgets. The state also sets the local educational policies, especially regarding curriculum and textbooks, within which local school districts must operate. Higher education is not neglected either. The superintendent sits ex officio on the Board of Regents of the University of California, the Trustees of the State University System, and the Board of Governors of the state's community colleges.

Insurance Commissioner

The office of an elected insurance commissioner was created by an initiative, Proposition 103, in 1988. All auto-insurance rate increases and methods of pricing insurance must be approved by the commissioner in a fashion similar to the way the Public Utilities Commission sets electricity or telephone rates and determines com-

---

12. At the local, school district level, the procedure is just the opposite: The board is elected and the super-intendent is appointed.

READING 6.1

Lawyers, Firms Donate Heavily to Garamendi;
Many Contributors Regularly Practice Before His Agency;
Any Conflicts Denied

State Insurance Commissioner John Garamendi, whose vigorous regulation of the insurance industry has proven to be a financial bonanza for lawyers and firms throughout the state, has received nearly $500,000 from many of those whose work is directly influenced by his agency.

The attorney-donors, who have given 25 percent of the $2 million cash contributions to Garamendi over the last two years, range from Democratic powerhouse O'Melveny & Myers to a well-known insurance defense firm, Buchalter, Nemer, Fields & Younger.

Although Garamendi . . . has made it a personal policy not to accept money directly from insurance companies, he has accepted substantial contributions from attorneys who represent the Department of Insurance, as well as from attorneys who represent insurance companies.

SOURCE: "Lawyers, Firms Donate Heavily to Garamendi; Many Contributors Regularly Practice Before His Agency, Any Conflicts Denied," *Los Angeles Daily Journal,* November 25, 1992, p. 1. Reprinted by permission.

---

pany profits. In setting rates, the commissioner is required by the California Supreme Court to allow insurance companies a "fair and reasonable" return. The insurance commissioner also has the duty to determine the financial health of insurance companies and to take over those that are insolvent.

The insurance industry in California involves many billions of dollars. Regulation of such an expensive industry subjects the regulators to the temptations described in Reading 6.1 from the *Los Angeles Daily Journal,* a newspaper for lawyers.

The ethical dilemmas inherent in having an elected insurance commissioner were revealed in the 1994 election for this position: Charles Quackenbush, whose principal campaign contributors were insurance companies, defeated Art Torres, who relied heavily on contributions from personal injury attorneys who pursue cases against insurance companies.

Members of the State Board of Equalization

The Board of Equalization consists of four elected members and the state controller, who serves ex officio. The state is divided into four Board of Equalization districts by the state legislature; each district must have approximately equal population, and each is represented by one member of the board elected on a partisan basis.

The Board of Equalization must ensure that property throughout the state is assessed according to uniform criteria. To accomplish this, the board trains county assessors. The Board of Equalization also does some assessing itself, but only of the property of railroads and public utilities. In addition, the board administers certain taxes, such as the sales, gas, cigarette, and liquor taxes. In income-tax matters, the Board of Equalization rules on appeals from Franchise Tax Board decisions.

In the late 1980s the board's exercise of its power to assess public utility property and to hear appeals from the Franchise Tax Board became extremely controversial. Board decisions can cost utilities, banks, and corporations many millions of dollars, hence the affected interests made substantial campaign contributions to board members, with board member Conway Collis receiving $1 million in a thirty-month period. The result was favorable property-tax assessments for utilities such as Pacific Gas and Electric (PG&E), General Telephone, and Southern California Gas, among many others. According to one former board member, "Would this country permit the U.S. collector of internal revenue to be an elected public official? The idea is absurd. Yet, in California, we have this system where the tax collectors have the power to extract campaign monies from the people over whom they have jurisdiction."[13] In 1990 the state legislature passed an ethics bill that required a board member to disqualify himself or herself from voting on matters coming before the board that involve an interest which has contributed more than $250 to the board member in the previous twelve months. (Requiring someone else to be ethical is rather easy; the legislature's ethics bill did not restrict itself in this manner.)

BOARDS AND COMMISSIONS

Numerous commentators have noted that one of the most significant developments in the structure of state government over the past thirty years has been the rise of appointive government. The range of activities regulated by independent boards and commissions filled by gubernatorial appointment is truly amazing. Boards or commissions make regulations that affect the cost of heating a home, the size of a telephone bill, the location of new power facilities, private development along the coastline, approval of auto-emission–control systems, the location of highways, protection of endangered species, licensing of professions, and administration of the state's system of higher education. This development suggests certain conclusions: Government control over private economic activity has increased; although the governor (through appointees) can leave his or her stamp on a wider range of policy-making areas, fewer decisions are being made by elected officials; because appointed officials never run for election or re-election, the decision-making power of the public has been reduced accordingly. Because the governor appoints nearly all of the members of these boards and commissions, the individuals usually chosen share his or her point of view on the matters under the boards' jurisdictions. However, once on a board, an appointee

---

13. William Bennett, quoted in Gale Cook, "Has Politics Tarnished the State Board of Equalization?" *California Journal* (January 1989): 33.

cannot be directed by the governor. In fact, a board member's term may outlast the governor's tenure. A description of some of the more important commissions follows.

Public Utilities Commission

The Public Utilities Commission (PUC) may have more impact on where Californians' dollars go than do most elected officials. The commission has five members who serve six-year terms. The terms of the members overlap; thus, at any one time individual members of the commission have usually been appointed by different governors. All commissioners must be confirmed by majority vote of the state Senate before taking office.

The PUC has the important task of setting the intrastate (within California) charges for gas, electricity, water, and telephone companies. In addition, it sets the rates of railroads, airlines, buses, trucks, and movers of household goods. Although all of the companies regulated by the PUC are privately owned, they must obtain PUC permission to increase their rates. The PUC also decides how much profit these companies are allowed to make. Furthermore, through its regulatory power, the PUC is able to encourage specific policies. For example, efforts by the commission to encourage energy conservation have received nationwide attention.

Critics of the PUC assert that the commission is too generous in granting rate increases for residential gas and electricity customers. These critics further argue that the utilities are mismanaged. This charge has often been leveled at Northern California's PG&E; moreover, in 1986, the PUC accused Southern California Edison and San Diego Gas & Electric of imprudent and lax management in constructing the San Onofre nuclear power plant. The commission required the utilities' shareholders, rather than consumers, to absorb $344 million in costs. This penalty was the largest ever assessed on a California utility for unreasonable spending on a construction project. Spokespeople for ratepayer groups want the legislature to forbid the utilities to pass on to current customers the cost of constructing new power plants, because these plants will primarily benefit future customers.

California Coastal Commission

The Coastal Commission was established by an initiative in 1972. Its goal is the planned, long-range development and protection of California's magnificent 1,000-mile-long coastline. Among the issues for commission consideration are public access to the coast (including actually being able to see the coast), wise land use, space for recreation, and development and conservation of vegetation and marine life. The sixty-eight cities and counties along the coast develop local land-use plans for approval by the state commission. After these plans have been approved, the commission must oversee the implementation of the plans, rule on local amendments to the plans, and hear appeals from local coastal development decisions. Moreover, these local plans are updated every five years and reviewed by the commission.

Finally, federal law provides that offshore oil development that might affect the California coastline or its submerged lands must be reviewed by the Coastal Commission. The commission studies proposals for oil and gas drilling in the outer continental shelf and informs the federal government whether these plans conflict with state law. However, the Coastal Commission cannot intervene and block federal oil and gas lease sales if the tracts are more than three miles offshore.

Two-thirds of the Coastal Commission's voting members are appointed by legislative leaders; during the 1980s, the speaker of the Assembly and the president pro tem of the Senate repeatedly appointed to the commission important political fund-raisers whose voting on development projects was conditioned on campaign contributions. Commission members regularly received information privately from parties who had dealings with the commission. Legislative leaders also attempted to influence commission votes. For example, after a commissioner appointed by the president pro tem of the Senate announced that he would not vote on a pending project as the pro tem wished, the commissioner was replaced in the middle of a meeting on that project by a staff aide of the pro tem. An appointee of the Speaker was seated on the Commission and was immediately chosen chairperson only hours before the vote on a highly controversial development project. Mark Nathanson, another appointee of Assembly Speaker Willie Brown, pleaded guilty to using his Coastal Commission position for bribery, extortion, and racketeering. Nathanson solicited $975,000 from various coastal landowners, including actor Sylvester Stallone, in exchange for permits to develop their properties. After an intensive study of commission operations, the *Los Angeles Times* concluded that coastal protection is a noble goal, but that the Coastal Commission is "an ideal gone astray."[14]

State Water Resources Control Board

The Porter–Cologne Water Quality Control Act created the State Water Resources Control Board (SWRCB) and nine regional water-quality-control boards. Each of the nine commissions develops a regional water-quality plan tailored to its region's needs that takes into account population growth, land use such as agriculture, industrial development, and environmental and economic impacts. In effect, the regional boards are regional governments (as described in Chapter 9) under the ultimate authority of the State Water Resources Control Board, which ensures that a statewide perspective will guide water-quality policy. The state board hears appeals from decisions of the regional boards. The SWRCB also administers the Clean Water Grant Program, an expensive public works plan that assists local governments in building wastewater-treatment facilities to process public waste discharge.

In recent years, the State Water Resources Control Board has come under increasing criticism for its handling of toxic chemicals and pesticides that are entering the

---

14. "Coastal Commission—An Ideal Gone Astray," *Los Angeles Times*, September 7, 1987, pt. 1, p. 1.

water supply, especially into aquifers deep underground that supply an important part of state water needs. The sources of these poisons are leakage from underground chemical storage tanks and hazardous waste dump sites, as well as pesticide flows from irrigated farmlands. The SWRCB has been accused of not monitoring the regional boards closely enough to ensure that they are preventing the contamination of state water.

To correct some of the problems, the legislature has enacted significant measures. For example, one law requires owners of underground tanks to register their tanks with the SWRCB, which then sends the information to counties and cities for enforcement. Another law requires the SWRCB to set leak-proof rules for under-ground tanks, especially by establishing tank-construction standards and determin-ing proper leak-detection devices. Finally, the regional water-quality-control boards have been required to inspect open toxic ponds, lagoons, and pits to make sure that they are safe and double-lined. Any that are closer than one-half mile to a drinking-water supply are to be closed.

Air Resources Board

The Air Resources Board (ARB) is the air-pollution-control agency for the whole state, and its special concern is auto emissions. The ARB surveys air quality statewide, approves vehicle emission-control systems, and may order the recall and repair of cars that fall short of emission standards. The ARB has ordered car manufacturers to replace without charge to customers any smog-control parts that malfunction during a car's first 100,000 miles. In addition, car manufacturers must install in all cars a small, inexpensive computer that can tell whether the car's engine is burning as cleanly as it was designed to run. The ARB has also ordered tailpipe-emission standards that are the toughest in the world: Standards are to be progressively tightened until every new car would be at least 70 percent less polluting than 1994 cars. As early as 1998, electric-powered cars must be 2 percent of all new cars sold; the percentage will rise to 10 percent by 2003. The ARB has also required that gasoline be at least 30 percent cleaner by 1996. Gasoline prices will rise by 17¢ per gallon by 1996. When local air-pollution agencies are unable to control nonvehicular sources of air pollution such as oil refineries, the ARB will do so. (Chapter 1 also describes some of the ARB's enforcement programs.)

Governing Boards for Higher Education

The Regents of the University of California (UC), the Trustees of the California State University System (CSU), and the Board of Governors of the state's community colleges are the governing boards for higher education in California. The University of California has twenty-seven Regents appointed by the governor and confirmed by the state Senate; they serve twelve-year, staggered terms. Among the ex officio members are the governor, the speaker of the Assembly, and the superintendent of public instruction. The Regents govern the huge UC system, but the governor and the legislature maintain substantial financial control. The CSU Trustees, unlike the UC Regents, were not created by the state Constitution but by the state legislature and are therefore under greater control of the legislature and the state Department of Finance, which can disallow any expenditure by the CSU system even after its budget has been approved by the legislature and the money has been appropriated. The Board of Governors of the community colleges assists the seventy community college districts in the state, each of which is locally administered. State interest in the community colleges is heightened by the fact that the state government spends more money on the community colleges than on either the UC or CSU systems.

In the early 1990s, the UC Regents secretly voted large retirement benefits for high-level administrators at a time when student tuition was rising sharply. These actions prompted the UC Student Association to demand that the appointments of nine Regents be taken from the governor and given to students, the alumni association, and the faculty. Legislators demanded that they be given the power to appoint Regents. Consumer advocate Ralph Nader called for the statewide election of Regents. Considering the fact that the Regents control a $6 billion budget, including many lucrative scientific-research contracts, would legislatively appointed Regents become political fund-raisers like members of the Coastal Commission? If Regents run for office on a statewide basis, would they receive campaign contributions from vendors selling goods and services to the UC system in a manner similar to the way lawyers contribute to the insurance commissioner?

Commission on California State Government Organization and Economy ("Little Hoover Commission")

The Commission on California State Government Organization and Economy, usually called California's "Little Hoover Commission," was established to promote efficiency and economy in state government. It issues many valuable reports on state-government operations; for example, the commission's highly critical reports on state policing of privately run board-and-care homes for elderly, mentally ill, and retarded persons prompted the legislature to pass a series of reform measures. The Little Hoover Commission has documented poor management of state real-estate holdings. The state owns more than 6 million acres of land valued at $2 billion but lacks a current, complete inventory and is losing millions of dollars in income each year. The commission has also documented deficiencies in the state's programs for abused and abandoned children in the foster-care system.

This chapter has described some of the more important appointive boards and commissions in California state government. As we saw in Chapter 4, many others exist, some performing unneeded tasks or even functions that are detrimental to the interests of consumers. The Little Hoover Commission, itself an appointed commission, regularly identifies superfluous boards and commissions.

READING 6.2

The "Do as I Say, Not as I Do" Award Goes to . . .

What State Government agency has been penalized by Southern California air quality officials for failing to take adequate steps to promote car-pooling by its employees? Cal-Trans—whose role includes promoting car-pooling by the public.

The South Coast Air Quality Management District announced that CalTrans' Los Angeles office is spending $31,500 on in-house ride-sharing programs as a settlement for having failed to properly submit an annual up-date of its trip-reduction plan to the AQMD. Although a CalTrans spokesman said the agency's violation was technical, CalTrans has agreed to make five additional minivans available to employees for van-pooling and is devoting staff time to promoting in-house ride-sharing efforts.

SOURCE: "The 'Do as I Say, Not as I Do' Award Goes to . . ." by Paul Feldman, *Los Angeles Times,* March 5, 1993, p. A3. Copyright 1993, Los Angeles Times. Reprinted by permission.

GOVERNMENT IN THE SUNSHINE

Openness in California state government is promoted by the Bagley–Keene Open Meetings Act and by the California Public Records Act. The Bagley–Keene Act requires that state agencies and their advisory committees open their meetings to the public unless a closed session is specifically authorized and that the public be given adequate advance notice of meetings. (A similar law, the Ralph M. Brown Act of 1953, applies to local governments; it will be discussed in Chapter 9.) The Bagley–Keene Act provides that the public must receive a meeting agenda ten days before a meeting and that no decision may be made on any business that was not included on the published agenda. The ten-day-notice requirement does not apply in the event of an emergency that threatens the public health or safety, such as a disaster, public-employee strike, or disruption of public facilities. State agencies may meet in closed session (executive session) to hear charges brought against a public employee, to discuss personnel matters and salary issues, and to discuss pending lawsuits with an agency lawyer. Closed sessions must also be announced ten days in advance. Any member of a state agency who attends a meeting that violates the Bagley–Keene Act is guilty of a misdemeanor. Members of the public may also bring suit to void decisions taken in violation of the act.

The California Public Records Act establishes the right of the people to inspect any public document that is not specifically exempted. The act applies to both state and local governments. Public documents include not only written documents but also photographs, maps, recordings, and computer tapes. The Public Records Act

© 1993 Mal Ent., Inc.

exempts notes and memoranda that government agencies prepare before making a decision, records pertaining to pending lawsuits, personnel files, bank records, trade secrets, and police files. Before a state or local agency may keep a document secret, it must prove in court that the public interest in keeping the document secret "clearly outweighs" the public interest in disclosing the document.

The thrust of both the Open Meetings Act and the Public Records Act is to allow the public to have access to its government. California government belongs to the people of California: It is not the property of administrators and state employees.

STATE CIVIL SERVICE

Excluding those who work for institutions of public higher education, California has approximately 165,000 state employees. Known variously as "civil servants" or "bureaucrats," these state workers are employed in positions such as clerical workers, California Highway Patrol officers, driver's license examiners, CalTrans road crew members, fish and game wardens, state foresters, park rangers, prison guards, hospital workers, and many others. These people do the day-to-day work of running California government and are the "face" of government most frequently encountered by average citizens. Civil servants administer the programs established by the governor and the legislature, hence they exercise a delegated authority. Elected officials use laws to identify problems, set objectives for administrators to meet, and appropriate money to finance the programs. Civil servants are left "to fill in the details" and use their technical expertise to achieve the goals set by the law. Filling in the details may also involve filling out lots of forms.

Doug Menuez / Reportage

State employees work at many different jobs—for example, as park rangers.

As noted earlier, California is not a high-patronage state. Approximately 98 percent of all state employees received their positions through competitive examinations or by demonstrating competence for their position, and not through loyalty to an elected official or political party. The California civil service system is directed by the state Personnel Board, which conducts examinations for initial appointment and for promotion.

In 1977 state workers won the right to select a labor union as their exclusive bargaining agent in wage disputes and other employment matters. Under the collective-bargaining act, the Public Employment Relations Board was established to supervise the law and to investigate and rule on unfair labor practices. In early 1983, in one of his last official actions as governor, Jerry Brown signed an agency-shop agreement that allows unions representing state workers to collect fees from nonmembers. The fees are roughly equal to union dues and produce more than $6 million more each year for the California State Employees Association (CSEA). At the time that the agreements were signed, the CSEA represented only 46 percent of the state workers covered by the agreement.

The 1977 collective-bargaining law forbade public-employee strikes, but in 1985 the state Supreme Court ruled them to be legal. Ten other states allow strikes by public employees, but in every state except California it has been authorized by the legislature and not the courts. The state Supreme Court held that "unless or until it is clearly demonstrated that such a strike creates substantial and imminent threat to the health or safety of the public," strikes by state or local workers are legal (*County Sanitation District #2 of Los Angeles County v. Los Angeles County Employees Association,* 38 Cal. 3d 564). Police and firefighters are exempted from the ruling, however.

SUMMARY

The executive branch of California state government is huge. Including public higher education, it consists of 275,000 state employees, as well as the governor, other state constitutional officers and their staffs, and numerous boards and commissions.

The purpose of those who work in the executive branch is to execute duties prescribed by state law and the state Constitution. With the important exception of rules and regulations issued by administrative agencies, the executive branch does not make law. In Chapter 7 we turn to the lawmaking branch of the state government, the state legislature.

DISCUSSION QUESTIONS

1. For more than one hundred years, all of California's governors have governed under a state Constitution that has given them much the same powers it gives the governor now. Yet some, like Earl Warren, have been powerful and are remembered, and others are forgotten even by historians. Thus, the powers written into the state Constitution do not by themselves make a governor strong, influential, or effective. What factors can make an average governor into a great governor?

2. This chapter has provided evidence for the argument that state constitutional officers might find advantage in not cooperating with one another rather than working as a team. At the national level, the attorney general, secretary of state, and others serve at the president's pleasure. This fact encourages, but does not guarantee, harmony. Would you rather have state officials elected (so that you can say who they will be), but run the risk that they will work against each other once elected? Or would you rather give up your chance to choose in order that state officials might work together more harmoniously?

3. What are some of the boards and commissions established to regulate economic activities? What are some of the areas of regulation? Which of these boards and commissions provide environmental protection?

4. State employees are important people whose role in California government is often overlooked. Why are civil servants influential in the lives of average Californians? Because of this state's merit system of employment, state workers are usually highly qualified individuals, but it is also extremely difficult to fire those who are not. Under a patronage system, public employees are highly responsive to the governor, who is supposed to be the head of the administrative branch, because he or she has hired them and can easily fire them. Should California return to the patronage system that it had early in this century?

Chapter 7
Legislature

*L*egislative bodies, including the California legislature, perform several important functions: (1) representation of the interests of constituents and response to constituent requests for assistance on governmental matters; (2) deliberation and lawmaking; (3) resolution of conflict and the building of consensus; (4) education of the public; and (5) control of the administration—that is, overseeing administrators, especially through passage of the budget and through investigations.[1] This chapter describes how the California legislature is organized to perform these functions. We will also consider the legislature's leadership, legislative procedure, drawing district lines, and legislative reform.

LEGISLATIVE ORGANIZATION

The California legislature is a **bicameral,** or two-chamber, body. It consists of a lower house, called the *Assembly,* which has eighty members, and an upper house, called the *Senate,* which has forty members. Members of the Assembly serve two-year terms, and senators serve four-year terms. Should a vacancy occur in the state legislature, the governor must call a special election to fill the vacant seat.

Being a senator is considered more prestigious than being a member of the Assembly. The following are some of the reasons the Senate is so attractive:

1. The Senate has fewer members than the Assembly. Hence, the spotlight is easier to catch, and power is easier to wield.

---

1. Legislatures also have judicial functions, such as impeachment, judging the qualifications of members, and expelling members accused of wrongdoing. In addition, they must confirm many of the executive's appointments, such as those to boards and commissions.

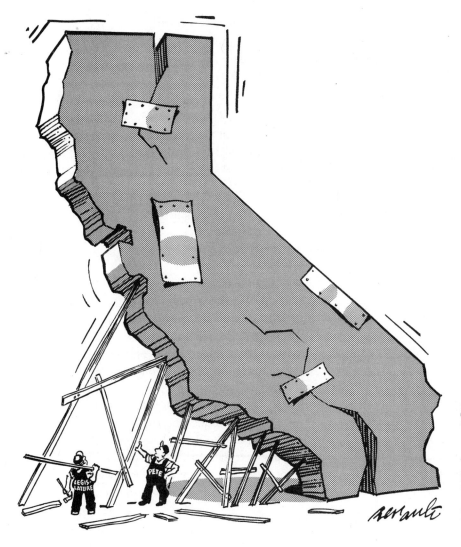

Dennis Renault / The Sacramento Bee

The state of the state

2. Senate terms are longer than Assembly terms, so that senators run half as often as Assembly members. Also, the election year that falls in the middle of a four-year term provides an excellent opportunity to run for higher office (such as attorney general, controller, or member of the U.S. House of Representatives) without having to give up the Senate seat. Senators may serve two four-year terms, but Assembly members may serve only three two-year terms.

3. Senate districts are twice as large as Assembly districts. In fact, state Senate districts are even larger in population than congressional districts and larger in population than six entire states. Representing many people confers distinction.

4. The Senate itself has more duties than the Assembly. The Senate confirms or rejects the governor's nominees to various boards and commissions.

5. In addition, the state Senate reflects some of the glory of the U.S. Senate, after which it was patterned.

Because of term limits (described later in the chapter), power may shift from the Assembly to the Senate. Term limits will lead to turnover and therefore to less experienced members in each chamber, but the Senate will have the benefit of many experienced former Assembly members. This means that the Senate will eventually have more members with greater legislative experience than will the Assembly. In time, the Senate will come to have a greater institutional memory than will the Assembly. The shift of power to the Senate is also hastened by the weakening of the Assembly speakership (which is described later).

Compensation

Whatever the differences in status, the salary and benefits in both chambers are the same: $75,600 per year salary, $109 per day living expense allowance while the legislature is in session, round-trip travel expenses for official business (such as sessions of the legislature and committee meetings); credit cards for telephone and gasoline expenses; an allowance for a state-licensed automobile; and generous health benefits. Is this amount of remuneration excessive? If legislators were paid too little, successful people would not take these positions, and the caliber of the legislature would decline; low salaries also would lead to dependence on lobbyists for favors. Even though the salary and per day (per diem) allowance amount to $100,00 per year, some members of the California legislature (for example, lawyers, doctors, and businesspeople) take a considerable reduction in salary in order to enter public life.

Sessions

Since 1967, California has had a year-round, full-time legislature. Not much time is lost between election day and the beginning of work: Sessions begin on the first Monday in December of even-numbered years. The session must end on November 30 of the following even-numbered year.

Special sessions are called by the governor to deal with pressing topics and can run concurrently with regular sessions. Laws passed in a special session go into effect in ninety days, whereas laws passed in regular session usually go into effect the following January 1. The special-session approach is sometimes used to accelerate the effective date of bills requiring only a majority vote for passage. At least one special session has been held concurrently with the regular session in every session since 1981.

Don Eastman / Photo 20–20

The serene exterior of the capitol masks the fierce rivalries inside the building.

LEADERSHIP IN THE LEGISLATURE

Senate

The lieutenant governor is the president and presiding officer of the state Senate. He or she recognizes those who wish to speak and makes parliamentary decisions; for example, the lieutenant governor can rule motions out of order. Because the lieutenant governor is normally not present in the chamber (as we have explained, he or she can vote only in the unlikely event of a tie), the president *pro tempore* ("for the time being") presides. The president pro tem, as he or she is usually called, is elected from the majority party. The president pro tem becomes acting governor when both the governor and the lieutenant governor are absent from the state. Senate leadership is collective: The president pro tem administers the Senate along with the four elected members—usually two from each party—of the Senate Rules Committee. The Rules Committee names committee chairpersons, appoints members to committees, and refers bills to committee.

Assembly

The Assembly is presided over by the Speaker, who may be the second most important person in California government and politics and who, therefore, is a potential contender for the governorship. (When the Speaker is absent, a Speaker pro tempore acts as a substitute.) As presiding officer, the Speaker rules on parliamentary procedure. The Speaker's knowledge of parliamentary tactics and judicious use of procedure can spell life or death for some bills. The Speaker's most important power is in appointing the chairperson and all members of all committees. To aid one's constituents or to further one's policy goals, an Assembly member often prefers to serve on a particular committee. For example, a member from a farm area may want to be on the Agriculture Committee or a teacher may want to be on the Education Committee. The Speaker places those whom he or she favors on preferred committees: Friends and supporters are rewarded; others are brought into line or penalized.[2]

We must also note a less than honorable reason for wanting to serve on a particular committee. Members of committees that review legislation on banking, mortgage lending, insurance, horse racing, and alcoholic beverages get immense campaign contributions from those interests. A member may want to serve on these committees not out of interest in banking or insurance but to squeeze money out of the interest groups. Hence, these committees are known around the capitol as **"juice" committees.**

The Speaker is a powerful fund-raiser, which is the position's source of great strength. Interest groups often funnel their campaign contributions through the Speaker, who distributes the money to majority party members running in close election races. The Speaker benefits from this arrangement much more than do the interest groups because the Speaker decides how to distribute large sums of money to members, who may not know how much money each interest group has contributed. The Speaker's influence thus pervades the Assembly because his or her fund-raising ability has enabled the majority party to remain in power. In the 1990 and 1994 elections, Speaker Willie Brown spent more than $7 million on Assembly races. Such fund-raising takes a great deal of the Speaker's time; Brown lamented, "I have to spend every day of my life raising a minimum of $3,000 a day. . . . That means almost all of my public time has to be devoted to fundraising."[3] Because both the Speaker and the Senate president pro tem contribute much more to legislative candidates than do the state's political parties, these legislative leaders have been described as "the real political parties in California."

---

2. The Speaker also makes many appointments to nonlegislative and high-paying positions on important powerful commissions such as the Coastal Commission, the Commission on Judicial Performance, and the Integrated Waste Management Board, among others.

3. "Willie Brown Decries Time Spent on Raising Funds," *Los Angeles Times,* May 4, 1985, pt. 11, p. 6.

Sherry Bebitch Jeffe has conducted a comprehensive study of state legislative leadership.[4] Speakers of the California Assembly can be considered in terms of *interpersonal style* (how each Speaker relates to peers, subordinates, rivals, advisors, the governor, the media, lobbyists) or in terms of *functional style* (how each Speaker perceives the function of leadership). All Speakers between 1961 and 1994 followed a "directive" interpersonal style that was firm, tough, aggressive, assertive, partisan, autocratic, confrontational, and centralized in approach. Jeffe's interviews with all surviving former Speakers and former legislators and staff members revealed Leo McCarthy (1974–1980) to have been the best example of a directive interpersonal style. On the other hand, a Speaker's functional style must be administrative if not programmatic as well. An administrative Speaker may concentrate on reforming legislative procedure and organization, as did Robert Monagan (1969–1970), or stress raising money for campaigns, as has Willie Brown (1980–). In contrast, the programmatic Speaker focuses on policy issues in order to influence social change in the future. Jeffe believes that Jesse Unruh (1961–1968) is the model of the programmatic Speaker, but he was also an influential administrative Speaker.

The Changed Speakership

As a result of the 1994 elections, the Republicans apparently won a 41–39 majority of Assembly seats. After twenty-five years of Democratic Party control of the Assembly, the Republicans thought they were finally ready to elect a Republican Speaker, former minority leader Jim Brulte. However, Republican Paul Horcher had received a committee vice-chairmanship from Speaker Willie Brown in the previous session. Because the Republican caucus had preferred another Republican for the vice-chairmanship and urged Horcher not to take the position in the previous session, Horcher was a party outcast when the new session began in December 1994. When the vote to choose a Speaker was taken, Horcher switched his party affiliation to Independent and voted for Willie Brown as Speaker, thus resulting in forty votes for Brown and forty votes for Brulte. With the chamber deadlocked and unable to proceed, Brown eventually manipulated the expulsion of one Republican member by ruling that the member could not vote on the issue of his own expulsion, then expelled him 40–39, with thirty-nine Democratic votes plus Horcher in favor of expulsion, and thirty-nine Republican votes in opposition. However, the California Constitution (Article IV, Section 5) provides that a member may be expelled only by two-thirds of the membership. Disgruntled Republicans in Horcher's district later mounted a successful recall of the renegade legislator, but political instability continued in the Assembly.

In 1992, the Michigan House of Representatives deadlocked at 55–55, ending twenty-six years of Democratic Party rule. Although Michigan's chamber is just as

---

4. Sherry Bebitch Jeffe, "How Leadership Styles Influence Political Effectiveness," *Western City* (May 1986): 14–19.

rancorous as California's and probably more partisan, it was able to work out a shared-power arrangement in which each party's leaders agreed to alternate control each month. When one party controlled power on the floor, the other party controlled legislative committees. Each party got the same number of staff members and the same budget for legislative operations. Much to the surprise of the Michigan legislators, this odd arrangement led to an amazingly productive legislative session. Even if such a balanced arrangement is not formally adopted by the California legislature, clearly a great deal of cooperation will be necessary to get anything done when there is an approximately equal number of seats for each party. The party balance could tip back and forth over the two-year session depending on vacancies resulting from deaths, members running for higher office, or recall elections. A two-thirds vote is required to pass the state budget. Because this is the legislature's single most important task, considerable cooperation will be required of all involved, including the governor, to get this job done.

Even if the 1994 election had not produced a nearly even balance of power between the parties, the once-immense power of the Speaker was due to change. Term limits mean that no one can be Speaker for a long period of time, as Willie Brown has been. Future Speakers will have much less time to develop the pervasive influence that centralizes power in the speakership. Assembly leadership could become collective, as is Senate leadership. Power could shift to a committee or even to the majority-party caucus. As we saw in Chapter 3, term limits mean that members are constantly "jumping ship" to run for the state Senate, or Congress, or some other office. There are repeated special elections to select successors, which introduces continuing instability in the Assembly. Sherry Bebitch Jeffe believes that the speakership may return to the interpersonal style that was common before 1961.[5] Then, the Speaker's power rested on his ability to maintain smooth social relations with members and to promote the collegiality that sustains governing coalitions. Such coalitions tend somewhat to blur partisanship or at least to tone down the fierce partisan wrangling that characterized the Assembly in the 1980s and early 1990s.

The Speaker's chief assistant and personal representative on the floor is the majority floor leader. The minority party also elects its own leader, the minority leader. Before 1995, Speaker Willie Brown frequently chose not to allow the minority leader to name Republicans to Assembly committees, hence the latter's powers were decreased significantly because the minority leader could not reward or punish his own party members. Such bare-knuckle tactics are less likely in the future if the speakership is more collegial and depends on coalitions to pass legislation.

---

5. Sherry Bebitch Jeffe, "A Preview of Life in Sacramento Under Term Limits," *Los Angeles Times*, December 11, 1994, p. M1.

LEGISLATIVE PROCEDURE

In this section we outline the stages of the legislative process through which a bill becomes law. After a brief summary of the different stages, we will describe each in greater detail.

1. The bill is introduced.
2. The bill is given its first reading (by number, title, and author only) and then referred to committee.
3. A committee acts on the bill.
4. The bill is given a second reading on the chamber floor; amendments from the floor may be considered.
5. A third and final reading is made. The chamber votes its approval or rejection.
6. If approved, the bill is sent to the other chamber, where steps 1 to 5 are repeated.
7. A **conference committee** resolves differences in the bills passed by the two chambers.
8. The bill goes to the governor for signing.

Introduction

Bills come from many sources. The subject matter may be an issue studied by the author for some time or suggested by a constituent. More good laws than many people realize are suggested by citizens with ideas for improving life in California. As we noted in Chapter 4, interest groups suggest many bills. The governor also plays a large part in setting the legislature's agenda (see Chapter 6). The governor and other state constitutional officers are an important source of legislation, as are the agencies and departments of state government. Local governments receive their powers from the state. Not surprisingly, they or their statewide organizations have many proposals for new legislation. Committee staff members, who are competent and influential, also have many recommendations. The Judicial Council (see Chapter 8) is a significant source of bills for reforming the state's court system.

Whatever the source of a bill, only a member of the legislature can introduce it (after the bill has been checked by the legislative counsel). Members introduce bills simply by giving a signed copy to the clerk of the Assembly or to the secretary of the Senate. When bills and resolutions are introduced, they are identified by letters that designate the chamber in which they originated and the type of legislation they contain. Table 7.1 (page 176) shows the letter codes by which bills and resolutions are identified and tells what these codes mean. Bills usually cannot be acted upon for thirty days after they have been introduced.

Legislators sometimes introduce bills that they do not especially want to have passed. If they have been pressured by a constituent or an interest group or the media, they act to relieve that pressure. Legislators may also be trying to get publicity or to

Table 7.1 Codes for Bills and Resolutions

CODE	DEFINITION	MEANING OF CODE
AB	Assembly bill	Bills introduced in the Assembly are numbered AB 1, AB 2, and so on.
SB	Senate bill	Bills introduced in the Senate are numbered SB 1, SB 2, and so on.
ACA	Assembly constitutional amendment	
SCA	Senate constitutional amendment	
ACR	Assembly concurrent resolutions	
SCR	Senate concurrent resolutions	These enable the two houses to take common action—for example, to establish a joint committee, to provide for joint rules, to recess or adjourn, or to praise important individuals.
AJR	Assembly joint resolution	
SJR	Senate joint resolution	Through this resolution, the legislature states its view on a matter before the U.S. Congress.
HR	House resolution	
SR	Senate resolution	This resolution is used when a single chamber wants to adopt a rule for itself or when a legislator wants to honor a constituent.

stake out a philosophical position or to encourage campaign contributions from a particular group. Sometimes they also introduce bills in skeleton form because the bills can serve as vehicles for dealing with related matters that may come up late in the session.

First Reading and Referral The state Constitution requires that each bill receive three readings. This first reading is perfunctory only. After the bill is read, the Rules Committee then refers it to a specific committee.

A bill's success depends on whether the receiving committee is hostile or friendly. Bills often treat issues that fall under the authority of more than one committee; in addition, committee jurisdictions sometimes overlap. These factors mean that bill referral is an important and extremely political process. These reasons, in addition to the power to assign choice office suites, make the Rules Committee in each chamber a powerful body.

Committee Deliberation More than 7,000 measures were introduced in each of the past five sessions of the California legislature. To deal with such a volume of proposals, the legislature divides itself into **standing committees** (see Table 7.2, page 178). When a bill is referred to committee, the committee studies it and holds hearings at which interested parties give testimony. For example, the bill's author, representatives of the Department of Finance, the legislative analyst (whose duties we will describe later), and lobbyists may appear and give their views. Ultimately, the committee may (1) kill the bill by not reporting it out, (2) report it out to the whole chamber without recommendation, (3) report it out with a "do pass" recommendation, or (4) report it out with amendments. This committee stage can be crucial because many bills never emerge from committee. Although a bill can be forced out of committee by majority vote of the entire membership, this tactic is rarely used—only one bill has been successfully discharged from committee since 1960 because it directly challenges the Speaker's power. In 1988, a bill was discharged from the Assembly Public Safety Committee. The bill applied the death penalty to murderers of children under age 14. The committee was dominated by liberal death-penalty opponents appointed by Speaker Willie Brown. A coalition of moderate Democrats and Republicans claimed that the Speaker was attempting to enforce a liberal agenda that was not supported by most Californians and that bills with strong public support were being buried in committees packed with Brown's liberal appointees.

After first passing a policy committee, appropriations bills (or those seeking to spend money) must then go to the fiscal committees: the Assembly Ways and Means Committee or the Senate Appropriations Committee.

Second Reading and Floor Consideration Once a committee has reported a bill out, the chamber must vote on any amendments made by committee or proposed on the floor.

Third Reading If a bill can make it through both the committee and the amending process, then it has a good chance of passing. An absolute majority vote of the membership (forty-one votes in the Assembly and twenty-one in the Senate) is needed to pass legislation. Urgency statutes, appropriations bills (such as the budget), and amendments to the state Constitution all require a two-thirds majority of the *total* membership (fifty-four votes in the Assembly and twenty-seven in the Senate). The requirement that the budget be passed by a two-thirds majority allows the budget to be held hostage by the minority party or even a smaller group of legislators. Because the majority party usually does not have the fifty-four votes or twenty-seven votes needed to pass the budget, the minority party can exact budgetary concessions in exchange for its votes. Individual legislators can also withhold their votes until pet

Table 7.2 Legislative Committees

ASSEMBLY COMMITTEES (27)	SENATE COMMITTEES (22)
Aging and Long-Term Care	Appropriations[b]
Agriculture	Banking and Commerce[a]
Constitutional Amendments	Budget and Fiscal Review[b]
Consumer Protection	Business and Professions
Economic Development and New Technologies	Constitutional Amendments
Education	Education
Elections and Reapportionment	Elections
Environmental Safety and Toxic Materials	Energy and Public Utilities
Finance, Insurance, and Commerce[a]	Governmental Organization[a]
Governmental Organizations[a]	Health and Human Services
Health	Housing and Urban Affairs
Housing and Community Development	Industrial Relations
Human Services	Insurance and Indemnity[a]
Intergovernmental Relations	Judiciary
Judiciary	Local Government
Labor and Employment	Natural Resources and Wildlife
Local Government	Public Employment and Retirement
Natural Resources	Revenue and Taxation
Public Employees and Retirement	Rules
Public Safety	Toxics and Public Safety Management
Revenue and Taxation	Transportation
Rules	
Transportation	
Utilities	
Veterans Affairs	
Water, Parks, and Wildlife	
Ways and Means[b]	
Agriculture and Water Resources	

[a]One of the so-called juice committees
[b]Fiscal committee

projects for their districts are included in the budget. Only three other states require a two-thirds vote for passing the budget, and the U.S. Congress needs only a simple majority to pass most legislation.

As California lurched from one annual budget crisis to another in the 1990s, the two-thirds vote requirement for passage of the budget became more and more controversial as one editorial writer after another called for its abolition. However, those calling for abolition seemed to assume that agreement or consensus existed on how the public's money should be spent. Dan Walters notes that:

> . . . political paralysis is not confined to the budget. There are literally dozens of issues on which the Legislature can't come to terms, none of them requiring a two-thirds vote. The years-long deadlock over workers' compensation is an excellent example. Thus, the problems that have plagued adoption of the budget in recent years should be seen more as a symptom of a larger malaise.
>
> California has had the two-thirds vote for many decades, but it has not been until recently that it has had serious deadlocks over the state budget. That would imply that something other than the two-thirds vote is the primary cause of gridlock—such as the chronic gap between revenues and baseline spending requirements or the equally chronic decision of California voters to have the executive branch controlled by one party and the legislative by another.[6]

A *California Journal* study of key votes in the 1989–1990 session showed the legislature to be polarized along liberal versus conservative lines.[7] Almost half of the membership voted either 94 percent liberal or 94 percent conservative on forty significant bills. Only 23 percent of the members could be characterized as moderate—for example, Democrats who take a liberal position less than 80 percent of the time or Republicans who take a conservative position less than 80 percent of the time. The Assembly was even more ideological than the Senate. Because the California electorate is hardly as polarized as its elected officials, the representative function of the California legislature and its function of building consensus may not be working too well.

If we explain the voting on third reading in liberal versus conservative terms, we use an "ideological" explanation of why bills pass. Journalist Dan Walters provides a "special-interest" explanation that is cynical but close to being accurate: "[T]he objective merits of a bill have almost nothing to do with its fate. Success or failure depends almost solely on obtaining an author with the right Capitol connections, hiring the right lobbyists, lining up the most palatable list of endorsers and lubricating the process with timely 'contributions' of money."[8]

Second Chamber Action A bill now follows substantially the same course of action in the other chamber. If the second house makes no changes, the bill is sent to the

---

6. Dan Walters, "Two-Thirds Not Budget's Villain," *Sacramento Bee,* May 3, 1993, p. A3.
7. Andrew Hackett, "Who's Liberal; Who's Conservative," *California Journal* (March 1991): 138–140.
8. Dan Walters, "Politicos Aided a Tax Dodger," *Sacramento Bee,* December 11, 1991, p. A3.

governor for consideration. Should the second chamber amend the bill (a strong possibility), then it is sent to the house of origin with a request that the original chamber accept the changes that have been made. If the house of origin refuses to accept the changes that have been made in its bill, a conference committee must be called.

Conference Committee The Assembly Speaker and the Senate Rules Committee each appoint three members of their respective houses to serve on the conference committee for a bill (one member from each chamber must have voted against the bill). Conference committees have great leeway in working out an agreement between the chambers: Except in the case of the budget bill, a conference committee may change other items besides those disputed by the chambers. When a majority of each delegation has approved the conference committee's work, the delegations return to their respective chambers and present the conference committee's bill to their houses on a take-it-or-leave-it basis. If the two houses accept the bill exactly as presented to them by their conferees, then the bill goes to the governor for his or her consideration. Should one or both of the chambers refuse to accept the conference committee's actions, a new conference committee must be appointed (three conference committees on the same bill is the limit).

Governor Considers the Bill If the governor signs the bill, it usually takes effect on the following January 1, once a ninety-day waiting period has elapsed from the date the bill was signed. The governor has twelve days in which to sign or veto the bill. If the governor does nothing, the bill becomes law without his or her signature. If the governor vetoes the bill (which happens 12 percent of the time), the legislature may override that veto by a two-thirds vote (which rarely happens).

Procedure for the Budget Bill Legislative procedure for passing the budget bill follows a similar, but somewhat different, course. Introduction of the governor's budget proposal—something required by the state Constitution within the first ten days of January each year—is the beginning of a lengthy process that is supposed to result in adoption of a budget by July 1, the start of the new fiscal year.

Table 7.3 provides a step-by-step guide to the process that was followed until the fiscal crises of the 1990s.

The huge deficits of the 1990s required that normal procedure for the budget bill be supplemented by what has become known as "Big Five Budgeting." The Big Five are the governor and the Democratic and Republican leaders of both chambers who meet in closed-door, face-to-face negotiations to build consensus in the tough task of crafting a budget for hard times. The Big Five has replaced the marathon sessions of the Assembly–Senate conference committee (noted in Table 7.3), which have lost importance as the state's task has become more one of "spreading the pain rather than handing out the goodies."[9]

---

9. "Budget Talks Going On Behind Scenes," *Los Angeles Times,* July 24, 1992, p. A31.

Table 7.3 Budget Process Followed Before the 1990s

- *January:* The proposal is introduced separately in the Senate and Assembly, usually by the chairmen of the Senate Budget and Fiscal Review Committee and the Assembly Ways and Means Committee.
- *February:* Those fiscal committees usually take no action until late February, to allow the state legislative analyst—the Legislature's nonpartisan fiscal adviser—time to review the proposal.
- *March–April:* Budget subcommittees in the Senate and Assembly conduct independent hearings on spending proposed for areas including health, welfare, labor, government services and prisons.
- *May:* Subcommittee reports are collected by the Budget and Fiscal Review Committee and the Ways and Means Committee and incorporated into separate versions of the state budget adopted by the full committees.
- *June:* Budgets are adopted by the two houses by required two-thirds majorities. Differences are worked out in marathon sessions of a two-house conference committee, which is working under the pressure of a June 15 deadline for the Legislature to adopt a final spending plan, a deadline missed more often than it is met.
- The compromise version of the budget is adopted by the two houses, again on two-thirds votes.
- The Legislature sends the budget to the governor, who has 12 working days to sign it. The governor can veto any individual line item appropriations that the Legislature has added to his proposal, but he cannot restore proposals that the Legislature deleted. The Legislature, by a two-thirds vote, can override the vetoes.

SOURCE: "The Budget Process," by David Puckett, *Los Angeles Times,* January 11, 1985, p. I, p. 28. Copyright 1985, Los Angeles Times. Reprinted by permission.

DRAWING DISTRICT LINES

The Two Arenas of California Politics

In California, political battles between Democrats and Republicans really take place in two different arenas, the first of these being the "competitive statewide arena in which the battles for president, governor, and senator are contested."[10] We say that the statewide political arena is competitive because in almost any election year an

---

10. Eugene C. Lee, "The Two Arenas and the Two Worlds of California Politics," in *The California Governmental Process,* ed. Eugene C. Lee (Boston: Little, Brown, 1966), pp. 47–48. The discussion of California's two political arenas does not apply to low-visibility statewide races such as those for state treasurer or secretary of state.

attractive candidate from either major party has a reasonable chance of winning. Because these races rely heavily on television and radio advertising, they are high-visibility elections that are candidate-centered rather than party-centered. Furthermore, the weak party loyalty and voter independence of so many Californians usually make these races unpredictable. By contrast, true competition is definitely not likely in the second arena of California politics, the frequently one-party districts of state legislators and U.S. representatives. Between 1980 and 1994, only 34 incumbent state legislators out of approximately 1,450 who ran for re-election lost. These legislative districts did not become safe for one party by accident but rather by plan. These lopsided districts are the result of a **gerrymander.**

A gerrymander occurs when the majority party in the state legislature draws district boundary lines in such a manner that the party will increase its number of seats. **Redistricting** must take place after each U.S. census, which is held every ten years (1980, 1990, and so on). The state legislature draws not only its own district lines but also those of California's members of the U.S. House of Representatives.

Figure 7.1 gives a simplified but accurate example of how the process works. Assume that the state consists of only four districts (rather than eighty for Assembly members or forty for members of the state Senate or fifty-two for U.S. House members). Further assume that we are the Democratic majority in the state legislature and that Democrats (represented by O) tend to live near each other, as do Republicans (represented by X). Because we have been required by the U.S. Supreme Court's one-person, one-vote rule to make all districts of equal population (*Reynolds v. Sims,* 377 U.S. 533 [1964]), we could choose Plan 1 shown in the figure. In that way we could isolate the Republicans in one district and write the district off, and no Democrat would have to worry about a serious race in the other three districts. But a better and more profitable way to draw lines is shown in Plan 2. The tactics illustrated here force the minority party to waste its votes, either by isolating or breaking up its strength. In actual practice, both plans are used. An example of the effectiveness of the gerrymander in wasting votes of minority party members is the 1984 elections for the U.S. House of Representatives. All California Republican candidates for the U.S. House got more votes than all the Democratic candidates, but the Republicans were able to win only seventeen out of the forty-five seats. Such a result is a denial of majority rule.

In contrast to the partisan gerrymander, an **incumbent** gerrymander establishes district lines to protect incumbents of both parties by preserving the status quo. This strategy is used when each party has a roughly equal number of legislators—without such a compromise plan, no redistricting bill could be passed. Situations of divided control, in which different political parties control the Assembly and Senate or in which the governor is a member of a political party different from the one that controls the legislature, may lead to an incumbent gerrymander. In the 1970 and 1990 redistrictings, Republican governors and legislatures controlled by the Democrats could not agree on redistricting plans, so district lines were drawn by court-appointed judges.

| Plan 1 | | Plan 2 | | | |

Plan 1

XXXXXXXXXXXXXXXXXXXXXXXXX

OOOOOOOOOOOOOOOOOOOOOOOO

OOOOOOOOOOOOOOOOOOOOOOOO

OOOOOOOOOOOOOOOOOOOOOOOO

Plan 2

XXXXX	XXXXX	XXXXX	XXXXX
OOOOO	OOOOO	OOOOO	OOOOO
OOOOO	OOOOO	OOOOO	OOOOO
OOOOO	OOOOO	OOOOO	OOOOO

Figure 7.1 Two redistricting plans

The drawing of district lines is deadly serious business because nothing worries a politician more than the composition of his or her district. When the legislature turns its attention to redistricting, it breaks the entire state down into units of as few as 200 people, feeds data about voters into giant computers, and begins strategy making. Gerrymandering is not only a science, but also an art. A political party must show great creativity to accomplish its ends. The result is that many districts have strange and unusual shapes. The author has heard of some districts bearing a distinct resemblance to a flying goose. In 1980, the Democratic majority in the legislature put eight incumbent Assembly Republicans in four districts, and six incumbent senate Republicans in three districts.

In most legislative districts in this state, the political party balance is tilted so much in favor of the majority party, the minority-party candidate has no chance. People are frequently outraged when they learn of this blatant attempt to stack the deck. However, keep the following points in mind. Unless a reform proposal, like the bipartisan reapportionment commission described below, is actually approved by the voters as an initiative, then change in redistricting procedures is difficult to achieve. State legislatures draw district lines and probably will not give up this important power voluntarily. Party politicians, like most people, act out of self-interest. They are not altruistic; they do not put the welfare of others before their own. We may deplore self-interested behavior, but we should not be surprised by it.

Remember also two key points. First, the party that draws district lines at the beginning of the decade can mightily affect legislative politics for the next ten years. Second, for most legislative districts in California, the important election is not the general election but the primary of the *majority* party. Whomever voters select in the primary election will almost always win in November.

Why would anyone run in a district without hope of winning? Robert Huckshorn did an extensive study of losers in legislative races and found that the most important reason was to enhance the prestige of a political party or to promote a particular

Wright / Palm Beach Post

political **ideology,** liberal or conservative.[11] A candidate must "show the flag" or "give the voters a choice," not simply stand by and let an incumbent run unopposed. Many candidates view the race as an opportunity to educate (inform) the American people about liberalism, conservatism, environmentalism, and so forth.

Huckshorn indicates that another reason that many run is "for the sheer love of the game." Others "like to talk and to be listened to and there is no better forum than the political stump." A final reason is "personal prestige or personal gain," especially on the part of young attorneys who hope to enlarge their practices. We could add that a candidate might run a hopeless race now as preparation for a real chance later. For example, a person might be a 1996 sacrificial lamb in a noncompetitive congressional district because he or she is eyeing a 1998 race for a competitive Assembly district in the area. By means of a 1996 effort, the candidate learns how to campaign and how to put together a campaign organization, as well as increase vital name recognition in the area. By running the hopeless race, our hypothetical candidate may have paid some dues and earned the right to get a real chance.

An incumbent can be defeated in certain circumstances. The demographic characteristics of the district may gradually change. The incumbent may become involved in a scandal. The incumbent's margin of victory may have been declining in recent

---

11. Robert J. Huckshorn, "Political Defeat," in *Practical Politics in the United States,* ed. Cornelius P. Cotter (Boston: Allyn & Bacon, 1969), pp. 176 –196.

elections just as a strong challenger appears. The challenger might spend an extraordinary amount of money or be a particularly effective campaigner who can make his or her name well known in the district. Salient issues or political tides of the day might favor the challenger—for example, the challenger's gubernatorial or presidential candidate might be extremely popular. In addition, term limits require that no incumbent can run every six years in the Assembly and every eight years in the Senate. An **open-seat race** gives the minority party a better chance of winning.

The decreased competition that results from gerrymandering raises serious questions in democratic theory. When California voters participate in a legislative election the outcome of which has been virtually determined in advance, are they participating in a sham? Are legislators elected in safe districts less responsive to the wishes of their constituents? The greatest worry of an entrenched incumbent may be a serious challenger in the party primary, but how frequent are these? Today's incumbent may have initially achieved nomination in a crowded primary field in which he or she received only a small **plurality** of the vote. Are less capable legislators selected by such a system?

Concerns such as these prompt reform groups such as Common Cause and the League of Women Voters to favor an initiative that would establish a bipartisan reapportionment commission to draw district lines. Fairness in commission deliberations would be promoted by requirements for partisan balance and for an extraordinary majority (two-thirds) to make important decisions. The ten-member commission would consist of four members chosen by the Democratic and Republican caucuses in the Assembly and Senate, two members appointed by the Democratic and Republican state chairpersons, and four members (two from each party) selected by Court of Appeal justices. Partisan maneuvering would be inhibited by requiring that the final plan be approved by seven members, including three of the judicial appointees. Should the reapportionment commission become deadlocked in its deliberations, the state Supreme Court could appoint court masters to draw district lines. However, reapportionment commission initiatives supported by Common Cause, the League of Women Voters, or the Republican Party were defeated in 1982, 1984, and 1990.

The 1991 Redistricting

When districts had to be redrawn after the 1990 census, Republican Governor Pete Wilson and Democrats in the legislature could not agree on a redistricting plan. Therefore, the state Supreme Court, aided by special masters, had to draw the lines. This sequence, which was drawn-out and acrimonious, is likely to be repeated if redistricting occurs again during divided control of state government. Here is a look at the process.

As the Democratic Party began the redistricting process in the summer of 1991, it faced four difficult problems that seriously complicated its task: (1) The Democratic percentage of voter registration was declining; (2) there was slower population growth in Democratic areas than in Republican areas; (3) minority-group communities were demanding districts in which one of their members could be elected, even if it meant the replacement of an incumbent white Democrat; and (4) amendments to the federal Voting Rights Act had been enacted in 1982 that made redistricting a much more difficult process than in previous years.

Although California is a "minority-majority" state as noted in Chapter 1, its legislators are overwhelmingly white. Latinos were particularly disadvantaged at the time of redistricting because they made up 26 percent of the state's population but only 6 percent of the state's legislators. One way that the Democratic Party was able to control both chambers of the state legislature for more than two decades was by splitting minority communities (which have numerous Democratic voters) into as many districts as possible. The usual result was that white Democratic politicians were able to defeat their Republican challengers. Arguing that the interests of the Latino community are more important than the needs of the Democratic party, Latino groups such as the Mexican American Legal Defense and Education Fund (MALDEF) demanded more districts with a majority of Latino voters. They were joined by Republicans, who hoped that adjoining districts would be easier to capture.

The arguments of Latino groups were strengthened by 1982 amendments to the federal Voting Rights Act that required minority populations existing in significant numbers to be grouped together in ways that maximize their political influence. Any redistricting plan that failed to follow the Voting Rights Act could be challenged in court by Latino groups.

Further complicating the picture was the desire of Governor Pete Wilson for "competitive" districts that would benefit not only the Republican party as a whole, but also and especially Wilson's wing of the party. Districts in which the Democratic registration is approximately 54 percent to 61 percent of the total Democratic and Republican registration are quite competitive between the parties. Wilson believed that such districts are winnable for the Republicans, especially "moderate" Republicans of his own stripe. Wilson's fear was that districts with large GOP majorities would elect conservative Republicans hostile to him.

The Democrats pushed their reapportionment bills through the legislature without a single Republican voting for them. Governor Wilson promptly vetoed the bills, claiming that they sought "unfair partisan advantage." With the legislative and executive branches checkmated, the California Supreme Court had to appoint three retired judges called "special masters" to draw up a remapping plan for the court to adopt. The special masters and their staff of professors and computer technicians drew districts complying with the Voting Rights Act that also tried to keep cities, counties, and geographic regions intact. Most important, the special masters were not influenced by whether the districts drawn would benefit a particular political party or incumbent. In Assembly districts, twenty-two of eighty districts included homes of two or more incumbents, with one district containing homes of three incumbent Republicans.

RATING THE CALIFORNIA LEGISLATURE

Although a group of specialists on state government in the early 1970s rated the California legislature as the nation's best state legislature, the institution has come under increasing criticism in recent years. An FBI investigation in the 1980s and 1990s into corruption led to the convictions of several legislators. California's state legislators are said to be too responsive to interest groups, which in turn has led to two problems: a lowered moral tone of the legislature and institutional gridlock. *Sacramento Bee* columnist Dan Walters lays the blame at the foot of Speaker Willie Brown:

> The tone of the Capitol changed dramatically and nowhere is that change more noticeable than in the shift from McCarthy to Brown in the speakership.
>
> McCarthy not only established the example of focusing on legislative product but set a tone in his private life as well, giving up his San Francisco law practice and living on his salary as a legislator.
>
> Brown set a different mark. He pointedly retained his law practice and used his political clout as Speaker to represent corporate clients in dealings before local agencies, especially in San Francisco. Those private interests spilled over occasionally into state affairs as well.
>
> Brown's high-flying, wheeler-dealer demeanor emitted an unmistakable signal: It's all right to trade on your political position for private gain. And when that attitude was coupled with a voracious appetite for campaign funds, the change of atmosphere was radical. . . . Brown has used his speakership to pressure special interest pleaders into coughing up millions of dollars for his own campaign war chest and those of other Democratic politicians and causes. In their private conversations, Sacramento lobbyists term the Speaker's highpowered fund raising a "shakedown."[12]

On the other hand, William Endicott, also of the *Sacramento Bee,* casts a wider net. He points to the huge sums of money that must be raised for California legislative races that tend to "blur the distinction between right and wrong, between public interest and self interest—and between bills that are passed on merit alone and bills that are tied to campaign contributions and other favors. [Also,] the legislature has evolved over the last twenty years from a part-time collection of amateur politicians into a full-time collection of political professionals for whom politics is an end in itself and whose primary goal is staying in office."[13] The part-time citizen-legislators before 1967 had other occupations that provided their main livelihoods; if they were defeated for re-election, they could always return to those occupations. Today's full-time professional legislators usually have no other source of income, and many

---

12. Dan Walters, "Capitol Aura: Anything Goes," *Sacramento Bee,* February 10, 1985, p. A3, and "Willie Brown and Moriarty," *Sacramento Bee,* March 31, 1985, p. A3.
13. William Endicott, "Why Our Legislature Doesn't Work," *Sacramento Bee,* August 7, 1988, Forum, p. 2.

have known no career other than politics. For them, re-election is a major crisis—and they will do what is necessary to win.

Raising a great deal of money from interest groups is the necessary ingredient for re-election, and this has led to heightened group influence over the legislature and, according to some commentators, to institutional gridlock. California state government, especially the governor and legislature, are said to be stalemated; because of the diversity of interest groups in this state, groups can prevent significant policy change but cannot effect new policies. Water policy is the prime example, but so are property-tax relief and such recent issues as campaign finance reform, personal injury liability, auto-insurance costs, basic health insurance for low-income workers, and finance of infrastructure. The citizen-legislators, in contrast to today's professional legislators, may have been more willing to cast a politically difficult vote that was necessary to break the gridlock and solve the state's problems. If casting necessary votes caused problems for an amateur politician, then he or she could say, "A plague on all your houses," and return to a "real" occupation.

Institutional gridlock results not only from the selfishness of interest groups, but also from the fact that no consensus exists about what needs to be done to solve California's problems. In much of the 1950s and 1960s, there was substantial agreement about how to deal with issues such as growth, water, or higher education. But California of the 1990s is much more populous and diverse than forty years ago. The state is more diverse not only racially and ethnically, but also ideologically. Even if consensus could be achieved about the ends of California government, which the author doubts, then would the governor and the legislature agree on the means to achieve those ends?

A lesser but still significant problem is the wild end-of-session rush that closes each legislative session. In the final week of the 1989–1990 session, for example, the legislature passed more than 1,500 bills, which was more than twice as many bills as it had passed in the previous eight months. Legislators "deliberated" approximately three minutes per bill. In this frantic and convulsive atmosphere, the unscrupulous lobbyist sees a prime opportunity to sneak through unnoticed a questionable bill. In the jargon of the capitol, this is known as "low-balling." Only years later will the public or the taxpayers get the real "bill."

LEGISLATIVE REFORM AND TERM LIMITS

Responding to some of the concerns just mentioned, the legislature passed ethics legislation in the early 1990s that has the following effects:

CONFLICT OF INTEREST

- provide fines for state and local legislators who vote on matters affecting their own financial interests

- limit the acceptance of gifts by state and local elected officials if acceptance would create a conflict of interest

HONORARIA AND SPEAKING FEES
- completely ban speaking fees

REVOLVING-DOOR LOBBYING
- prohibit legislators and state executive branch officials from lobbying for one year after leaving office

SALARY-SETTING COMMISSION
- create the California Citizens Compensation Commission, with its members appointed by the governor, to set salaries for all state elected officials

OPEN SESSIONS
- allow closed sessions of the legislature only for the following reasons: to consider firing a public employee or to hear charges against a member of the legislature; to consider matters affecting the safety of the legislature; to meet with the legislature's lawyer regarding pending lawsuits; and to allow party caucuses.

In 1990, the voters passed Proposition 140, a constitutional amendment that limited legislators' terms, reduced the legislature's spending on its own operations, and ended retirement benefits for future legislators. The electorate was clearly angry about recent corruption convictions of legislators, the cost of state operations, and the legislature's inability to solve many state problems. Members of the Assembly are now limited to three two-year terms, and senators may serve only two four-year terms. A striking aspect of these limitations is that they are lifetime limitations: After a member of the Assembly or Senate has reached the maximum number of terms for that chamber, he or she may never return to that chamber. We can assess the probable effects of term limits as beneficial, detrimental, or "it depends on how you look at it."

The beneficial aspects of Proposition 140 include increased competition for open seats: Incumbents will no longer be able to hold onto their positions for long periods of time. Term limits bring new people and possibly new ideas into the system. More women and minorities are likely to be elected to office. The new legislators may have more energy and enthusiasm because they will have only a short time to accomplish their goals of enacting good public policy. Competition will probably increase throughout the entire California political system: Local officials such as mayors or county supervisors will find new openings in the state legislature; members of the legislature who have "maxed out" will run for the U.S. House of Representatives.

The detrimental ramifications of term limits include the consequence that the voters are not allowed to continue in office a legislator who is doing a good job if he or she has served the maximum number of terms. With increased turnover, inexperienced legislators may have difficulty dealing with complex problems such as water supply, environmental issues, or Medi-Cal. New legislators may become overly dependent on staff members or lobbyists. The key fact is that there are no term limits on lobbyists, who may become the institutional memory for the legislature. (However, this chapter has shown that previous legislators were *already* unable to solve many major problems *and* were too dependent on staff or lobbyists to begin with.) Term limits may also give an advantage to wealthy interest groups. Because of increased legislator turnover, a greater number of lobbyists will need to be employed to spend more time with legislators. This costs money. Because term limits have the incidental effect of turning over staff members as well as legislators, interest groups will have to provide much of the research once done by staff members. This also costs money, thus benefiting wealthier groups.

Term limits could also mean that the new legislators will be looking for a better job in higher office or private employment as soon as they begin their current positions. As the effects of Proposition 140 have begun to settle in, the state has seen nonstop special elections. Because the legislator is term-limited, the legislator quits his or her seat to take a better position, which triggers a special election. The seat is won by another elected official who then vacates his or her former seat, causing yet another special election, and on and on. This "musical chairs" situation causes a great deal of instability, particularly in the Assembly. Finally, there is the possibility of increased corruption. If one can hold his or her position for only a short time, better "make hay while the sun shines."

Proposition 140 can also be assessed differently depending on the values the commentator wishes to promote. Term limits may increase the number of Republicans elected to the state legislature because the greater number of open seats created by term limits are more likely to be seats formerly held by the Democratic Party, which controlled both chambers of the state legislature between 1970 and 1994. Term limits also weaken the Assembly speakership because the speaker will no longer be a member with extensive tenure and experience. This could be viewed as beneficial if one believes that the Speaker was formerly too powerful. On the other hand, if there are many new legislators at the beginning of each term, Assembly members may want strong leadership in order to keep legislative operations from flying off in eighty different directions. Finally, Proposition 140 reduced the amount of money spent on staff salaries and operating expenses by 38 percent. If one believes that the legislature's former payroll of 2,400 employees and a $200 million per year cost for operations was excessive, then this reduction is beneficial. On the other hand, one could argue that the state's 33 million people and its daunting public policy problems require that legislators have the highest quality research staff expertise and also sufficient personnel available for constituent service.

LEGISLATIVE STAFF

Highly qualified advisors, such as the legislative counsel or the legislative analyst, protect the legislature from depending excessively on the executive branch for vital information.

Legislative Counsel

The legislative counsel, a lawyer, helps members of the legislature draft bills. No bill may be introduced unless it is accompanied by a digest prepared by the legislative counsel. The digest shows the changes the proposed bill would make in existing law. The legislative counsel's office, which consists of 225 employees, including 80 lawyers, also advises members on the constitutionality of bills.

Legislative Analyst

Though unknown to most Californians, the legislative analyst is one of the most important figures in California government and politics: He or she provides advice to the legislature on anything with a fiscal implication, which can cover virtually every major bill. The legislative analyst's most important task is to analyze the budget bill presented by the governor. Because this examination is done item by item, the analyst's annual *Analysis of the Budget Bill* is a massive document more than 1,600 pages long. The legislative analyst and a staff of some fifty people have enough technical knowledge to serve as the legislature's counterweight to the governor's Department of Finance. Because the legislative analyst's chief aim is to make government more efficient, he or she usually recommends cuts in the governor's budget; this office is basically oriented toward economy in state government. The legislative analyst also prepares analyses of all ballot propositions to be submitted to the voters. These analyses appear in the pamphlet sent to each voter before the election.

When Proposition 140 passed and its legislative staff reductions of 38 percent took effect, the legislature reacted in a very irresponsible manner. Rather than eliminate any of the political operatives described under "Additional Staff" below, the legislature cut the personnel of the legislative analyst by one-half. When it came to choosing between expert advice to make government more economical and political aides to get themselves re-elected, the legislators chose self-interest first. The legislative analyst is even more vital as a result of term limits: Because legislators will come and go in rapid turnover, the legislative analyst may be an institutional memory to counter lobbyists.

Bureau of State Audits

Formerly known as the office of the auditor general, this office audits state agencies to make sure that money appropriated by the legislature has been spent for the purposes intended. The state auditor frees the legislature from reliance on the Department of Finance for the accomplishment of this task. Some commentators argue that this postaudit is more important than the preaudit performed by the state controller. The state auditor also evaluates the administration of programs authorized by the legislature, especially with an eye to efficiency, economy, and the possibility of fraud.

In response to staff reductions mandated by Proposition 140, the legislature irresponsibly abolished this office. It was later resurrected as part of the Little Hoover Commission (see Chapter 6), where it is no longer part of the legislature's staff budget.

Additional Staff

In addition to nonpartisan support available to all members from the legislative counsel, the legislative analyst, and the state auditor, three other kinds of staff support are also available: committee consultants responsible to committee chairpersons and to committee members of the minority party; partisan or caucus consultants reporting to the political parties in each chamber; and each member's personal staff.

Committee consultants conduct research for the committee that employs them and organize the committee's hearings. Because of the extremely high volume of legislation introduced each session, the bill analyses prepared by committee consultants and read by legislators significantly affect the content of legislation. In addition, each political party in each chamber employs approximately thirty professionals whose job it is to make sure that their employers get re-elected. These caucus consultants develop party positions and partisan strategy, write speeches, and, during election years, take leaves of absence to work in campaigns. In effect, they are publicly financed campaign organizations. Finally, each legislator has a personal staff working in his or her Sacramento office and in district offices to assist with legislative business and to respond to constituents' requests for assistance. The generally high quality of constituent service provided by these staffers is especially effective in getting members re-elected. As primary and general elections draw near, these individuals may take leaves of absence to become full-time campaign workers.

From this brief look at the support available to the legislature, we can conclude that (1) the California legislature is not understaffed, as are many state legislatures; (2) many employees are quite capable, especially those working for the legislative counsel, legislative analyst, and state auditor; (3) many are engaged in election-related rather than legislation-related activities, especially those employed by political parties; and (4) the legislative operation is expensive. Numerous factors have contributed to the current size of the legislature's staff operation: the complexity of modern issues; the election of issue-oriented legislators; constituents' increased demands for service; members' desires for re-election; and the determination, especially by past legislative leaders such as former Speaker Jesse Unruh, to have a modern, professional legislature. Critics charge that staff members may add to the workload rather than lighten it. Large staffs are faulted for generating unnecessary legislation. Other commentators assert that legislators rely too heavily on staff members for information about the content of bills—that is, others do their homework for them—and consequently legislators may not adequately understand the policies they enact into law. Finally, committee consultants may be changing from nonpartisan subject-matter experts into partisan aides whose main function is to ensure the re-election of the committee chairpersons who appointed them.

SUMMARY

Many of the key issues of California politics are thrashed out in the California legislature. This point is what we had in mind when we noted earlier that a function of the legislature is resolving conflict and building consensus. When the legislature makes its decision, which is usually embodied in the form of a statute or appropriation, it legitimizes a course of action. This chapter has described the means used to perform those ends: the legislature's organization, leadership, procedure, and staff support. But the legislature is not the final legitimizing agent. Those dissatisfied with the legislature's decision may carry the battle to the courts. The California court system is our next topic.

DISCUSSION QUESTIONS

1. Why would someone run for the Senate rather than for the Assembly?
2. What are the sources of bills?
3. Name the stages of the legislative process through which a bill progresses on the way to becoming a law.
4. The legislative process in California might be described as an obstacle course. Can you name some key points at which a bill can be killed? If so many danger points exist, why do any important bills get passed at all?
5. Describe the duties of the legislative counsel, the state auditor, and the legislative analyst.
6. Who is your Assembly member? Who is your state Senator?
7. The term limits required by Proposition 140 will have dramatic effects on California government. Which effects are likely to be beneficial, and which detrimental? Should the U.S. Congress adopt term limits?
8. Academic commentators and journalists have leveled various criticisms against the California legislature. What is the substance of these accusations? Are they accurate?

Chapter 8
Courts

*T*he California court system settles civil disputes and responds to criminal violations of state laws. The court system, which is also referred to as the **judiciary** or as the judicial branch of government, consists of two types of courts: **trial courts** and **appellate courts.** Only in the former do trials actually take place. Trial courts are said to have *original jurisdiction,* because cases originate there. A party that loses in the trial court may want to appeal to a higher court. The purpose of appellate courts is to hear appeals from trial courts.

The California courts, beginning with lowest, are listed below:

TRIAL COURTS

    Municipal courts

    Superior courts

APPELLATE COURTS

    Courts of appeal

    Supreme Court

The California court system is widely considered to be one of the nation's best. Such high quality is promoted by the Commission on Judicial Appointments, the Commission on Judicial Performance, the Judicial Council, and the Commission on Judicial Nominees Evaluation.

MUNICIPAL COURTS

Municipal courts have jurisdiction in both **civil law** and **criminal law** cases. Civil law cases usually involve disputes between private persons or private organizations and are concerned with whether one of the parties has been injured and what legal remedies would be appropriate for compensation. Breach of contract or defamation of character are examples of civil law cases. In a civil law case, the party bringing the suit is called the **plaintiff.** The party being sued is the **defendant.** Criminal law deals with crimes; cases are always brought "by and in the name of" the people of California. Questions to be determined are whether the defendant has injured society and what punishment is necessary.

The civil jurisdiction of municipal courts extends to cases involving up to $25,000 in contested cash or property. Because this sum is low for most civil cases in California, most of those cases are heard at the superior court level. The criminal jurisdiction of the municipal courts encompasses infractions and misdemeanors, or less serious crimes. The vast majority of municipal court criminal cases are traffic cases. (Similar courts in other states are often called traffic courts.)

Preliminary examinations in cases concerning felonies, or serious crimes, are conducted in municipal court. At these hearings, which are not trials, the judge determines whether a law has been broken and whether sufficient evidence suggests that the accused is the lawbreaker. If both of these requirements are met, then the accused is turned over to a superior court. Municipal courts also act as **small claims courts,** where individuals or corporations disputing less than $5,000 represent themselves before a judge. This procedure allows minor disagreements to be settled without lawyers' fees. Some municipal courts hold small claims court at night so contestants will not have to lose a day's salary. Unfortunately, small claims court often serves as a bill-collection agency, where utility companies and large retail stores try to collect allegedly delinquent bills.

Municipal court judges are elected in nonpartisan elections for six-year terms. The state has approximately 630 municipal court judges. Vacancies (through death, retirement, and so forth) are filled by the governor. The overwhelming majority of municipal court judges originally reached the bench by gubernatorial appointment. A judge who has decided to resign or retire will usually relinquish the post before the end of the term if he or she has confidence in the governor's ability to select a satisfactory replacement. The replacement serves the last year or so of the term and then runs for re-election as an incumbent. If the incumbent is unopposed—as is usually the case—then his or her name will not appear on the ballot. Therefore, in practice, municipal court judges (in fact, all California judges, as we will see) are appointed to a position that they hold for as long as they wish. Some judges are defeated in elections, but not many.

The role of the governor in staffing the courts is therefore extremely important. George Deukmejian made more than 1,000 appointments, and Jerry Brown more than 800. Ronald Reagan made 645 appointments, and Pat Brown made 621. An intensive study of factors that governors deem significant in choosing a judge revealed that support of the local bar association is crucial.[1] However, each governor places

---

1. Philip Dubois, "State Trial Court Appointment: Does the Governor Make a Difference?" *Judicature* 69 (June–July 1985): 20–28; Sara Fritz, "Brown's Judicial Picks Often Contributors Too," *Los Angeles Times,* April 5, 1992, p. A1.

The three "equal" branches of government

great emphasis on different additional factors. Pat Brown weighed heavily whether the potential appointee had the support of local business, labor, and political leaders, and especially if the individual was a personal friend or acquaintance of Brown's. Reagan valued the support of local business leaders and an influential legislator. Jerry Brown sought the advice of local political leaders, influential legislators, and racial and minority groups; Brown also selected lawyers who contributed heavily to his various campaigns for governor or president. The appointees of both Browns had been active in party organizations or political campaigns before their selection, and Reagan's choices had been active in bar and business associations. Each governor selected approximately 80 percent of his appointments from among members of his own political party.

Governor George Deukmejian's appointment procedure relied on a local screening committee in each area of the state that consisted of persons in whom the governor had confidence. The screening committee considered a candidate's experience, reputation, and political–judicial philosophy. It was extremely important that those appointed be acceptable to local law-enforcement authorities. Approximately 65 percent of those selected were former prosecutors, such as assistant district attorneys. Even a candidate's health was considered: Each prospective judge had to allow his or her physician to be interviewed by the administration. If a lawyer could meet these standards, then his or her name was sent to the state bar association's Commission on Judicial Nominees Evaluation (described later in the chapter).

Until 1994, California had justice courts. The justice courts had the same purpose as municipal courts but were located in rural areas. The justice courts were changed to municipal courts in 1994.

SUPERIOR COURTS

The superior courts are California's major trial courts. There must be at least one superior court for each county. The importance of the superior courts is indicated by the range of their original jurisdiction, which includes all civil cases over $25,000, all cases having to do with juveniles, guardianship cases, probate (wills), divorces, and felonies. In large counties with many judges, superior court judges specialize in and hear only certain kinds of cases, such as probate or juvenile ones. Although superior courts hear appeals from municipal courts, they are *not* appellate courts; they are trial courts.

Superior court judges are elected for six-year terms in nonpartisan elections. California has approximately 800 superior court judges (more than 220 in Los Angeles County alone). Vacancies are filled by the governor, who may wish to elevate a municipal court judge to the superior court. By filling a vacancy in this manner, the governor turns the original vacancy into two appointments.

COURTS OF APPEAL

The state is divided into six appellate districts. Each district has a court of appeal with one or more divisions to hear appeals from the superior courts in its district. The courts of appeal also review decisions of quasi-judicial bodies.

The courts of appeal are important; the vast majority of their decisions are not reviewed by the supreme court and thus are final. The chief function of these courts is to enable the losing party in superior court to appeal the case. Appellate courts filter the flow of cases going to the supreme court and thus reduce the highest court's workload. The courts of appeal correct errors in trial court cases. For example, they review questions decided by the trial judge such as the admissibility of evidence or interpretations of law. However, courts of appeal do *not* review questions of fact—that is, who did what during a crime.

At appellate hearings the justices consider only transcripts of superior court proceedings and listen only to brief oral arguments by counsel. Because the purpose of the hearing is to determine whether proper legal procedures were followed by the lower court and whether the correct law was applied, witnesses are not interrogated and evidence is not introduced. Despite popular misconceptions to the contrary, the courts of appeal reverse few criminal convictions from lower courts.

The eighty-eight justices of the courts of appeal are elected for twelve-year terms. Vacancies are filled by the governor; the name of the appointee appears on the ballot in the next gubernatorial election.[2] The ballot item asks, "Shall ——— be elected to the office for the term prescribed by law?" Because voters vote yes or no, no appellate court justice ever faces an opponent. If the justice receives more yes votes than no votes, then he or she is elected. Should the no votes exceed the yes votes, then a vacancy is created for the governor to fill.

CALIFORNIA SUPREME COURT

The California Supreme Court, consisting of seven justices, is one of the most prestigious state supreme courts in the nation. Its decisions in such areas as civil rights, the death penalty, abortion, product liability, and school finance have received national attention and have frequently influenced the U.S. Supreme Court's disposition of these issues. The California Supreme Court is a national leader because it advocates the "independent-state–grounds" doctrine, which was pioneered by Justice Stanley Mosk. Justice Mosk believes that when the state Supreme Court is interpreting provisions that are identical in the U.S. Constitution and the California Constitution, then the Court may use the state Constitution as grounds for a more expansive, but not a more restrictive, interpretation of constitutional rights. In areas such as search and seizure or the interrogation of criminal suspects by police officers, the California Supreme Court has taken a more liberal view of individual rights than has its federal counterpart. The theory is that "when the U.S. Supreme Court sets forth a rule on a constitutional issue, it is establishing a minimum standard. An individual state always has been free to establish a stricter rule."[3] Critics argue that the independent-state–grounds doctrine will cause basic rights to vary from state to state and that lower-level courts can use the doctrine to circumvent rulings of the U.S. Supreme Court. Ironically, California voters have used the initiative process to overturn state Supreme Court decisions made on independent state grounds in such areas as busing, police searches, criminal convictions, and the death penalty. As the California Supreme Court has become more conservative since 1986 (see below), it has relied less on the

---

2. At the first gubernatorial election after his or her appointment, the appellate justice is elected only for the remainder of the term to which he or she has been appointed. After this remainder has been served, the justice may then run for a full twelve-year term.

3. Ronald Blubaugh, "The State Supreme Court's Declaration of Independence," *California Journal* (May 1976): 154.

independent-state–grounds doctrine and has followed the leadership of the U.S. Supreme Court on many issues.

The California Supreme Court has discretionary authority to hear appeals from the courts of appeal and the superior courts. Because of the Supreme Court's extensive caseload, the vast majority of these petitions must be denied. However, appeals in death-penalty cases automatically go directly from the superior court to the state Supreme Court. Death-penalty appeals compose such a significant amount of the current court's caseload that it has fallen seriously behind in deciding other kinds of cases. In recent years, several justices have retired from the Supreme Court after relatively brief service; "burnout" from having to decide so many difficult death-penalty cases may be the cause. Some legal scholars have suggested an enhanced role for the courts of appeal in death-penalty cases as a way of relieving the Supreme Court's heavy workload. The courts of appeal could be allowed to make the final determination regarding the correctness of the jury's verdict of guilt in the first degree and also the correctness of its finding of special circumstances. This change would allow the Supreme Court to concentrate on the most important issue: life imprisonment without the possibility of parole or the death penalty. Justice Mosk has long favored the even more fundamental reform of increasing the size of the court to eleven justices and splitting it into two five-member divisions, one to hear criminal matters, and the other to hear civil cases. The Chief Justice would retain administrative responsibility for supervising the court's total workload and could sit in either division to replace a justice who is disqualified or ill.

The state's highest court (and also the courts of appeal) has original jurisdiction to issue the following *writs,* or orders: **prohibition,** which prohibits a lower court from having a case before it because the proceeding exceeds the lower court's jurisdiction; **habeas corpus,** which requires that a detained or jailed person be brought before a judge so that the judge may determine whether the detention is legal; and **mandate,** which compels a lower court or a public official to perform an official duty that the law specifically requires. Examples of the use of the writ of mandate, which is the most frequently used writ, are compelling the governor to call a special election to fill a vacancy in the legislature; requiring a local registrar of voters to examine the sufficiency of signatures on recall petitions; and commanding a city engineer to issue a building permit for a residence.

Supreme Court justices serve twelve-year terms. They are elected in the same manner as justices of the courts of appeal. The governor fills vacancies, generally selecting justices who share his or her views on legal and political issues. Once a justice is appointed, he or she is outside the governor's control. As an example, Governor Reagan appointed Donald Wright as chief justice and soon came to regret it. Reagan believed Wright to be a conservative, but Wright turned out to be a liberal. In general, legal and political issues are quite similar; for instance, consider capital punishment, busing, and obscenity. Obviously, a person does not give up lifelong political convictions when he or she dons the black robes. But a judge's decision also depends on the facts of the case at hand, on legal precedents, and on whether the judge believes a given issue should be decided by the courts or by the governor and the legislature—the branches designed to resolve strictly political differences.

The process followed by the California Supreme Court in deciding a case is somewhat complicated. The Court must first determine whether it wishes to review the lower court's decision. A *conference* memorandum is prepared by the court clerks, who research the case and recommend for or against granting review. At its weekly conference, the Court must then decide whether to accept the case. Acceptance requires at least four affirmative votes. Provided that review has been granted, one of the justices voting for review prepares a *calendar* memorandum, "stating the facts, applying the law, and recommending a ruling—a document that closely resembles a draft opinion."[4] The justices then take a preliminary vote on the calendar memorandum: Some justices may approve the calendar memorandum; others may suggest additions or deletions as a condition of approving it; still others may write a concurring calendar memorandum that agrees with the majority memorandum but bases the ruling on other grounds, or they may even write a dissenting (minority) calendar memorandum. After a majority of justices has agreed on a single calendar memorandum, oral arguments by the lawyers for each side in the case are scheduled. A final vote is then taken, and one of the justices agreeing with the majority calendar memorandum is assigned the task of writing the Court's opinion. This process, which involves numerous editings, rewritings, and extensive negotiating, culminates in a final opinion (or opinions) that is made public and becomes the decision of the Court.

As described later, the defeat of three liberal justices in 1986 and the appointments of Governor Deukmejian changed the orientation of the California Supreme Court, which had been a liberal stronghold for nearly four decades. Although the current Court's decisions generally support a conservative point of view, the justices are far from completely predictable, and they have issued unexpected decisions on several occasions.

In the criminal law area, the court under the leadership of Chief Justice Malcolm Lucas interpreted the Victims' Bill of Rights (discussed later in this chapter) as requiring trial judges to review a wide range of court records to determine whether a convicted felon had previously committed a residential burglary. The effect of the decision is to allow longer prison sentences for habitual criminals (*People* v. *Guerrero*, 44 Cal. 3d 343 [1988]). The Victims' Bill of Rights was also interpreted as allowing statements unlawfully obtained by the police to be used by the prosecution to impeach a defendant's credibility if the defendant chooses to testify during the trial. In so deciding, the California Supreme Court adopted the legal standard followed by the U.S. Supreme Court and rejected a California decision made during the Rose Bird era that was based on independent state grounds (People v. May, 44 Cal. 3d 309 [1988]). However, the Lucas court surprised nearly all observers when it ruled unanimously that a key section of Proposition 115 (described later) was an unconstitutional revision

---

4. "How Secret Should State High Court Decisions Be?" *Los Angeles Times,* November 23, 1978, pt. 1, p. 3.

of the state Constitution (*Raven v. Deukmejian*, 52 Cal. 3d 336 [1990]). The voters had approved Proposition 115, which provided that California courts may not use the doctrine of independent state grounds to grant criminal defendants greater rights than those afforded by the U.S. Constitution. The provision was clearly designed to overturn many of the liberal decisions of the Bird court. The current Court ruled that this section of the initiative was an unconstitutional attempt to revise the state Constitution by the initiative process. The Court held that the Constitution may be revised only by the legislature or by a constitutional convention.

The current Court overturned two Rose Bird–era decisions when it ruled that the prosecution is not required to prove the defendant's intent to kill the victim in order to establish the "special circumstances" necessary for the death penalty (*People v. Anderson*, 43 Cal. 3d 1104 [1987]). The intent-to-kill requirement had been the single greatest basis for reversals of death sentences by the Bird court. In *People v. Escobar*, 3 Cal. 4th 740 [1992]), the Court reversed another important Bird-era decision. It held that when a rapist, kidnapper, or other criminal inflicts "significant or substantial" harm on the victim, the defendant can receive a longer prison term. The Bird court had required a higher degree of harm: "severe or protracted" harm. The California Supreme Court has followed the leadership of the U.S. Supreme Court by ruling that death-row inmates who challenge their convictions may not file numerous successive habeas corpus petitions (*In re Clark*, 5 Cal. 4th 750 [1993]). Unless the inmate can show a "fundamental miscarriage of justice," he or she is limited to a single state petition. The Lucas court was concerned that inmates had abused the appeals system and had unreasonably delayed executions by repeatedly filing new appeals. Finally, the current Court has ruled that a person may be convicted of murder for causing a pregnant woman to miscarry and her fetus to die even if the fetus could have been legally aborted under California's abortion law (*People v. Davis*, 7 Cal. 4th 797 [1994]).

The current Court has also affirmed superior court death-penalty decisions far more often than did the Bird court (97 percent for the current Court; 13 percent for the Bird court), but serious trial court errors will cause a lower court decision to be reversed. For example, a unanimous Supreme Court ordered a new trial for an African-American defendant when several prospective black jurors were dismissed because of their race (*People v. Snow*, 44 Cal. 3d 216 [1987]).

In the civil law area, the California Supreme Court, consisting of five out of seven Deukmejian appointees, showed remarkable independence when it voted unanimously that the governor's appointment of a state treasurer must be approved by both chambers of the state legislature. This decision was a particularly bitter defeat for former Governor Deukmejian (*Lungren v. Deukmejian*, 45 Cal. 3d 727 [1988]). In a decision that caught almost all observers by surprise, the Court unanimously upheld Proposition 103, which sought to reduce automobile and homeowners' insurance rates by 20 percent. Insurance companies may receive an exemption from the rollback of rates if they can demonstrate to the insurance commissioner that the rate reduction would prevent them from receiving a "fair and reasonable" return (*Cal Farm Insurance*

The execution chairs at San Quentin Prison.

Courtesy of San Quentin Prison

v. *Deukmejian*, 48 Cal. 3d 805 [1989]). Because it was widely anticipated that the Court would declare the whole measure unconstitutional, the state Supreme Court insulated itself from the political charge of having a fixed bias on issues that so plagued the court under Rose Bird. The Court issued a decision of particular interest to students when it ruled that public university students cannot be forced to pay fees that fund campus political groups (*Smith* v. *Regents of the University of California*, 4 Cal. 4th 843 [1993]). The state Supreme Court held that mandatory activity fees violate the First Amendment prohibition of coerced speech because such fees force students to pay for political activities that they might oppose. Students who object to the use of their fees for political activities are entitled to a refund.

Although "judging judges" is never a precise science, it is accurate to say that the current Supreme Court is clearly more favorable to law-enforcement authorities and to the death penalty than was its predecessor.

JUDICIAL ELECTIONS

The state's voters grew restless in the late 1970s, perhaps because of controversial court decisions in the areas of busing, abortion, and the rights of criminal suspects. Maybe even more important was the belief of many voters that judges decide legal issues more on the basis of personal political values than on long-established judicial principles, even though, as we mentioned earlier, these values are not easily separated.

In any event, more voters began to express dissatisfaction with incumbent judges. Table 8.1 (page 204) shows the percentage of votes against Supreme Court justices elected from 1962 to 1994. The 1966 election marked a turning point because in that year many voters were angry at the Court for striking down Proposition 14, passed in 1964, which had established the right to refuse for personal reasons to sell real estate to any individual—that is, to practice discrimination. Before 1966, from 9 to 12 percent of the voters usually voted against Supreme Court justices. Since 1966, the negative vote has stayed in the high 20 to low 40 percent range and almost reached a majority against Rose Bird in 1978 and Cruz Reynoso in 1982. But then the unprecedented happened in 1986: Justices Bird, Reynoso, and Joseph Grodin were turned out of office by the voters. No court of appeal or Supreme Court justice had ever been defeated in the fifty-two years that California had used the judicial-retention election system, but three justices were rejected in a single day. The depth of the voters' dissatisfaction is indicated by the fact that Bird lost by 32 points, Reynoso by 20 points, and Grodin by 14 points. A *Los Angeles Times* statewide exit poll of voters found that Cruz Reynoso, the first Latino ever appointed to the Supreme Court, even failed to receive a majority of votes from Latino voters.

The key issue in the defeat of Justices Bird, Reynoso, and Grodin was clearly the death penalty. According to a Field Poll taken before the election, 83 percent of all Californians favored the death penalty. Public opposition to the Chief Justice crystallized more than a year before the election and then spilled over to the other two justices as election day approached. Opponents of the Chief Justice, led by the California District Attorneys Association, pointed out that Rose Bird voted to reverse all sixty-one death-penalty conviction cases that came before the Court during her tenure. As a result, a new trial was ordered on all or part of each of the sixty-one cases, or the convicted person's sentence was changed to life imprisonment. Hence, the opposition asserted that Bird was refusing to enforce California's death-penalty law. Supporters of the Chief Justice argued in response that proper procedures were not followed by the trial courts in these death-penalty cases, which led to a denial of the defendants' constitutional rights. Furthermore, the supporters said that it is the

Table 8.1 Votes (%) Against State Supreme Court Judges, 1962 to 1994

1962		1964		1966[a]	
Gibson	9.2	Peek	11.8	McComb	20.8
Traynor	10.3			Traynor	33.6
Tobriner	11.0			Burke	35.3
				Mosk	36.9
				Peek	37.8
1970		**1974**		**1978**	
Wright	19.4	Wright	24.3	Richardson	27.5
Burke	21.7	Mosk	25.7	Newman	35.8
Sullivan	26.8	Clark	25.9	Manuel	37.2
Peters	27.6	Tobriner	27.2	Bird	48.3
1982		**1986**		**1990**	
Richardson	23.8	Lucas	20.6	Lucas	31
Broussard	43.5	Panelli	21.4	Kennard	32
Kaus	44.3	Mosk	26.5	Baxter	34
Reynoso	47.4	Grodin	56.6	Panelli	34
		Reynoso	60.5	Arabian	44
		Bird	66.2		
		1994			
		Werdegar	39		
		Kennard	42		
		George	43		

[a]Since the constitutional revision of 1966, Supreme Court justices appear on the ballot only in gubernatorial election years.

duty of the Supreme Court to protect procedural values such as due process of law, a necessary duty that may not be popular with the public.

Another important issue that arose in the 1986 campaign for and against Justices Bird, Reynoso, and Grodin concerned the nature of the California judicial-retention election system itself. Defenders of the justices argued that to maintain the independence of the courts, court of appeal and Supreme Court justices should be retained in office unless they are "incompetent" in the sense of being unethical or in the sense of being unable or unwilling to perform their judicial responsibilities. Critics of the justices responded that California already has the Commission on Judicial Performance for assessing justices' competence, and that the voters may vote against a justice simply because they dislike his or her decisions. These contentions raise significant issues concerning an *elected* judiciary (rather than one appointed for life). If voters can deny reconfirmation to a justice based on dislike for his or her decisions, then will judges continually look over their shoulders as they make decisions? On the other hand, electing judges is intended to keep judges responsive to the needs of the governed and reflects a trust in the good sense of the public. According to one observer, if the courts engage in the "business of reforming and remaking society," they "lose their claim to protection from political ire of those coming out on the short end of the judicial rulings. . . . People who make policy ought to be accountable to someone in a democratic society."[5]

These significant issues may not be resolvable because they address the very nature of an elective judiciary. However, much of the 1986 campaign was waged on a considerably less enlightened level. Opponents of the justices included the California District Attorneys Association, the California State Sheriffs Association, the California Police Chiefs Association, Republican elected officials, farmers, and business and liability insurers who disliked Justice Bird's decisions in personal injury cases. They accused the three liberal justices of being "Jerry's judges" (a reference to their appointment by former Governor Jerry Brown, who was exceptionally unpopular at the time), and they utilized relatives of murder victims in television commercials to make emotional appeals for the death penalty. Governor Deukmejian called for the defeat of the three sitting Supreme Court justices, which was a highly unusual act for an incumbent governor. On the other hand, retention of the justices was favored by most Democratic elected officials, many law school professors, lawyers who represent plaintiffs in personal injury cases, and lawyers who defend persons accused of crimes (the California Trial Lawyers Association). They charged opponents of Rose Bird with being "bullies" and declared that Governor Deukmejian was trying to "pack" the court.

As a result of the defeat of the three justices, Governor Deukmejian appointed their replacements, which changed one of the nation's most liberal state supreme courts into a conservative one. Because Deukmejian had already appointed two justices to the Court before the election, a court majority in favor of the death penalty and many conservative legal doctrines was created.

If we turn to the trial court level, the high point for challenges to sitting judges was 1978: Twenty-eight superior court judges and forty municipal court judges were challenged. The comparable figures for 1970 were six and five challenged. In 1980

---

5. Gideon Kanner, "Standard for Judging Judges: There Is No Such Thing as a Free Lunch," in California State Senate Office of Research, *The Chief Justice Donald R. Wright Memorial Symposium on the California Judiciary* (Sacramento, 1986), pp. 12–13.

the number of challenged judges declined to fifty; two years later the number was thirty-eight, and it has continued to decline. The challengers have usually been assistant district attorneys who stress law-and-order issues and fault incumbent judges for being soft on criminals. Other reasons for challenging trial judges are unpopular decisions rendered by a particular incumbent (for example, ordering busing of school children to improve racial balances in schools) or an embarrassing scandal involving the judge. This competition has raised the cost of judicial campaigns, as incumbent judges and challengers turn to campaign-management firms. That supposedly nonpolitical, impartial judges must rely on seasoned political professionals has profound implications for the California judicial system. Competition and campaign expertise mean that judicial candidates must raise large sums of money from business companies and businesspeople, court-reporting firms, bail bondsmen, and especially other lawyers. The danger was expressed by one Fresno superior court judge: "What would you think if you were a litigant in my court and you knew the opposing counsel had contributed to my campaign? Wouldn't you wonder about the fairness of my decision if I ruled in his favor?"[6]

JUDICIAL COMMISSIONS

Commission on Judicial Appointments

The Commission on Judicial Appointments must confirm the governor's appointments to the courts of appeal and the Supreme Court. Its members are the Chief Justice of the California Supreme Court, the senior justice of the court of appeal, and the attorney general. Two of the three members must vote to confirm the nominee. Only once has the commission rejected a governor's nomination, although opposition from the commission has occasionally forced the governor to withdraw the name of a controversial choice. The members of the commission are supposed to base their votes on whether they find the nominee to be "qualified" or "unqualified," although in practice the decision is sometimes based on the nominee's political philosophy.

Commission on Judicial Nominees Evaluation

The state bar association appoints the twenty-five-member Commission on Judicial Nominees Evaluation, which is supposed to make confidential recommendations to the governor on the fitness of lawyers being considered for nomination or appointment as judges. The governor is required by law to submit the names of possible nominees for judgeships to the commission, which rates them "exceptionally well-qualified," "well-qualified," "qualified," or "not qualified." Although the governor may nominate or appoint whomever he or she chooses, the commission can embarrass

---

6. Quoted in Dena Cochran, "Paying for Judicial Races," *California Journal* (June 1981): 220. Incumbents usually outspend challengers by a margin of at least two to one.

the governor by making public its evaluation if someone it has judged to be unqualified is appointed.

The commission makes its evaluation after surveying at least seventy-five lawyers who know the candidate, and after interviewing the candidate. Because the commission meets in secret and does not disclose its sources of information, candidates (especially those who are rated as unqualified) liken it to a star-chamber proceeding. Moreover, there have been instances of commission members leaking "unqualified" ratings before the governor has received the evaluation.

Commission on Judicial Performance

The Commission on Judicial Performance is an eleven-member body that can retire, remove, or censure a judge whom the commission has found to be unfit. The constitutional ground for compulsory retirement is a "disability that seriously interferes with the performance of the judge's duties and is or is likely to become permanent." The grounds for removal or censure are more complex: "willful misconduct in office, persistent failure or inability to perform the judge's duties, habitual intemperance in the use of intoxicants or drugs, or conduct prejudicial to the administration of justice that brings the judicial office into disrepute." As an example of the latter, a municipal court judge was once removed from office for committing numerous "inexcusable and reprehensible" acts, including expressing "his disbelief in the testimony of a defendant by creating a sound commonly referred to as a 'raspberry' . . . and making a vulgar gesture (giving the 'finger' or *digitus impudicus*) in reprimanding a defendant for coming in late in a traffic matter" (*Spruance* v. *Commission on Judicial Performance*, 13 Cal. 3d 778 [1975]).

In the case of a Supreme Court justice, the Commission on Judicial Performance makes its recommendation to a panel of seven court of appeal justices selected by lot, and this panel then issues the order. In 1977 Supreme Court Justice Marshall McComb was retired because of senility.

In 1994 the voters passed a little-discussed constitutional amendment that made various changes in the commission, some of which are worthwhile and others of which are potentially quite dangerous. On the positive side, all commission proceedings must be open to the public once formal proceedings have begun against a judge. More troubling, however, was the change in the appointing authority for commission members: Rather than having a majority of members being judges appointed by the Supreme Court, the 1994 constitutional amendment made eight of the eleven members nonjudges appointed by elected officials (the governor, the Assembly Speaker, and the state Senate Rules Committee) without any review or confirmation process. When we consider that any judge in the state can be removed by the commission and that judges frequently must make decisions that affect powerful political interests and that the same political party could control both the governorship and the legislature, political interests could use the commission to punish judges who rule against those interests.

Judicial Council

The Judicial Council, headed by the Chief Justice, consists of twenty-one members; the twenty other members are appointed by the Chief Justice, the state bar association, the Assembly, and the Senate. The purpose of the council is to improve and make more efficient the California court system. Reassigning judges is one way to speed up the justice system. The Chief Justice may temporarily transfer a judge from a court with a light caseload to a court that is behind in its **docket**, or calendar. A judge from a lower court may be assigned to a higher court, but a judge from a higher court may not be assigned to a lower court without his or her permission. Retired judges may also be called into service. Many reassignments are made each year.

At each session of the state legislature, the Judicial Council reports to the legislature on the condition of the courts and suggests various court reforms. The council also sets rules of procedure for the state's courts and conducts seminars for new judges. The Judicial Council appoints an administrative director of the courts who conducts research on the court system.

JURIES

Two kinds of juries are found in California—trial juries and grand juries.

Trial Juries

Trial juries, or **petit juries,** determine the facts in civil or criminal cases and render verdicts in favor of one of the parties. Juries in felony cases must consist of twelve persons, and their decisions for conviction or acquittal must be unanimous. In misdemeanor cases and in civil cases, fewer than twelve jurors may be used if both parties consent. Both parties may also waive jury trial completely and have the case tried by a judge. Juries in civil cases may render a verdict on the basis of a three-fourths vote and a preponderance of the evidence. The state Supreme Court has ruled that counties may not rely solely on random selection of jurors from official lists of registered voters as the only method of selecting jurors. Such a selection procedure produces a disproportionately small number of African-American and Mexican-American jurors. Some counties also select potential jurors from lists of registered voters and motor-vehicle license rolls.

Many authorities have found fault with the jury system, claiming that jurors are influenced by emotional and nonrational factors (and that judges are not so influenced). One noted author has written, "To my mind a better instrument than the usual jury trial could scarcely be imagined for achieving uncertainty, capriciousness, lack of uniformity, . . . and unpredictability of decisions."[7] The alternative to a jury trial would be a judge trial, or bench trial, which some people believe produces wiser

---

7. Jerome Frank, *Courts on Trial* (Princeton, NJ: Princeton University Press, 1950), p. 123.

decisions. Jury trials in civil cases are also charged with being much more time-consuming than bench trials and thus contributing to court congestion. However, jury trials have their defenders, too. Juries of people with no legal training are thought to possess a commonsensical or natural feeling for justice that might be absent from a judge trial. Long ago, Alexis de Tocqueville wrote that jury service is "one of the most efficacious means for the education of people which society can employ."[8] Also, some people argue that trial by a jury of one's peers in a criminal case protects an individual from oppression by the state. A detailed study of the American jury system contradicts the charges of unpredictability and capriciousness: Judges and juries agree on the verdict 78 percent of the time in criminal cases; in the minority of cases in which they disagree, the jury leans heavily toward leniency.[9] In civil cases, 78 percent agreement is also found, and in instances of disagreement, a jury is slightly more likely than a judge to decide in favor of the plaintiff in personal injury cases.

Whether one favors judge trials or jury trials, a key point to remember is that most cases never go to trial. Criminal cases are most likely to be resolved by **plea bargaining** (pleading guilty to a lesser offense), and civil cases are also likely to be settled out of court. Reading 8.1 (page 210) explains the basic sequence of events in criminal cases.

Grand Juries

Grand juries consist of nineteen people (twenty-three in Los Angeles County) impaneled in each county for one year. Members are usually nominated by county judges; selection is by lottery. Grand juries have two primary functions: to return indictments and to investigate local (primarily county) government.

Grand juries return **indictments,** or charges, against suspected lawbreakers when requested to do so by the district attorney. Indictment by a grand jury means that sufficient evidence has been presented to justify a trial on criminal charges. Occasionally, though, when evidence is deemed insufficient, grand juries do not return indictments. Grand jury proceedings in criminal cases are dominated by the district attorney. Proceedings are secret, and no judge is present. The possible suspect may not have an attorney present in the room, nor may he or she question any witness or object to the prosecutor's evidence. However, rather than go through a grand jury, district attorneys usually favor making the formal charges themselves by means of an **information,** a sworn statement in superior court, or by a **complaint** filed in municipal court.

Grand juries also review the operations of local government, watching especially for wrongdoing and illegal spending by public officials. The grand jury's investigation of local government is hampered by jurors' lack of expertise in this area, by lack of staff, and by jurors' terms of only one year. By the time the incumbents have penetrated the maze of local government, all but four of them probably must be replaced by new jurors. At the end of its term, a grand jury must file a report, which may suggest reforms, on the condition of local government.

---

8. Alexis de Tocqueville, *Democracy in America,* ed. Phillips Bradley (New York: Vintage Books, 1945), 1:296.
9. Harry Kalven, Jr., and Hans Zeisel, *The American Jury* (Boston: Little, Brown, 1966), pp. 58–64.

READING 8.1

What Happens If You Get Arrested?

The material considered so far all assumes that somebody else has been arrested. But what if it is *you* who gets arrested?

1. **Arrest and Miranda warning.** When a police officer takes into custody a person whom the officer wants to interrogate or arrests any minor, the officer will give that person the warnings required by the U.S. Supreme Court in *Miranda v. Arizona*, 384 U.S. 436 (1966). These warnings are that you have a right to remain silent; that anything you say may be used against you in a later trial; that you have a right to an attorney; that if you cannot afford an attorney, one will be provided at no cost.

2. **Arraignment.** The arraignment takes place in municipal court; it is intended to inform you of the charges against you and to advise you again of your constitutional rights.

   If the crime charged is a misdemeanor, the city attorney or district attorney files a complaint. An attorney to represent you will be appointed if you have not already retained one. You will be asked whether you plead guilty or not guilty. In the event that you plead guilty, you will be sentenced. If you do not plead guilty, the judge must determine whether probable cause exists to detain you. Bail will be set or you will be released on your own recognizance (if you have sufficient ties to the community).

   If the crime charged is a felony, a date will be set for a preliminary examination and your attorney will probably make a Penal Code section 1538.5 motion, which avers that the police have illegally seized the evidence used against you.

3. **Preliminary examination.** The district attorney must present to the judge sufficient evidence to establish that a crime has been committed and that there is sufficient cause to believe that you committed a felony. If sufficient evidence is presented, you will be bound over for trial. The D.A. will then file an information in superior court or will seek an indictment.

4. **Readiness hearing.** The judge will inquire of attorneys for each side whether the case is ready for trial. Your attorney will make a Penal Code section 995 motion, which asks the judge to dismiss the case because of insufficient evidence. Plea bargaining will take place now if it has not already taken place extensively.

5. **Trial.** In the minority of cases that have not been plea-bargained, the formal trial will take place. You are entitled to a jury trial unless you formally waive it.

CRIMINAL JUSTICE ISSUES

Public concern over crime, particularly violent crime, has been one of the leading issues in recent years. In 1991, California ranked third in the violent-crime rate among the fifty states and the District of Columbia. Table 8.2 ranks California on different crime issues. Note that the state ranks consistently high on almost all issues, especially auto theft.

Table 8.2 California's National Ranking on Different Criminal Justice Issues[a]

ISSUE	RANKING
Overall Crime Rate	4
Violent Crime Rate	3
Murder	6
Rape	20
Robbery	3
Aggravated Assault	5
Property Crimes	8
Burglary	11
Larceny and Theft	20
Motor Vehicle Theft	1
State Correctional Population as a Percent of Adult Population (1990)	9
State and Local Police Personnel	13
State and Local Corrections Personnel	11
Per Capita State and Local Police Expenditures	3
Per Capita State and Local Corrections Expenditures	4

[a]The data are for 1991 and have been calculated per 100,000 population unless indicated otherwise. The District of Columbia is included in the ranking.

SOURCE: Kathleen Morgan et al., eds., *California in Perspective, 1993* (Lawrence, KS: Morgan Quinto Corporation, 1993). Reprinted by permission.

Two factors that make protection of the public much more difficult are *recidivism* and *drug-related crime*. **Recidivism** is demonstrated by the fact that more than three-fourths of the convicts released from California prisons are rearrested within three years, frequently for serious crimes that physically or psychologically harm their victims. Many parolees are also returned to prison for violating the conditions of their parole, such as testing positive for drug use. As an example of drug-related crime, nearly eight out of every ten people arrested for felonies in Los Angeles and San Diego tested positive for drug use within the previous two days. Law-enforcement authorities in Sacramento County estimate that 60 percent of their workload is drug-related: the arrest of persons manufacturing and trafficking in drugs; crimes committed to finance the habit, such as burglary, robbery, or auto theft; violent crimes committed by those under the influence; and violent crimes resulting from competition among drug dealers.[10]

10. Steven White, "Criminal Behavior Pegged to Drug Abuse," *California Journal* (January 1990): 28. See also James Sweeney, "Arresting Drugs," *Golden State Report* (February 1990): 33.

California sends more people back to prison for violating the conditions of parole than all other forty-nine states combined. These prisoners are called "technical violators" because they have been returned to prison not for a second conviction, but because they have violated parole—for example, by failing drug tests. Between 1978 and 1988, parole violators as a percentage of total prison admissions increased from 8 percent to 47 percent.[11] State policy regarding parole violators has been criticized by both liberals and conservatives. Liberals note that most parolees leave prison with no marketable skills, no high school diploma, an elementary school reading level, and a drug problem. They argue that these problems should have been addressed while the prisoner was still behind bars, especially through a drug-treatment program. Conservatives, on the other hand, assert that drug therapy is extremely expensive and that few clients avoid relapse. They say that returning technical violators to prison makes prison overcrowding much worse and is expensive because it costs $25,000 per year, or $70 per day, to incarcerate one prisoner.

The California prison system is seriously overcrowded. In 1995, 120,000 inmates were housed in facilities designed for a prison population of 66,000. As the legislature and the judiciary responded to the public's concern about crime in the 1980s and the 1990s, more people were sent to prison and for longer terms. The prison population increased by more than 300 percent in one decade. But prisons to house those persons sentenced were not built. The problem is difficult because prison construction is expensive and, in addition, few people want a new prison built in their community. The dangerously overcrowded situation leads to a constant threat of violence against both guards and inmates. Putting two prisoners in a cell built for one (double-celling) is common. Toilet facilities are poor, cells are dirty, lighting is inadequate, and prisoners feel that there is not enough exercise time. Many prisoners arrive with communicable diseases, especially tuberculosis. To make matters worse, today's prisoners are younger and more violent. In contrast with inmates of earlier years, they are more likely to have been sentenced for a violent crime than for a property crime. Many have makeshift weapons, and racially oriented gangs are commonplace. Although guards are predominantly white, racial minorities constitute more than two-thirds of the prisoners. As recently as 1970, racial minorities were only 30 percent of the prison population. Because of the rapid increase in Department of Corrections staff hiring, experienced and well-trained supervisory management people are in short supply. All of the foregoing factors indicate that the potential for a serious prison uprising is clearly present.

In the last decade and a half, California has made three significant changes to its criminal laws: the Victims' Bill of Rights (1982), Proposition 115 in 1990, and "three-strikes-and-you're-out" legislation in 1994. Paul Gann, coauthor of the tax-cutting Proposition 13, in 1982 persuaded voters to pass a ballot initiative known as the Victims' Bill of Rights. Provisions of this far-reaching measure address the use of seized evidence, bail, plea bargaining, restitution for victims, and other issues.

---

11. Joan Petersilia, "Crime and Punishment in California," *California Policy Seminar Brief* 11 (May 1993): 6.

The Gann initiative allows the use in a criminal trial of evidence seized by police through eavesdropping and wiretapping. The measure negated approximately fifty state Supreme Court rulings that required stricter rules of evidence for California trials than are required by the U.S. Supreme Court. Persons who have previously been convicted of a serious felony receive an extra five years of sentence if they are convicted of another serious felony. This provision may be the most important part of the law because it results in more guilty pleas by defendants who are afraid to risk going on trial, being convicted, and then having their prior conviction give them a longer term for the current offense. In fact, sentences enhanced by a prior conviction must be served one after another rather than concurrently.

Pretrial bail is no longer guaranteed and is to be granted only if the accused person is not a threat to public safety. When a judge grants or denies bail, he or she must state why in the court record. Critics charge that this section of the initiative reverses the presumption that a person is innocent until proven guilty.

In addition, the Victims' Bill of Rights gives victims or their surviving next of kin the right to attend all sentencing and parole hearings and to make a statement. Probation officers are required to notify them of the date of the hearing.

In 1990 the voters approved another initiative intended as a follow-up to the Victims' Bill of Rights initiative. Proposition 115 adopts the federal practice of allowing the judge rather than the attorneys to examine prospective jurors. This change speeds up trials considerably because attorneys may question jurors only to challenge them for cause, not as part of the attorneys' peremptory challenges. In addition, this comprehensive measure expands the death penalty, creates the crime of torture, repeals the right to a preliminary hearing after grand jury indictment, and allows police officers to use statements of victims or crime witnesses at preliminary hearings so that these people do not have to appear in person at the preliminary hearings. The practical meaning of the Gann crime initiative became evident only after many court challenges; Proposition 115 will be similarly tested in the coming years. The human motivation for crime is complex, as is the human motivation for any act. Reading 8.2 (page 214) provides one perspective on criminal motivation.

In 1994, reports of two separate murders of young girls coalesced public support behind "three-strikes-and-you're-out" legislation. A young girl in Fresno was murdered by a man with a long record of previous crimes. This was soon followed by the murder of Polly Klaas, who was abducted from a slumber party at her Petaluma home and murdered by a man who had been released from prison just months earlier. Governor Wilson and legislative Republicans pushed through the legislature the following reforms of the state's criminal law: Under "strike one," anyone convicted of a violent or serious felony must serve at least 80 percent of his or her sentence (under the previous law, a prisoner could use "good-time" credits to reduce up to 50 percent of his or her sentence); under "strike two," a person convicted of a second serious or violent felony will be sentenced to twice the prison term for that crime; under "strike three," anyone convicted of a third felony must be sentenced to a

READING 8.2

The Bloodiest Criminals May Still Be Sane

Criminals don't have to be suffering from a disease to commit heinous crimes, according to a mental health expert. Most of the men and women behind bars actually suffer from a "character disorder."

In other words, they lack a conscience.

"I would feel terrible if I bashed a lady over the head for a quarter, but these people don't," said Dr. Steven Shon, state Department of Mental Health assistant to the director for clinical services. "That is why they can shoot somebody, maim, rob, whatever and they think, 'So what?'"

For instance, state doctors determined last year that rapist-mutilator Larry Singleton had a character disorder rather than a serious mental illness. As a result, the man who raped and chopped off the arms of 15-year-old Mary Vincent was released from prison in April despite an outcry from Californians.

Lawmakers held a public hearing and protested the diagnosis. A recently enacted Cali-

fornia law would have allowed the state to hold Singleton in a mental hospital if he had been diagnosed as suffering from a serious mental illness that was not in remission. Shon said doctors couldn't make that diagnosis because Singleton neither suffered from delusions nor any of the other symptoms of a serious mental illness.

"There is a flaw in thinking that because Singleton chops off a girl's arms, he must be crazy," Shon said. "Just because someone does something awful, doesn't mean they are crazy. But we as a society see that thing as so abhorrent, that we create a reason. We say, 'Gee, he must be crazy.' . . . But we (doctors) don't have any magic pill or magic wand that can take violence out of them. Violence in itself is not anything we have answers for."

SOURCE: From "The Bloodiest Criminals Still Can Be Sane," *Sacramento Bee,* August 8, 1988, p. A13. Copyright Sacramento Bee, 1990. Reprinted by permission.

minimum prison term of 25 years to life. The third felony can be any of 500 felonies on the books in California and does not need to be either serious or violent. Two controversial aspects of the law are that strikes one and two could be juvenile crimes committed by 16- and 17-year-olds even if they are not tried as adults and do not have a right to a jury trial; furthermore, the third strike could be a relatively minor nonviolent crime.

"Three-strikes" legislation is likely to be extremely costly, according to the California Department of Corrections. Twenty new prisons will need to be built before the year 2000, *in addition to* the twelve that had already been planned before the measure's passage. The corrections part of the state budget has been the fastest growing item in the budget in recent years, and it will grow even larger in the future. More money will also be needed for judges, prosecutors, and public defenders because criminal defendants are less likely to plea bargain and more likely to demand a trial as a result

Wayne Stayskal / *Tampa Tribune*

of the tough provisions of three strikes. Given California's serious fiscal problems, paying for three-strikes legislation may be a major headache in the future. Proponents of the legislation argue that California will save money in the long run because, at least for the time that they are in prison, habitual criminals will not be able to commit crimes that victimize innocent Californians. The Rand research group estimates that three strikes will reduce the number of serious crimes (such as aggravated assault, rape, robbery, and burglary) by 338,000 per year over the next quarter century. This reduction is 28 percent below the number of serious crimes predicted if the legislation had not been approved.

California also has attempted gun control, which has been accompanied by considerable controversy. After a gunman armed with a military-style assault rifle killed five children and wounded twenty-nine in a Stockton schoolyard in 1989, the legislature made California the first state to ban this type of weapon. As a result of the legislation, it is illegal in California to manufacture or sell firearms with a high rate of fire or firepower capacity. Such weapons that were registered with the California Department of Justice before 1991 may be legally possessed.

In 1990 California became the first state to impose a fifteen-day waiting period for the purchase of recreational rifles and shotguns. This state has long required authorities to run a background check for a criminal record or for mental instability when a person seeks to purchase a handgun. The "cooling-off" period for rifle

Lady Justice

purchases was intended to prevent crimes of passion in which family members are killed. This legislation may actually be more far-reaching than the ban on assault weapons because it will affect millions of ordinary citizens who buy firearms for sporting purposes or for self-protection. The National Rifle Association argued unsuccessfully that the law would inconvenience law-abiding citizens but would not prevent criminals from getting firearms because the latter can always get them from illegal sources.

As indicated earlier in the chapter, the state Supreme Court's decisions in the *Anderson* and *Clark* cases mean that the death penalty could be imposed more frequently in California. In 1992, Robert Alton Harris became the first person executed in California in a quarter of a century. This action was soon followed by the execution of David Edwin Mason in 1993. Although California has an extraordinarily large number of prisoners on death row and the public overwhelmingly supports the death penalty, federal appellate court justices sitting in California are likely to block executions. If there is an execution in California, arguments will rage about the justice, fairness, and humaneness of death as a punishment. Opponents of capital punishment make five principal arguments:

1. No conclusive scientific evidence exists that the death penalty acts as a deterrent to murder.

2. When capital punishment is imposed on a widespread basis, some innocent people will be put to death. If a mistake is made, it is irrevocable and completely unjust.

3. Poor people cannot mount an adequate defense and are more likely to be convicted of capital crimes.

4. Blacks who kill whites are much more likely to receive death sentences than are other murderers.

5. When the State of California legalizes the taking of human life by execution, it cheapens the value of human life.

Death penalty proponents make five generally countervailing arguments:

1. The death penalty acts as a deterrent under many circumstances.

2. When capital punishment is imposed, there will be more innocent victims of future murderers saved than innocent murderers executed by mistake.

3. Certain crimes are themselves so grievous an affront to humanity that the only adequate response is the penalty of death.

4. If there is no death penalty, an outraged public will turn to vigilante justice.

5. If life is to be valued, then it must be known that one who takes the life of another forfeits his own.

Neither side in this emotional debate is likely to persuade the other, and the debate will arise again and again as each convicted murderer is put to death in future years.

Los Angeles, April 1992: Riot or Rebellion?

In April 1992, some Los Angeles residents erupted in five days of violent disorder that was the most costly civil disturbance in terms of human life in recent American history: Fifty-one people were killed and 2,400 were wounded. Unlike the 1965 Watts riots, violence was not confined to an isolated area. The event that triggered the eruption was the acquittal of four white police officers for unlawful brutality in the beating of Rodney King, an African-American man whom they were attempting to arrest after a high-speed automobile chase. A private citizen had videotaped the beating, and the videotape received worldwide attention because it showed the officers repeatedly beating King with their batons and kicking him while he was on the ground. An all-white jury did not believe that the videotape told the whole story and believed that King was combative and ignored the officers' orders. Hours after the acquittal verdicts were announced, thousands of rioters torched buildings, looted and ransacked stores, assaulted passersby, and engaged in sniper fire.

Downtown Los Angeles, South Los Angeles, Hollywood, and the Westside soon resembled a smoke-covered combat zone. More than 1,600 buildings were severely damaged or burned out, usually by gasoline. Governor Wilson sent in 12,300

During the 1992 Los Angeles riots, California National Guard soldiers responded to sniper fire near Florence Avenue and the Harbor Freeway.

members of the California National Guard and the California Highway Patrol. President George Bush ordered 3,300 federal troops and 1,000 riot-trained federal law officers. "A city that had long boasted about the richness of its Third World flavor came to mirror the worst of some war-torn neighbors to the south. Military equipment rolled down boulevards, men with automatic weapons stood sentry, and a dusk-to-dawn curfew kept residents indoors."[12]

More than 17,000 arrests were made, including 2,600 felony arrests. A *Los Angeles Times* study of 700 people convicted of riot-related felonies found that 60 percent had prior felony convictions. Demographically, 50 percent were black, 43 percent Latino, 4 percent white, and 3 percent "other." Eighty percent of the Latinos were foreign-born. Two-thirds of the rioters were unemployed, and only 13 percent earned as much as $1,000 per month. The demographic characteristics of the rioters were generally reflective of the demographic characteristics of the riot-damaged areas. According to James Q. Wilson of the University of California at Los Angeles, one of

---

12. All quotations in this section are from the *Los Angeles Times*, May 2, 1992, p. A1; June 18, 1992, p. B3; October 22, 1992, p. A31; May 2, 1993, p. A1.

the nation's leading experts on crime, "If the immediate area is composed mostly of Latinos . . . Latinos are going to be the ones police are going to pick up." It is perhaps an ironic commentary on California life that a special investigatory commission created by the L.A. Police Commission reported that "live television coverage of the initial outbreaks of violence was a catalyst for further looting and violence" because television reported the slow response of the Los Angeles Police Department to the disturbance.

Often in politics, the more things change, the more they remain the same. The comments of political activists after the 1992 disturbances were almost identical echoes of comments made after the Watts riots more than a quarter of a century earlier. Conservatives stressed the necessity for all people to be law-abiding, especially in the event of governmental decisions that one strongly opposes. Liberals pointed to what they feel are the "root causes" of riots: racism, police brutality, chronic poverty, the need for jobs, and the lack of economic opportunity in poor areas. They issued the customary calls for more spending on social programs. Minority group spokespersons said that 1992 Los Angeles did not have a riot, but a rebellion. It was a "revolt of the poor" against inequality, and there would be "no justice, no peace"—meaning that rioting would recur—unless the police officers involved in the King affair were convicted. However one views these different claims and counterclaims, this much is clear: The areas most severely hit by the violence were the poorest areas of the city. A hard life for the people living there got measurably harder as jobs were lost in burned-out stores and small businesses, limited housing became even scarcer, and grocery stores and gas stations became harder to find. If Rodney King was beaten and kicked when he was already down on the ground, the looters, firebombers, and snipers gave the same treatment to the residents of the poorest areas of the city.

SUMMARY

In this chapter, we have discussed California's trial courts and its appellate courts, with special emphasis on the pivotal role of the California Supreme Court. Perhaps the most difficult issues faced by any court are criminal justice issues. We have noted drug-related crime, prison overcrowding, recent reform proposals, and clearly the most serious issue of all, capital punishment.

DISCUSSION QUESTIONS

1. How do trial courts differ from appellate courts? Which California courts are trial courts, and which are appellate courts?

2. In what ways do the Commission on Judicial Appointments, the Commission on Judicial Performance, the Judicial Council, and the Commission on Judicial Nominees Evaluation serve to improve the California court system?

3. Describe the two kinds of juries found in trial courts.

4. If a judge's views on legal issues have much in common with his or her views on political issues, would it be better to have California judges run as candidates of a political party? Or should this state adopt the federal practice of executive appointment of judges for life, subject only to removal by impeachment?

5. A dramatic change of personnel on a court can change that body's decisions. If the liberal Supreme Court under Rose Bird had remained in office, how might it have decided the recent cases discussed in this chapter?

6. If the saying "Justice delayed is justice denied" is true, how do you rate the California court system? Would you like to try to sell the idea of swift justice to an indicted suspect whose attorney is trying to prepare an effective defense?

7. Whether to use the death penalty as a punishment is one of the most momentous decisions that any society has to make. What are the leading arguments for and against capital punishment? Based on the arguments made by each side, what can we conclude are the core values that each side seeks to promote?

8. What is "three-strikes-and-you're-out" legislation? Considering *both* the problem this legislation is intended to correct and the fiscal implications of the legislation, are the benefits likely to outweigh the costs?

Part Four

LOCAL GOVERNMENT AND STATE AND LOCAL GOVERNMENT FINANCE

Government in California encompasses not only the state but also counties, cities, special districts, and regional agencies. Cities and counties make up the grassroots government that has been celebrated since the time of Thomas Jefferson. In Part 4, we focus on local government and many of the quality-of-life issues we have discussed in this book. Consider some of the recent clashes in local government over such issues as land use and zoning, management of growth, traffic congestion, and location of public housing for low-income people. One of the hottest issues in California in recent years—the property tax—was directly related to local government. Few issues incensed Californians more than rapidly increasing property-tax bills.

Local government is important in the lives of Californians because at the local level the **police power** of government is exercised vigorously. By "police power," far more is meant than simply law enforcement. Police power is the authority of local (or state) government to pass laws regulating the health, safety, welfare, and morals of the people. Because this authority is so broad (little is excluded from the definition), Californians concerned about the quality of life and about gaining control of the institutions that shape their lives should pay special heed to local government.

Local government in California encompasses 58 counties, more than 470 cities, more than 1,000 school districts, and approximately 3,400 other special districts. Local governments may exercise only the powers granted to them by state law or the state constitution. Each of the 50 state governments is thus a **unitary system of government.** The legal relationship between local government and the state government was stated long ago:

> Local governments owe their origin to, and derive their powers from, the [state] legislature. It breathes into them the breath of life, without which they cannot exist. As it created, so it may destroy. . . . Unless there is some constitutional limitation on the right, the legislature might, by a single act, if we can suppose it capable of so great a folly and so great a wrong, sweep from existence all of the [cities] of the state, and the [cities] could not prevent it.[1]

Realistically, the state legislature is not going to abolish the city of San Francisco or even the city of Lodi. California has been one of the most permissive states in the amount of latitude granted to local governments. However, Proposition 13 of 1978 dramatically reduced local property-tax revenues and caused local jurisdictions to depend financially much more on the state government. As a result, power increasingly shifted to the state level, especially to the legislature, which must decide how much money will be allotted to counties, cities, or special districts.

In Chapter 9, we will describe the various local governments in California and discuss the financial issues these governments face. In Chapter 10, we will look at the state budget and state taxes, principally the income tax and the state sales tax. As an example of the fiscal centralization noted above, we will see that state aid to local governments is the largest item in the state budget; in fact, it is about three-fourths of the entire state budget. As Chapters 9 and 10 will point out, local governments are tied to state budget purse strings in a myriad of ways. In an ironic twist of fate, the state has recently been looking to local government as a source of money to help solve the state's financial problems.

---

1. *City of Clinton v. Cedar Rapids and Missouri R. R. Co.,* 24 Iowa 455 (1868).

Chapter 9

Counties, Cities, Special Districts, and Regional Agencies

*I*n June 1978, California voters passed Proposition 13 (the Jarvis–Gann amendment). Although the amendment dramatically reduced the property taxes on which counties, cities, and special districts so heavily depended, its effects were not felt immediately by local government. Unfortunately, that happy situation has changed. The huge state surplus that the state legislature used to bail out local governments is long gone. In fact, the state government is now coveting some local government money as a way to solve the *state's* financial problems. How local governments have reacted to this fiscal stringency and how the "settling in" of Proposition 13 has altered intergovernmental relations are two of the main themes of this chapter. We will now consider the various types of local governments in California.

COUNTIES

The first striking fact about California's fifty-eight counties is their diversity. In terms of area, San Bernardino County is the largest in the continental United States; covering 20,000 square miles, this county is 200 times larger than San Francisco County. In terms of population, Los Angeles County, with far more than 9 million people, is the largest in the nation. By contrast, Alpine County has approximately 1,200 people.

Counties provide many services. They are the administering agents for various state programs, including welfare (although almost all the money and regulations for the welfare program are prescribed by the federal and state governments). Counties provide health care. They also provide police and fire protection in **unincorporated areas,** or noncity areas, and within cities that contract for these services; the sheriff runs the county jail. Municipal and superior courts are funded by the state but operated by the county. Counties conduct elections for cities, and they also attempt to meet recreational needs. Outside cities (in unincorporated areas), county government serves as a general-purpose local government, performing services usually rendered by city governments such as building streets and roads, regulating land use, and providing zoning and law enforcement. The importance of the role of county government in unincorporated areas is indicated by the fact that almost 20 percent of Californians live in these areas. The county is an important keeper of records (wills, deeds, birth certificates, and so forth).

County Budget

Eleven percent of the typical county budget is allotted to cover general government costs. Counties must provide for a legislative body (the board of supervisors), an assessor, and many other officials (either elected or appointed). Salaries must be paid, and retirement plans must be provided for all county employees. The largest portion of a county's budget is for public assistance. The percentage spent on welfare varies somewhat from county to county, but 40 percent is an average figure. Although the county administers the welfare program, the bulk of the money is provided by the federal government and the state government. To relieve financial pressures on counties because of Proposition 13, the state government assumes all county costs of medical care for poor people, a program known as Medi-Cal.

Public protection of persons and property constitutes some 26 percent of budget costs. By *public protection* we mean the district attorney, the sheriff, the coroner, the county jail, and the probation department, as well as juvenile detention, fire protection, and activities such as building and safety inspection.

Counties spend 13 percent of their budgets on health and sanitation. In addition to operating the county hospital and mental-health facilities, counties treat alcoholism, venereal disease, and other problems on an outpatient basis. The AIDS epidemic has had and will continue to have an effect on county government because many AIDS victims are treated in county hospitals. Inspection of milk and control of pests and rodents are other functions.

Construction and maintenance of roads, bridges, and other facilities account for 4 percent of the budget. Supported by the state's gasoline tax, 42 percent of the state's road mileage is maintained by counties. As more and more counties come to be covered with an unhealthy, low-hanging layer of gray smog, alternate means of transporting people (such as mass transit) become a county concern.

The county allots 1.2 percent of its expenditures for education, primarily for libraries but also for the county superintendent of schools. Finally, county governments seek to meet recreation and cultural needs. Approximately 1.3 percent of the money budgeted goes for parks, golf courses, and county beaches.

Table 9.1 Sources of County Revenue Before and After Proposition 13

SOURCE	FY 1977 PERCENTAGE	FY 1993 PERCENTAGE
General property tax	35.36	21.79
Sales tax	2.18	1.23
Other taxes	.64	1.27
Licenses, permits, and franchises	.87	.94
Fines, forfeits, and penalties	1.03	1.14
Use of money and property	1.56	2.39
From other governmental agencies:		
State	24.72	38.20
Federal	23.88	20.14
Other	.13	.57
Charges for current services	8.92	9.02
Other revenue	.71	3.31
	100.00	100.00

SOURCE: State Controller, *Annual Report of Financial Transactions Concerning Counties, Fiscal Year 1976–1977* (Sacramento, 1978), p. vii; State Controller, *Annual Report, 1992–1993*, p. vii.

Sources of county revenues are given in Table 9.1. Note that state and federal aid currently account for more than 58 percent of county revenue, and that reliance on the property tax has decreased since the pre–Proposition 13 period.

Types of Counties

General Law Counties Of California's fifty-eight counties, forty-six are *general law* counties. General law counties operate according to general laws, passed by the legislature and applicable statewide. Such laws might determine the structure of county government, or require that certain public services be provided, or allow for the levying of various taxes. The state legislature classifies counties by population size and then passes laws covering particular classes of counties, regardless of where those counties are located. Because two counties of similar population may have widely different characteristics and needs, a desire for more flexibility paved the way for a second type of county, a charter county.

Charter Counties Although only twelve counties are charter (or home rule) counties, approximately two-thirds of the state's population lives in these counties. The charter counties are San Bernardino, Los Angeles, Butte, Tehema, Alameda, San Francisco, Fresno, Sacramento, San Diego, San Mateo, Santa Clara, and Placer. Rather than general laws, a county's **charter**—a document similar to a constitution—determines how charter counties are governed. General law counties must have a five-member board of supervisors, but charter counties can have more than five supervisors; more charter counties, especially large ones, should use this opportunity. In addition to choosing supervisors by district, voters in general law counties must elect the following long list of officers: treasurer, county clerk, auditor, sheriff, tax collector, controller, license collector, district attorney, recorder, assessor, public administrator, and coroner. In charter counties, as a service to tired voters, these officials (with the exception of the assessor, sheriff, and district attorney) can be either appointed or elected. According to the short-ballot reform, officers whose functions are essentially technical and who do not establish basic policy for the county should be appointed by the supervisors. Many of the duties of these officials are combined, especially in charter counties.

To establish a charter, a board of freeholders must be elected. These citizens draw up a charter, which is then submitted to the voters for approval. Placer County adopted a charter in 1980. One great asset of a charter is that a county can tailor its government to its needs and preferences.

City and County of San Francisco Never known for being hidebound, San Francisco has a combined city and county. Unique in California, this arrangement was established in the city's charter. San Francisco is the only county to have more than five supervisors—it has eleven. The city–county has a mayor, who is elected separately from the supervisors; he or she has veto powers and substantial power over the budget and can appoint members of various powerful commissions (civil service commission, police commission, and planning commission). For a local executive in California, these are extensive powers.

County Officers

Board of Supervisors The legislative body for each county is its board of supervisors (see Figure 9.1). County supervisors serve four-year terms; they are elected in nonpartisan elections that coincide with the party primaries of even-numbered years. If one candidate receives a majority of the total primary vote, a runoff election is not needed in November. Vacancies on the board of supervisors in general law counties are filled by the governor; vacancies in charter counties are filled by the supervisors themselves or by the governor. The board of supervisors adopts the county budget; approximately 90 percent of its expenditures are mandated by the state. The supervisors may sit as an appeals board to hear appeals regarding property **assessments** made by the assessor and also regarding land-use decisions made by the county planning commission. Before the passage of Proposition 13, the board of supervisors set each county's tax rate on real estate, but the Jarvis amendment set the maximum

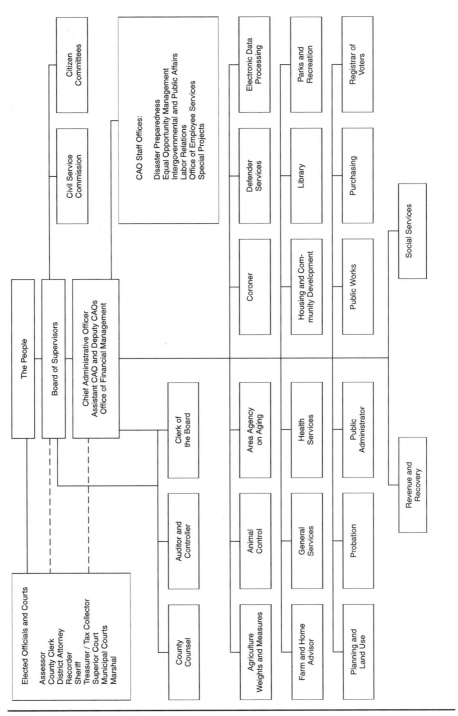

Figure 9.1 County organization

rate at 1 percent throughout the state. Finally, supervisors also oversee various county departments and decide the location of roads and bridges.

The small size of county boards of supervisors may be unwise in large counties. Five counties have more than 1 million people, two have more than 2 million, and one has more than 9 million residents. Supervisorial decisions have immense impact in these counties, but five supervisors, even if all are present at meetings, may be too few to provide adequate representation and to be an effective decision-making body. In 1992, Los Angeles County voters rejected a ballot proposition to increase the number of supervisors to nine (as well as a related proposal to create an elected county executive). Unfortunately, to control policy with smaller boards, interest groups need to win over only three people rather than four, five, or six. Supervisors in urbanized, populous counties are heavily dependent on campaign contributions.

Chief Administrative Officer California county government has no elected executive officer, but counties do have an official appointed by the board of supervisors; he or she is called the chief administrative officer (CAO) or county manager (in charter counties). The CAO or county manager prepares the budget for board approval, administers the budget after it has been approved, and provides the board of supervisors with information with which the board can make decisions that will be implemented by the county manager or CAO. A county manager is normally given more authority than a CAO in budget matters and personnel decisions, but both officials are there primarily to integrate and coordinate county government. The following descriptions of other county officials will make the need for such coordination obvious.

District Attorney The district attorney prosecutes (brings to trial) those accused of crime. He or she must also investigate all shootings involving police officers. If the county has no county counsel, then the district attorney will also represent the county in civil cases. The post of district attorney is an important stepping-stone to higher office, such as a judgeship or the state legislature.

Sheriff and Coroner The sheriff and deputies enforce the law in unincorporated areas of the county and in any cities that contract for law-enforcement services (under the Lakewood Plan described later). The sheriff's office provides bailiffs, or attendants, for the superior court and serves all processes and summonses. The sheriff also runs the county jail. In many counties, this office is combined with the office of coroner, which conducts inquests of all sudden, violent, or unusual deaths.

County Clerk and Recorder The county clerk performs many significant duties. He or she is the clerk of the superior court and of the board of supervisors, and keeps minutes and maintains documents for both. The county clerk also keeps many other important records such as marriage licenses, articles of incorporation, and various filings (the clerk collects fees for these services). In addition, the county clerk registers voters and conducts elections. The office of county clerk is often combined with the office of recorder.

Bettmann

Orange County's supervisors discuss the fiscal fallout from the county's 1994 bankruptcy.

Public Administrator, Auditor, County Superintendent of Schools, and County Assessor The public administrator administers the estates of people who die without clearly designating heirs. The auditor disburses checks (warrants) and reviews county books. The county superintendent of schools maintains statewide standards in local school districts, processes applications for teacher certification, and provides special programs for school districts such as migrant education and classes for handicapped children. Programs that cannot be economically provided by a small school district (for example, audiovisual services or data processing) are provided by the county superintendent of schools on a contract basis. The assessor determines the value of real estate in the county.

Local Agency Formation Commission Every county must have a **local agency formation commission (LAFCO)** composed of two members appointed by the board of supervisors, two appointed by mayors of cities in the county, and one appointed by the first four members of the agency itself. The purpose of the commission is to approve or disapprove proposals to form cities or special districts (described later in the chapter) and proposals to **annex** unincorporated territory to cities. The LAFCO conducts a fiscal review intended to make sure that the proposed city or special district will be financially healthy. Some factors that LAFCOs consider are assessed valuation, likelihood of future growth, population density, the need for governmental services, and the adequacy of current services. LAFCOs are supposed to use the fiscal review to prevent the creation of unnecessary new cities and special districts.

One fact is readily apparent about California county governments: They are not each run by one elected executive (as at the national level) but by many elected executives. With authority so divided and dispersed, responsibility for county action or inaction is difficult to determine. Because the board of supervisors will ultimately be held responsible, it should appoint officials—such as the auditor, tax collector, and coroner—who do not hold policy-making positions but technical, specialized, and ministerial positions. The supervisors should be given the power to appoint all county officers except the district attorney, who as public prosecutor should be responsible only to the electorate. However, were the state legislature to consider such action, the County Clerks Association, the County Treasurers Association, the County Recorders Association, and other such organizations would lobby hard against the bill in Sacramento. The dispersed nature of county government paved the way for Orange County's 1994 bankruptcy. A separately elected county treasurer, who was not directly controlled by the board of supervisors, engaged in risky and speculative investments of county money, borrowing $2 for every $1 that he had in his investment fund. When the treasurer's financial house of cards collapsed, Orange County plunged into bankruptcy.

FUTURE OF COUNTIES HIGHLY UNCERTAIN

As California county government nears the end of the century, its dual and perhaps contradictory roles become even more evident, especially in the financing of counties. The state's fifty-eight counties were established to be agents of the state government for the delivery of services required by the state, yet they are also supposed to be local governments responsive to the special needs of fifty-eight separate constituencies. By concentrating the power of the purse in Sacramento, Proposition 13 disconnected the raising of money by counties and the spending of that money by counties. County funds are substantially supplied by taxes levied by higher levels of government (state and federal); these higher levels allow counties little flexibility in determining expenditure priorities tailored to meet local preferences, which vary from county to county. Because of the pervasiveness of state mandates, local discretionary programs ranging from libraries to the sheriff's patrol services tend to be shortchanged. To make matters worse, county governments have only those revenue sources authorized by the state. Perhaps a better approach would be to allow counties any revenue source not forbidden by the state. Different strategies for solving county fiscal problems might be a state buyout of specific county programs, or the state dedicating part of one or more of its revenue sources to the counties, or the state giving counties authority to levy various taxes (for example, a higher sales tax). Because of the state's financial problems, none of these possibilities is particularly likely. Local governments need to plan over the long range, hence counties (and cities as well) need a stable source of revenue. But county governments are seriously dependent on state financial aid, which varies from year to year depending on the fiscal and political pressures to which the state government is subjected.

The highly uncertain future of counties is evident from the many recent proposals to restructure counties radically or to abolish them entirely. Some reformers would merge county government with state government, thus making counties merely administrative districts of the state. The rationale for this reform is that more than one-third of county government revenue already comes from the state and that 90 percent of their expenditures are already mandated by the state. Other reformers would abolish counties in highly urbanized areas because county services are allegedly duplicative of city services. Still other reformers would abolish counties in favor of strengthened regional governments (regional governments are described later in the chapter). Each of these proposals compromises local control and responsiveness partially or totally, and thus is likely to be controversial if it were to come to a vote of the state legislature or of the public. Counties have few friends in the state legislature: Republicans do not like them, and Democrats are unreliable allies. Republicans dislike county governments because counties dispense welfare and health care to poor people. Neither of these programs is a high-priority Republican program. Democrats, on the other hand, favor these programs but also want to spend money on education, environmental protection, and a host of other projects. As evidence of the "unwanted stepchild" status of counties, consider what happened to them in the 1992 and 1993 state budget crises. In 1992, the state government ended the bailout of local government that began immediately after the passage of Proposition 13 in 1978. The state transferred $1.3 billion from local governments ($525 million from counties) to school districts. The state did this to reduce the amount it had to allocate to schools. In 1993, the state transferred $2.6 billion in local property-tax revenue to school districts. This money included nearly $2 billion from counties and was nearly 25 percent of the property-tax revenue collected by counties, cities, redevelopment agencies, and special districts. Because the state was taking local government money (especially county money) to pay for state aid to education, the state was easing its own financial burden. The state government was also making *state* tax increases less likely, but *local* tax increases more likely. County officials called this procedure the "trickle-down theory of taxation."

CITIES

The vast majority of Californians live in one of the state's more than 470 cities. The term *cities* covers incorporated areas ranging from the city of Amador (in Amador County) with 160 people and Sand City (Monterey County) with 210 people to the state's metropolitan giants. Regardless of their sizes, cities influence the degree to which our lives are pleasant and improved by amenities, at least to the extent that government can make our lives pleasant. Cities supply police and fire protection; build and maintain streets and sewers; provide regulations such as building inspection, sanitation, and zoning codes; and furnish parks and libraries. Some cities operate public utilities.

The types of cities, following the same pattern as counties, include general law cities (numbering approximately 390), charter cities (numbering some 80), and the combined City and County of San Francisco. Although there are many more general law cities than charter cities, all of the state's large cities are charter cities. Because the state legislature has been giving general law cities more and more control over their own affairs, the difference between general law cities and charter cities is becoming unclear. However, what the legislature gives, it may also take away. The powers of charter cities are specified in their charters or in the state Constitution.

City Budget

The most important items in the city budget are police protection and the provision of electricity to the public. Other key budgetary items are fire protection, streets and storm drains, sewers, parks and recreation, libraries, and the provision of water. Table 9.2 shows sources of city revenue. Note that cities have a much more diversified revenue base than do counties. As the table shows, property taxes and state–federal aid have become less important and charges for current services much more important since the passage of Proposition 13. Examples of the latter are charges for sewer services, garbage collection, water, and especially electricity. A relatively new tax is the utility users tax, which is applied to a resident's electric, gas, or telephone bill, usually at a rate of 5 percent. City councils prefer this tax because it is collected by the utility companies as part of their monthly billings: Any taxpayer anger may be directed at the utilities and not at elected officials. Business license taxes are based on the total gross receipts of local businesses. Because cities apply the same percentage to businesses with a high net profit margin and those with a low net profit margin, the tax is burdensome for the latter. The transient occupancy tax, or hotel–motel tax, is popular because it is paid by tourists or other nonresidents.

Cities have also greatly increased their use of **exactions**, which are the streets, sewers, sidewalks, parks, and police and fire stations that cities demand from developers in exchange for a building permit. According to a report issued by the state Office of Planning and Research, these "are the legal, legitimate equivalent of extortion."[1] For example, to receive permission to build Rancho Carmel near San Diego, the developer had to provide $85 million in improvements, including a fire station complete with fire engines, a freeway overpass, traffic signals, and parks. Cities (and counties) have had to rely heavily on these fees as a result of Proposition 13, but these charges also add greatly to the cost of a new home because developers pass

---

1. Quoted in Ron Soble, "Government's Search for Money," *Los Angeles Times,* June 9, 1983, pt. 11, p. 5.

Table 9.2 **Sources of City Revenue Before and After Proposition 13**

SOURCE	FY 1977 PERCENTAGE	FY 1993 PERCENTAGE
General property tax	23.78	8.20
Sales and use tax	15.47	9.58
Business license tax	2.77	2.41
Other nonproperty taxes	7.84	6.97
Utility users tax	—	4.01
Licenses and permits	2.01	1.14
Fines and penalties	1.92	.97
Revenues from use of money and property	2.93	4.41
Other governmental agencies	29.89	10.28
Charges for current services (e.g., electricity, water, sewers, garbage collection)	8.64	39.96
Other revenue	4.75	12.07
	100.00	100.00

Note: The state controller has grouped together data from cities differing widely in population. The importance of each revenue source may vary considerably between very large and very small cities.

SOURCE: State Controller, *Annual Report of Financial Transactions Concerning Cities, Fiscal Year 1976–1977* (Sacramento, 1978), p. viii; State Controller, *Annual Report, 1992–1993*, p. viii.

the cost of exactions on to purchasers. The increased cost of houses as a result of exactions, which is often $30,000 or more, makes many homes unaffordable to first-time buyers. Moreover, is it fair to make one part of the community (those buying homes today) pay for what benefits the whole community?

User charges are another nontax source of income for cities. If a person visits a city museum or plays golf on a county course, he or she may pay a fee to help support that service. That those who receive a benefit should pay for it has long been urged by some scholars of taxation. (Other maxims of taxation in addition to the benefits-received principle will be discussed in Chapter 10.) Proponents of user charges argue that these charges are fair because no one is coerced into paying for a service that he or she does not receive and that user charges promote conservation: Water and electricity are conserved because they must be paid for, and conservation increases when the unit price rises with consumption. Opponents of user charges argue that

Mickey Pfleger / Photo 20–20

The protection of people and property is an important duty of city governments.

poor people may be denied some government services and that some benefits cannot be financed in this manner. Air-pollution-control programs or flood-control programs are so-called collective goods that benefit all citizens. These services could not be financed by user charges.

Incorporation

Cities come into being (incorporate) for numerous reasons: to maintain local control of local services, especially police protection and the issuance of construction permits; to get the power to zone land in order to maintain current land uses or to prevent undesirable uses; to avoid being annexed by another city; to assimilate and tax a local industry or shopping center; to collect sales tax revenue from a local shopping center or auto dealership; and to keep taxes down by negotiating money-saving service contracts with the county. Cities are sometimes formed not for people but for special interests. Industries may want to create a city containing little but industries so that the assessed valuation is high, because a low tax rate will still raise the amount of money needed for services. Vernon is a city of this type.

Cities not only may be born but also may die, as happens when the city stops electing officers. For example, the city that once served as the county seat of Alpine County ceased to exist.

Forms of City Government

The first form of city government we will discuss is the mayor–council city. Here, the city council possesses the legislative power. Executive power is wielded by a mayor, who may be either strong or weak, depending on the amount of power granted to the office. Strong mayors in mayor–council cities are directly elected by the people. They have veto powers and can appoint department heads. Most large cities have strong mayors, but in these cities many powerful independent boards and commissions may dilute a strong mayor's power. All major cities elect the mayor directly. Weak mayors in mayor–council cities are elected by the city council and are members of those councils. Because a weak mayor's duties are largely ceremonial, the post is often rotated annually among council members.

The second form of city government, and the most prevalent type in California, is the council–manager city. Here, council members serve on a part-time basis, and there is no mayor, but the council appoints a full-time city manager. Well-trained, highly paid, and usually very competent, city managers run most of California's cities, but ultimate power rests with the councils. Although they serve at the council's pleasure, most managers are given wide authority and discretion.

Because the city council may meet only once a week, the manager is held accountable for the details of city operation and administration, and he or she must run the city from day to day. City managers have the power to appoint and dismiss some department heads such as the police chief, prepare the agenda for council approval, and draw up the city budget for adoption by the council. The influence of a politically astute city manager can be immense, especially because council members are part-time elected officials and the manager is a full-time trained professional. Some observers have noted that because the manager and his or her staff have a "near-monopoly of technical competence," the policy-making process may be one in which the manager proposes and the council disposes.[2] Because the manager is responsible for running the city on a daily basis, he or she has far more information about city operations than does any council member, even those with long service on the council. A city manager with strong beliefs about policy may be in a position to "limit the range of possible policies that the council considers and to reduce the council essentially to the role of saying yes or no to his own policy recommendations."[3] However, this is not the case on highly controversial issues or on matters about which the council has strong preferences. Critics of the council–manager form of city

2. Ronald O. Loveridge, *City Managers in Legislative Politics* (Indianapolis: Bobbs Merrill, 1971), p. 100.
3. Demetrios Caraley, *City Governments and Urban Problems* (Englewood Cliffs, NJ: Prentice-Hall, 1977), pp. 233–234. See also Loveridge, *City Managers in Legislative Politics*, pp. 130–131.

government fear that the manager may not apprise the council of alternatives to his or her recommendations or present the disadvantages of proposals that he or she favors. Even though this form of city government vests great power in a person who has never stood for election, remember that the influence and tenure of managers varies from city to city, that the council hires and fires the manager, and that the ultimate power to pass ordinances and to appropriate money rests with an elected city council.

City Politics

City councils usually have five members (a few have seven) who are elected in nonpartisan elections for four-year terms. (The Los Angeles City Council has fifteen members, but it is a full-time legislative body.) Council members usually serve part-time and receive little or no salary. Most members are elected at large (the whole city votes for each member of the council), and elections are held separately from elections for partisan offices. Scheduling municipal elections separately from national and state elections and making local elections nonpartisan are intended to insulate these races from other contests so that local issues will be debated on their own merits. However, each of the arrangements also reduces voter turnout among lower-income groups or less-educated voters.

Methods of selecting local legislators (both city and county) have been increasingly criticized. Both at-large elections and elections by districts have advantages and disadvantages.

At-large elections allow the most capable candidates to be selected, regardless of where they might live. Those selected will put the interests of the whole city (or county) above district interests. Gerrymandering is impossible, and district boundaries need not be frequently redrawn to keep up with population shifts. However, racial or ethnic minorities concentrated in a particular area may be consistently outvoted by the majority. Also, at-large elections make for long ballots and increase voter **information costs**—that is, voters must inform themselves about many candidates rather than just a few. For example, if a city has election by district and five districts, each with seven candidates, then a voter must be informed only about the seven candidates in his or her district. If all council members are elected at large, voters must decide among thirty-five candidates. In addition, campaign costs rise because the whole city is the electoral arena, and people of modest means may not want to run for office. In any event, at-large elections may be feasible only in small or medium-sized cities.

Election from districts allows candidates to be more familiar with, and accessible to, the constituents. Minorities are more likely to place a member in the local legislature, and voters may be able to cast a more informed ballot. On the negative side, representatives are encouraged to care more about the interests of their districts than about those of the whole city. A five-member council uses the "rule of five" to apportion discretionary funds: divide the amount of money to be spent into five equal amounts, one-fifth for each district. Unfortunately, this procedure means that the areas of the city with the greatest needs may not get the largest amount of money.

In 1988 a federal appeals court ruled that the at-large election system used in the city of Watsonville violated the federal Voting Rights Act (*Cruz Gomez* v. *City of Watsonville*, 852 F.2d 1186 [1988]). Forty-nine percent of Watsonville's population (and 37 percent of its U.S. citizens) are Latino, but no Latino had ever been elected as a member of the city council as of the time of trial. Because at-large elections are used by 93 percent of California cities, many cities may have to change their election laws. Interestingly, an empirical study of at-large versus district elections in California found that "Asians have achieved a proportionate share of local political power under the traditional at-large city election system" and that district elections are not necessary for African-American political success in California.[4]

A compromise method of selection would require a legislator to live in the district he or she represents but be elected by the entire city. When a vacancy opens on a city council, "the remainder of the council may fill the vacancy by appointment or leave the vacancy unfilled until the next regular election or until a special election can be called. . . . It is a practice in some communities for a councilman electing not to seek reelection to resign from the governing board about two months before the end of his term."[5] The other council members may then select anyone they choose to fill out the last two months of the term, and the member chosen can run as an incumbent for a position on the council. Nearly a fourth of California's city council members may initially have reached office through appointment.

City Councils in Action

American government is celebrated as government of the people and by the people. The level of government most accessible to average citizens is city government. We urge readers to attend meetings of their city councils to see government in action. Here is the usual order of business:

> The council is called to order and the presence of a **quorum** of members is determined. A quorum is the minimum number of members who must be present for the council to conduct business officially.

> The minutes of the previous meeting are read, corrected or amended if necessary, and then approved.

> Petitions or memorials are called for. These may be presented by a group of local citizens who are present.

> Officers and committees present their reports.

---

4. James Fay and Roy Christman, "A New Electorate Gains Power," *Los Angeles Times,* November 4, 1991, p. B7, and "Political Success Lies in Coalition-Building," *Los Angeles Times,* November 6, 1991, p. B7.
5. George S. Blair and Houston Flournoy, *Legislative Bodies in California* (Belmont, CA: Dickenson, 1967), p. 74.

Unfinished business from the last meeting is taken up.

New business is called for. Ordinances (described later) are presented and voted upon at this time.

Announcements are called for.

Adjournment.

Enactments, or laws, passed by the city councils are called **ordinances.** Except for emergency measures, they do not become effective for thirty days. This delay allows dissatisfied citizens the opportunity to circulate referendum petitions.

A study of voting behavior on city councils in the San Francisco Bay Area found three patterns:

1. *unipolar,* a unanimity often induced by social pressure, in which "no lineups ever occur [and] . . . all members vote together" with only an occasional dissenter;

2. *nonpolar,* in which no stable voting alignments persist over time; and

3. *bipolar,* in which long-standing factions, stemming from liberal or conservative points of view, from the backgrounds of members, or from personal differences, vote as blocs.[6]

Local legislative bodies are covered by the Ralph M. Brown Act of 1953, the open-meeting law. The act requires that a meeting be open to the public if it is conducted by a city council, county supervisors, school board, or a committee or advisory group to which any of these bodies have delegated power. The public must receive notice at least one week before regularly scheduled meetings, and twenty-four hours before special meetings. In addition, local legislative bodies must post a specific agenda before both regular and special meetings, no new items may be added during the meeting, and no action may be taken on any item not on the agenda. This latter stipulation was prompted by newspaper accounts of the Los Angeles City Council's raising its members' salaries without allowing the raise issue to appear on its agenda, be posted in public, or even be discussed by the council. Closed sessions are allowed if an employee or officer is to be appointed, hired, or fired; if an employee or officer brings charges against another; if the council meets with its attorney to consider legal action; or if the council meets with its labor negotiators or with its real-estate agent to discuss the purchase of property. Items to be discussed during a closed session must be disclosed before the closed session. Local government actions taken in violation of the Brown Act may be challenged in court, but the complaining party must first ask the local legislative body to cure the purported defect. Criminal penalties are also available but are hard to enforce: A member of the city council must attend an unauthorized meeting with a wrongful intent to deprive the public of information.

---

6. Heinz Eulau and Kenneth Prewitt, *Labyrinths of Democracy* (Indianapolis: Bobbs Merrill, 1973), p. 174.

Contracting and Cooperation

California pioneered a practice called the **Lakewood Plan.** When the citizens of Lakewood decided in 1954 to incorporate, they also decided that their city would provide them with no services directly; instead, they would contract with the County of Los Angeles for all desired services. The **contract cities** idea was born. Today, Los Angeles County has approximately 1,500 contracts to provide 50 different services to cities. Lakewood, which now provides some of its own services, receives 41 separate services, ranging from helicopter service to road maintenance. Contracting with the county is thought to keep taxes down by avoiding large capital expenditures and maintenance costs of equipment.

Cities can also pool their resources to provide better services at reduced rates. Joint agreements may be formal or informal. Joint sewage disposal, police radio facilities, or water supply, along with cooperative purchasing, can avoid duplication and increase efficiency. Under the Joint Exercise of Powers Act, two cities that can take an action individually can also act jointly. Gonzales is one of three cities that jointly hires a building inspector; Westminster is one of four cities sharing fire training and communications operations (at a cost reduction of approximately 30 percent); Upland provides police radio dispatching for three other cities. By acting jointly, small cities may be able to take advantage of economies of scale.

Cities also contract for services with private suppliers. For example, Imperial Beach receives paramedical services and bus service from private companies, San Jose uses private contractors to cite parking violators, the Corona Fire Department contracts out the investigation of fires, and West Covina contracts out its recreation program. Service areas in which cost-conscious cities have been able to save the greatest amount of money are janitorial service, asphalt paving, street cleaning, lawn and street-tree maintenance, traffic-signal maintenance, and residential refuse collection.

The provision of governmental services by private suppliers has both advocates and critics. In the opinion of some, advantages include the following:

1. If a service is needed only infrequently, then it is more cheaply purchased as needed than provided by permanent personnel.

2. If the service requires expensive equipment, particularly equipment used only occasionally, then a private supplier is more economical.

3. If the service is provided by personnel who must possess specialized knowledge, training, or skill and who therefore can command extraordinarily high salaries, then local government should hire such people on contract.

4. If the persons providing the services must be unusually flexible or innovative, then such people should be sought outside the public sector.[7]

---

7. Rosaline Levenson, "Public Use of Private Service Contracts in Local Government: A Plea for Caution," in *Public–Private Collaboration in the Delivery of Local Public Services*, ed. Institute of Governmental Affairs (Davis: University of California, 1980), p. 23. See also pp. 20–22.

5. Private provision of a service can serve as a yardstick to evaluate public provision of the same service. (Ironically, however, in the 1930s the federal Tennessee Valley Authority set efficiency standards against which private power companies could be judged.)

6. A survey of procurement administrators in eighty-nine cities nationwide found that private contracting costs less than government delivery of services and results in better quality of service.[8]

7. Better service at lower cost may result from private firms' having incentive systems that reward managers for productivity increases. In addition, a private supplier may feel the need to be efficient because it can be replaced by another private company. A government agency that is the sole supplier of a service does not have the spur of competition.

Note that contracting is usually urged only in extraordinary circumstances or for fairly narrow purposes and is not normally advocated as the way to provide most mainline local government services.

Critics of private provision of governmental services stress the following arguments:

1. Any cost saving realized by contracting may be eliminated by the expense of monitoring the service contract. Furthermore, some contracts allow cost overruns.

2. Because the private supplier is a profit-making enterprise, it may scrimp on the quality of service in order to make more money.

3. Contracting may foster favoritism and corruption because the contractor that makes the most generous campaign contributions to mayors and city council members may be most likely to receive the service contract. By this means, an inefficient firm can prevail over superior competitors.

4. Representatives of public employee groups say that the services of private suppliers cost less because those suppliers pay lower wages and offer fewer benefits than does the public sector.[9]

The debate over private provision of public services is likely to intensify as financially strapped cities adjust to receiving less financial assistance from Sacramento.

---

8. Patricia Florestano and Stephen Gordon, "Public v. Private," *Public Administration Review* 40 (January–February 1980): 33.

9. Supporters of contracting, such as E. S. Savas, acknowledge that private firms provide fewer fringe benefits, but they assert that wages are slightly higher and that lower costs result because fewer people are needed to do the job, absenteeism is lower, and more modern equipment is used by private companies. See "Should Private Firms Do Government Work?" *Sacramento Bee*, November 16, 1981, p. C3.

HARD CHOICES AHEAD FOR CITIES

Life in California is for the most part urban life. The kind of environment that cities in California provide for their residents is therefore particularly important. The state's newer cities may have been incorporated because residents wanted to protect a lifestyle. Recall our discussion in Chapter 1 of attempts to manage rapid growth in a way that preserves beauty and natural resources. Many local planning commissions have become centers of intense controversy because they must decide how land will be used. Citizens who want to build on their land contend that their private property rights are infringed upon by restrictive zoning policies. Others retort that unless planners halt headlong development, many beautiful cities will be covered by asphalt parking lots, gas stations, and fast-food chains.

The attempts of some California cities to control or end growth have attracted considerable attention. Petaluma led the way by rationing building permits; Santa Cruz has set growth-rate limits; Belmont, Redlands, and Oceanside have restricted the number of new dwellings; Riverside has established minimum lot sizes (a measure that cuts population density but also excludes low-income people); San Francisco has limited new office space; and Walnut Creek has prohibited construction until traffic improves at seventy-five congested intersections. The latter part of the 1980s saw a flurry of antigrowth activity at the city and county levels. However, as the economy fell into a recession around 1990, there was very little growth to control. As the economy revives, this issue probably will again be a hot political topic.

Opponents of growth point to the loss of open space and agricultural land, and to air pollution, inadequate infrastructure (such as sewer systems) to support population expansion, insufficient water supplies and landfill capacity, and especially over-crowded schools and traffic congestion. One way that they seek to stop growth is by targeting highway improvements; antigrowth forces argue that streets and highways must already be in place before more growth is allowed (however, they also oppose spending more money for transportation improvements). For their part, those who favor growth claim that in a free country, people will move to where jobs are available. They assert that the only way to prevent growth is to destroy a local area's economy or for government forcibly to prevent people from moving to an area. In their own defense, developers say that they did not create the demand for housing or office space but are only responding to it.

The progrowth-versus-antigrowth debate has split the city of Los Angeles along geographic, racial, and class lines. On the Westside, especially in affluent white areas such as Westwood, residents are fiercely antigrowth. However, on the poorer Eastside such as South Los Angeles and Watts, people cannot get enough of growth and development. After the Watts riot, residents waited nearly twenty years for the area's first shopping center to open, an event that raised local spirits. Two longtime Watts residents were interviewed by the *Los Angeles Times;* referring to the Westside, one said, "To a child who has lived on ice cream his whole life, it is an annoyance to tell him there is going to be another 31 Flavors on the corner. But to a kid who can't have ice cream every day, it is a luxury. It is a treat." The other said, "We would love to have a Sizzler. We all have to go to Compton for a nice meal on Saturday or Sunday. We want one here."[10]

Antigrowth forces argue that city council members (and county supervisors) are overly dependent on the campaign contributions of developers and construction companies, and that these legislators are therefore too inclined to approve new construction. Clearly, campaign contributions play an important role in the process, but remember that Proposition 13 (described in the next chapter) froze the property-tax rate and hence limited the amount of tax revenue that real estate can generate. One of the few ways that cities and counties can get new sources of revenue is to approve development projects that generate tax revenue.

The arguments of each side in the growth-control debate have been subjected to careful academic study, with surprising results. First, growth continues under growth control because the controls only slightly restrain population growth and housing development. Second, despite what one might be led to believe by the law of supply and demand, growth controls did not make home prices rise.[11] The authors of the studies conclude that growth controls are not really effective in *limiting* growth; instead, controls *displace* growth. For example, the success of antigrowth activists in Ventura County may have shifted population to Riverside and San Bernardino counties. The result is longer commutes for workers, increased freeway congestion, and more auto emissions. At the same time, the state government has spent insufficient amounts of money building and maintaining freeways.

Streets and sewers, police stations and fire stations, and bridges are part of California's local infrastructure, which has fallen into serious disrepair. For example, California cities lose 80 billion gallons of water each year because of unrepaired leaks in municipal water systems. As a result of fiscal limitations, and the necessity to fund operating budgets, local officials have neglected to maintain the immense public investment in these facilities, which are essential to preserve the state's economic health. Budget-conscious elected officials defer repair and maintenance as long as possible, especially past the end of their terms so that their successors can deal with the problem. That some of these facilities, such as sewers and water systems, are out of sight makes it easier to postpone necessary repairs. However, these postponed repairs cost more in the long run.

It is sometimes said that the most important decisions made by local governments relate to the use of land. Two central issues in this area are "the fiscalization of land use" and the proper role for community redevelopment agencies.

Cities and counties have always made decisions controlling the use of land: Some areas of the city shall be zoned as residential, others are commercial, industrial, or

---

10. Quoted in "Poverty Areas, Slow-Growth Advocates Not Natural Allies," *Los Angeles Times,* August 1, 1988, pt. 1, p. 3.

11. John Landis, "Do Growth Controls Work?" *California Policy Seminar Brief,* 4 (February 1992); Kee Warner and Harvey Molotch, "Growth Control: Inner Workings and External Effects," *California Policy Seminar Brief,* 4 (August 1992).

mixed use; some development projects are approved but others are denied. However, since the passage of Proposition 13, there has been a "fiscalization" of land-use decisions. This means that land-use decisions are less likely to be made with an eye toward the best use of land for the long-range development of the city or the proper balance between land for homes and land for commercial purposes. Now land-use decisions are more likely to be made primarily on the basis of how much money the land use can generate for the city (or county). Proposition 13 forced this kind of decision making because it limited the amount of property-tax revenues that any parcel of property can produce for the city or county. However, certain kinds of new development can produce huge amounts of *sales-tax* revenue for the city or county where the sales take place. This is why local governments readily approve the construction of shopping malls, high-volume discount warehouses, electronics stores, and car dealerships. Cities and counties may be much less likely to allow the construction of housing because it produces relatively small amounts of *property-tax* revenue yet requires large expenditures for streets, street lighting, sewers, parks, police protection, and so on. Shopping malls and auto dealerships are tax "gainers" for the city or county, but housing is a tax "loser." That is why cities and counties engage in fierce competition with one another to lure tax gainers. As noted earlier, these fiscal considerations also affect decisions on whether unincorporated areas with shopping malls or car dealerships decide to incorporate. These considerations are also behind many of the bitter annexation fights between cities as nearby cities attempt to reach out and annex an area with good potential for sales-tax revenue.

Some two-thirds of California's cities have redevelopment agencies (which are often the city council sitting in another capacity) that designate parts of their cities as "blighted." The existing property-tax base in the blighted area is noted by the agency as the base year, and increases in property-tax revenues from that base (called the *tax increment*) are used by the city agency to improve the area over twenty-five to thirty-five years. Other local governments serving the area continue to receive revenue from the base, but they receive no more than 2 percent of the tax increment unless the agency agrees to give them some of it. Using condemnation if necessary, the redevelopment agency purchases property in the blighted area, tears down old buildings, and signs agreements with developers for new construction in the area. New office buildings, hotels, shopping centers, housing projects, and warehouses have been built in this manner; examples include the Embarcadero Center in San Francisco, Bunker Hill in Los Angeles, and Horton Plaza in San Diego. In response to complaints that redevelopment has destroyed too many homes of poor people, the state legislature has required that 20 percent of the increment must be used to build low- and moderate-priced housing.

Community redevelopment has sparked numerous controversies in recent years. For example, areas determined by the redevelopment agency to be blighted in fact may lack only public improvements or be characterized by land lots of irregular form or shape. Tax-increment financing has also been used to improve areas in which development would have occurred anyway without it. In this instance, the city acting through its redevelopment agency denies counties and other local governments the property-tax revenues they would have gotten normally. Moreover, community growth that has been spurred by redevelopment places severe burdens on local school districts, which in turn want a cut of the tax increment. Redevelopment has also been used in growth areas to build projects that might have been financed through the normal city budget: streets, sewers, storm drains, parks, and other public facilities. Redevelopment is often seen by city officials as a way to get around the limitations of Proposition 13. In addition, the urban redevelopment agency can force the owner of a parcel of private property to sell his or her land to the city, which later sells the land to a different private party. This process, which can infringe on basic rights, takes place without a vote of the public and without supervision by the state government. Finally, redevelopment agencies have used their impressive powers of eminent domain and tax-increment financing to lure projects that produce large amounts of sales-tax revenue, thus contributing to the fiscalization of land use.

SPECIAL DISTRICTS

Special districts are units of government formed when citizens desire a service unavailable from the city or county. Excluding school districts, more than 3,400 special districts exist in California. They provide an amazing variety of services, including fire protection, water, street lighting, cemeteries, recreation and parks, and mosquito abatement. They range in size from the Happy Camp Cemetery District in Siskiyou County to the huge Metropolitan Water District (MWD) of Southern California.

Special districts are necessary when local governments do not have the power (or the willingness) to tax and to borrow in order to finance the service that citizens desire. Citizens in unincorporated areas may create a special district in lieu of annexing themselves to a city or incorporating. This would happen because they believe that annexation or incorporation will increase their taxes, or because they do not want the full range of services that cities provide. Finally, because adding another special district is a small-scale, incremental change, it is politically acceptable to existing governments.

The state's nonschool special districts outnumber the combined total of all other local governments by about two to one. However, nearly one-third of the nonschool special districts are classified as dependent districts; that is, their governing boards are either city councils or county boards of supervisors. Although dependent districts are not really autonomous units of government, they are counted in the total number of special districts. Some special districts charge for their services (enterprise districts), and others rely on property taxes (nonenterprise districts) to finance those services. Enterprise districts include those that charge for waste disposal or sell water or power.

Special districts have been called "the least understood, least cared about, and most used of any class of government in California." The problem is that special districts pile up . . . like an uneven stack of pancakes. Many a citizen . . . [is] located in eight or ten special districts, . . . the citizen is failing to receive the coordinated benefits of true municipal government . . . [and] his community's future is largely determined by the agglomeration of uncoordinated, single-interest special districts.

The boards of special districts do not consider themselves engaged in overall community planning, but willy-nilly they are: "When a water main is laid by a utility district, the spread of housing development is determined and assured—in an area that might best be reserved for a park."[12]

Special districts present a problem: They are nearly invisible. Californians do not know how many special districts serve them; many citizens do not even know that special districts exist. The levies of districts supported by property taxes appear on the *county* tax bill and are often not separately and specifically listed. Finally, turnout in special-district elections is very low, often less than 5 percent. Who knows the issues? (Everyone is for abating mosquitoes.)

The most prevalent special district is the school district. Currently, there are approximately 660 elementary school districts, 115 high school districts, 265 unified school districts, and 71 community college districts. Although two-thirds of the state's elementary and secondary school students attend school in unified districts, a very large number of school districts consist of only a single school.

REGIONAL AGENCIES

Many problems on the local government agenda span cities and counties and have a regional dimension; in California, actions taken in one community affect other communities. Because problems such as pollution, transportation, or land use spill beyond city and county boundaries, regional agencies have been developed to deal with regional problems. Examples are the Metropolitan Water District of Southern California, the Bay Area Air Pollution Control District, the Bay Area Rapid Transit District, and **councils of governments (COGs).** These units of government provide either a single service (such as water or transportation) or do regional planning. They are not "genuine multipurpose governments in the major metropolitan areas of the state, governmental bodies that . . . not only plan but also provide [a full range of] services directly to the citizens of the area."[13]

Of particular importance are two councils of governments, the Association of Bay Area Governments (ABAG) and the Southern California Association of Governments

---

12. The three quoted passages in this paragraph are from Wood and Heller, *Phantom Cities*, pp. 44–45. For an opposing view, see Robert B. Hawkins, Jr., "Special Districts and Urban Services," in *The Delivery of Urban Services,* ed. Elinor Ostrom (Beverly Hills, CA: Sage Publications, 1976), p. 182.

13. Randall Shores, "Regional Government: Its Structure, Functions and Finance," *California Journal* (January 1973): 15.

(SCAG). Each serves as a forum where the region's local governments can meet to discuss regional issues and use the council's large staffs for research and planning. ABAG consists of representatives of 9 counties and 96 cities in the Bay Area, and it is especially important in developing regional plans to protect the quality of the air and water. SCAG (composed of 188 cities and 6 counties) was patterned after its northern counterpart. It has been particularly active in the field of regional transportation policy. An important function of both ABAG and SCAG is to review local governments' applications for federal grants-in-aid. These councils of governments draw up comprehensive area-wide plans and then decide whether local requests for aid conform to these plans. COGs in nonmetropolitan areas perform many of the same functions as ABAG and SCAG. However, COGs have not been successful at land-use planning because they have been unable to stop urban sprawl, but they provide valuable services such as credit pooling, technical support, and research reports to their member governments.

THE MANDATES ISSUE

To alleviate its revenue problems, the state could require local governments to pay for public services mandated—that is, imposed on them—by the state. This strategy has been illegal since 1972, when the legislature required that the state reimburse local governments for any costs imposed on them by the state. However, the legislature excluded costs mandated by court decisions, the federal government, or the voters. In November 1979, Proposition 4 placed these rules into the state Constitution.

If the state does not fund a program it mandates, local governments can seek a court order excusing them from compliance or declaring the mandate unconstitutional. However, the legislature inserts into bills a disclaimer stating that no new costs are being required of local governments. The legislature most often asserts that only minor costs will result from a bill; the legislature also asserts that a bill will effect savings that will offset any new costs. In addition, mandated programs funded by local user fees are not reimbursed by the state. Because of the legislature's actions, the state Constitution should be amended to make unfunded mandates optional for local governments.

SUMMARY

In this chapter we have studied counties, cities, special districts, and regional agencies. These units of government were once thought to deal with only noncontroversial matters, but some of the issues mentioned in this chapter indicate otherwise. Local government finance in the post–Proposition 13 era, the election of city council members by districts or at-large, attempts by cities to manage growth, the creation of more special districts, and the changing roles of regional agencies—all of these matters, and many more, come before the thousands of citizen-legislators serving part-time on county boards of supervisors, city councils, special-district boards, and regional agencies. Those who select these representatives must understand the operation of California local government.

DISCUSSION QUESTIONS

1. Who is (are) your county supervisor(s)? Can you name your county treasurer? Because you probably cannot name the latter, do you think the supervisors should appoint this person?

2. Does your county or city have a charter? Does it need one?

3. Does your city have a city manager? What are the city manager's duties?

4. What are some of the arguments for and against municipal contracts for public services?

5. Suppose the streetlight in front of your house or apartment stopped working. What unit of government should you contact: city, county, or special district? Does uncertainty about whom to call indicate that responsibilities in local government are fragmented? On the other hand, does it matter who does the job as long as the job gets done?

6. Name some of the services provided by the 3,400 nonschool special districts in California.

7. What is the purpose of regional agencies? What functions do councils of government serve?

8. Do you favor user charges? Why?

9. Define the "fiscalization of land use." Why is it a problem for sound land-use decisions by local government?

10. Why are growth control and community redevelopment so controversial?

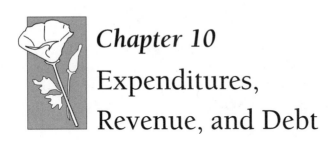

Chapter 10
Expenditures, Revenue, and Debt

Money is the focus of this chapter: how government raises it, borrows it, and spends it. A key consideration of this chapter is the state's chronic fiscal problems, which are likely to continue at least for the near future. Remember that fiscal matters are not solely dollars-and-cents decisions but basic political questions: Who should pay for government services? Who should receive the benefits of government services? To what extent should future generations be obligated by today's fiscal decisions?

STATE SPENDING

The budget submitted by Governor Pete Wilson for fiscal year 1996 was the largest state budget in the nation at $56.3 billion. The expenditures may be classified according to function as follows (figures indicate percentage of budget):

Elementary, secondary, and community college education	29.2
University of California and CSU Systems	10.6
Social welfare (aid to the elderly, blind, and disabled; AFDC); public health; mental hygiene	27.1
Agencies in the business, transportation, and housing fields	7.9
Prisons	6.7
Shared revenue (the state government collects certain taxes—for example, sales taxes, liquor license fees, and motor-vehicle taxes—part of which must be returned to local governments)	5.6

Resources such as conservation, reclamation, water	2.4
Environmental protection	1.3
Consumer services	1.3
Property-tax relief for homeowners and senior citizens	0.8
Other expenses, such as costs of the legislative branch, executive branch, and most of the judicial branch	7.1

Striking patterns can be seen in state spending. Education, health, and welfare make up more than two-thirds of all state expenditures. Furthermore, three-fourths of the state budget is aid to local government (such as school aid or local aid to the aged and disabled), hence only one of every four dollars in the *state* budget goes to finance *state* services. We mentioned in an earlier chapter that many expenditures are channeled to programs that continue from year to year, such as highway funds and aid to local school districts. Therefore, very little of a governor's budget is discretionary: The governor must request certain money and the legislature must spend it whether or not either side has much enthusiasm for the appropriation.

The amount of required spending appears to be increasing. In 1990 the voters passed an initiative statute that guarantees that $30 million per year for the next thirty years be transferred to a fund to acquire land for open space or for wildlife. In 1988 the voters passed Proposition 98, a landmark constitutional initiative sponsored by teachers unions that requires that elementary, secondary, and community college education receive a specified percentage of the state budget. Education thus became the only state spending program with a priority claim on state funds protected by the state Constitution. One of the lessons that the governor and the legislature learned from recent budget crises is that the finance of elementary–secondary–community college education is the first piece of the budget puzzle that must be dealt with because it is the largest piece of general fund spending at approximately 40 percent. In fact, what the state does with education funding determines how much is left to spend on everything else. Because the state's population is growing older, more money will need to be spent to provide medical care. A situation has been created in which there could be fierce competition between the beneficiaries of education versus health programs. Table 10.1 (page 250) compares California's spending on different programs to that of other states.

STATE REVENUE

The previous section of this chapter was entitled "State Spending," but it could just as accurately have been called "Where the Money Goes." In this section, we deal with where the money comes from. Not surprisingly, most of the money comes from you in the form of taxes.

Certain canons, or principles, of taxation are generally accepted:

Table 10.1 California Spending Rankings Among States

BUDGET ITEM	RANKING AMONG STATES
Highways	49th
Elementary and secondary education	42nd
Higher education	34th
Welfare	18th
Natural resources and parks	16th
Health and hospitals	14th
Corrections	5th
Total state and local spending	23rd

Note: Data are fiscal year 1992 and take into account personal income.

SOURCE: *Cal-Tax News*, October 15, 1994, p. 3.

1. Taxation should be based on ability to pay. In California, the income tax is **progressive**—that is, as a person's income increases, the tax rate as a percentage of income also increases. A **flat-rate tax** (for example, all taxpayers paying 10 percent) also implements the ability-to-pay principle because those with higher incomes pay more in absolute dollars, but it does not redistribute income from higher-income taxpayers to lower-income taxpayers as the progressive income tax is intended to do. Sales taxes, on the other hand, are **regressive**—that is, as a person's income increases, the tax paid as a percentage of income tends to decrease. For this reason, a higher percentage of a poor person's income goes to sales tax.

Different views about tax equity or tax fairness also come into play. Vertical equity means that those with more ability to pay actually do pay more—the progressive income tax furthers this view. Horizontal equity means that people in similar economic situations pay approximately equal taxes; we will note later that, because real estate is reassessed only when it is sold, Proposition 13 does not promote horizontal equity.

2. The state or local governments should have a diversified tax structure. Neither should rely too much on a single tax. California state government and city governments meet this criterion, but county government does not.

3. A person receiving a specific benefit should pay for that benefit. (The benefits-received principle was discussed in Chapter 9.)

4. Taxes should be economical to administer and collect.

5. Taxes should be easy to understand and as convenient to pay as possible. The taxes due from each taxpayer should be definite and sure of collection. Taxes should be difficult to evade. The sales tax usually meets this goal.

Prisons are the fastest-growing item in the state budget.

6. Taxes should produce sufficient revenue and should produce a stable stream of revenue for government that does not fluctuate greatly with the business cycle. The income tax meets the first part of this criterion but may not meet the second part.

Estimated revenues for fiscal year 1996 are from the following sources (figures indicate percentages of revenues):

Personal income tax	34.8
Sales tax	31.1
Bank and corporation tax	8.6
Motor-vehicle license fees	8.5
Motor-fuels tax	4.9
Insurance tax	2.2
Cigarette (stamp) tax, alcoholic beverage tax, fees on amounts wagered at horse races	1.8
Inheritance and gift taxes	1.0
Other, including the lottery, numerous fees, and bond sales	7.1

A significant part of state taxes is earmarked (designated) by law or by the state Constitution to be spent for specified purposes. For example, the gas tax must be spent to build and maintain roads, the state Constitution designates motor-vehicle

Scott Willis / San Jose Mercury-News

license fees for local governments, and lottery proceeds go to education. In fact, the percentage of **earmarked funds** is increasing; in 1988 the voters passed an initiative raising the cigarette tax and directing the proceeds to antismoking advertising and medical care for poor people. Earmarking has been criticized for several reasons:

1. It introduces rigidity into budgetary policy because the governor and the legislature cannot balance needs with the funds on hand. Hence, a program benefiting from earmarked funds may be receiving more money than it needs, while another program is underfunded.

2. A portion of governmental activities is removed from periodic review and control by the governor and the legislature.

3. When funding is guaranteed for a program, the interest groups benefiting from that program have no incentive to cooperate in reforming it.

4. When one interest group gets a percentage of the budget earmarked for its benefit, other groups decide to attempt the same thing in order to protect themselves.

5. If governments have to cut their budgets, cuts must fall on programs that are not earmarked.

PERENNIAL BUDGET CRISES

There is a dispute between Governor Wilson and different commentators about whether a *structural deficit* is the underlying cause of the state's perennial budget crises. California has a structural deficit if the state government's deficit persists *even after the state's economy rebounds.* According to Wilson, California's economy is changing significantly as manufacturing declines and as illegal immigration continues at high levels. He argues that immigration patterns have produced an "outflow of those who are producers" and a "tremendous increase in the number of consumers of [government] services."[1] A key assumption of Wilson's position is that illegal immigrants are a net detriment to California's economy. (Please see Chapter 2 for the "net-benefit versus net-detriment" dispute.) Other persons considered receivers of government services are the children of illegal immigrants, welfare recipients, medically indigent persons, prison inmates, and students (from elementary school to graduate school). The result is believed to be a taxpayer squeeze in which fewer taxpayers support more tax receivers: "In 1980, there were 6.9 taxpayers for each AFDC [welfare] recipient.

---

1. Pete Wilson, "There is a Limit to What We Can Absorb," *Time,* November 18, 1991, p. 54; "California's Taxpayers Face A Bigger Squeeze In the 1990s," *Sacramento Bee,* November 19, 1991, p. B7.

If these trends continue, by the year 2000 there will be only 2.94 taxpayers supporting each AFDC recipient." According to two academic observers, "The rate of growth in service-needy populations exceeds that of real per-worker incomes in the state, which ensures long-term fiscal crises."[2]

Wilson's position is vigorously disputed by those who say recurrent deficits are temporary phenomena resulting from a stagnant economy, reduced defense spending, and natural (or human-created) disasters such as droughts, earthquakes, fires, or riots. Democrats argue that Wilson lacks leadership for failing to increase taxes on business and wealthy persons. Others note that the voters have used the initiative process to reduce taxes (Proposition 13) or set aside spending for specific purposes (Proposition 98's education spending). This "ballot box budgeting" is thought to tie the state budget process into knots. Still others say that the state has unwisely taken on new spending responsibilities when it could not prudently do so: "Three-strikes-and-you're-out" legislation should prove to be very expensive. Some academic observers take aim at Wilson's taxpayer-squeeze argument: "There is general agreement that the ratio of service recipients to taxpayers (crudely labeled the dependency ratio) will rise over the next decade. But even under the most pessimistic forecast, the dependency ratio is lower than it was in 1960 and 1970. . . . California [has] prospered in past times of high dependency ratios."[3] In addition, it is inaccurate to classify people as *either* taxpayers *or* tax receivers: *All* people pay some taxes and receive some services.

Note that the information in Tables 10.1 and 10.2 provides little consolation to Governor Wilson. California is about average in both spending and tax burden.

The "Trigger" and the "Hammer"

To muddle through the 1994 budget crisis, the state agreed to the potentially very serious "trigger" and "hammer" budget-balancing process for 1995 and 1996. In the "trigger" part of the process, the legislative analyst must present to the state controller by November 15, 1995, an analysis which the state controller uses to estimate the state's general fund cash flow. If the controller and the legislative analyst agree that a shortfall of more than 1 percent exists, then the governor has until January 10, 1996, to present a plan to fix the problem to the legislature. If the legislature does not agree to the governor's plan or does not devise its own by February 15, 1996, then the "hammer" falls five days later and automatic across-the-board spending reductions are made in all programs that are not protected by the state Constitution or by federal law. Examples of protected programs are elementary–secondary–community college education (because of Proposition 98), debt service, and federally mandated appropriations. The trigger and the hammer are "bitter medicine" devices demanded by

---

2. John J. Kirlin and Donald R. Winkler, "California Policy Choices," in *California Policy Choices,* vol. 7, ed. Kirlin and Winkler (Sacramento: Sacramento Public Affairs Center, 1991), p. 1.

3. David Bowman et al., "Structural Deficit and the Long-Term Fiscal Condition of the State," in *California Policy Choices,* vol. 9, ed. John J. Kirlin and Donald R. Winkler (Sacramento: Sacramento Public Affairs Center, 1994), p. 30.

Table 10.2 California Tax Rankings Among States

TAX	RANKING AMONG STATES
Banking and corporation tax	4th
Personal income tax	17th
Sales tax	17th
Property tax	28th
Total state and local tax collections	20th

Note: Data are fiscal year 1992 and take into account state personal income.

SOURCE: *Cal-Tax News,* October 15, 1994, pp. 4–10.

international bankers because the state needed money from the bankers to bail it out of its financial difficulties. It is a sad commentary that only this pistol pointed at the legislature's head could give it the discipline to tackle the state's crisis.

CALIFORNIA TAX ISSUES

California's income tax law is probably the most progressive in the nation. The *Los Angeles Times* has found that the wealthiest 4 percent of Californians, those with incomes of $100,000, pay half of all personal income taxes.[4] In contrast, California's tax burden for those at the $35,000 income level ranks 40th out of 42 states that have personal income taxes.

The November 1992 ballot included Proposition 167, which was described by the *Los Angeles Times* as having "the most dramatic impact on California taxpayers of any measure since Proposition 13 [because it was] the largest package of tax increases in state history."[5] Proposition 167 sought to increase income taxes on individual taxpayers making more than $100,000 per year and to increase corporate income taxes by 20 percent. The measure also prevented the legislature from later lowering these taxes by less than a two-thirds vote. Proposition 167 also would have raised property taxes paid by businesses 10 percent to 20 percent by establishing a **split-roll** property-tax system in which owners of business property pay more taxes than owners of residential property. Proposition 167 would have established an oil **severance tax** for California—a tax on oil extracted from the ground. Finally, the proposition would have reduced the state sales tax.

4. "State Tax Facts—and Fiction," *Los Angeles Times,* October 10, 1993, p. A1.
5. "Tax Hike Measure Prompts High-Stakes Showdown," *Los Angeles Times,* October 15, 1992, p. A1.

Proposition 167 was put on the ballot by liberal activist Lenny Goldberg, public employee unions, the California Teachers Association, and senior citizen groups. Proponents argued that California faces one budget crisis after another and thus is in chronic need of revenue, and that businesses and upper-income persons are not paying enough taxes. The business community opposed the measure and argued that it would cost California jobs in the midst of the current severe recession, that the split roll would severely hurt small businesses (which are the major job producers), and that large business would pass increased taxes on to consumers in the form of higher prices.

Proposition 167 was defeated 58 percent to 42 percent for two key reasons: Californians are strongly opposed to tax increases, and the measure did not say how the money raised would be spent. The state had just gone through its record sixty-three-day budget stalemate, leaving the governor and the legislature with low public esteem. "Don't give the politicians more money to waste" was a potent argument against Proposition 167.

In most states, inflation increases government revenues. People are pushed into higher tax brackets as salaries are raised to meet increased costs of goods and services. State government gets something of a tax windfall. In fact, state government can get more money *without having to raise the tax rate.* California voters adopted a 1982 initiative measure to deal with this situation. (See Proposition 7 in Figure 5.1.) By establishing **indexing** of income taxes, California's income-tax brackets are adjusted for the effects of inflation. Indexing income taxes makes elected officials more accountable because a higher income-tax burden should result from overt state legislative action rather than from the silent consequences of inflation. Also note that as inflation raises the price of taxable items, sales-tax revenues also rise.

The sales tax is regressive, as we have noted. Low-income people pay a larger percentage of their income to sales taxes than do wealthy people. The sales tax violates the ability-to-pay principle. However, California mitigates the regressive effects of the sales tax by exempting medicine, food purchased in a store, and certain other items. Because it is used in conjunction with other taxes, the sales tax diversifies the tax structure. It is a good revenue producer and is easily understood, convenient to pay, and somewhat difficult to evade.

Another tax—and one less controversial than the others—is the motor-fuels tax (the gas tax). It is included in the price of gasoline, and so out-of-state tourists pay this tax too. The sales tax is also applied to gasoline, and it is computed not only on the cost of the gasoline itself but also on state and federal gasoline taxes, which makes it a tax on a tax. The proceeds from the sales tax on gasoline may be spent on mass transit, but the gas tax itself may be spent only on mass-transit guideways and on building and maintaining roads. When an owner registers a car, he or she must also pay a motor-vehicle license fee based on the age and cost of the car. This is really a local personal property tax on cars that is collected by the state in lieu of a city and county personal property tax on cars. Because the money is returned to the cities and

Death and taxes may be certain, but neither is popular.

counties, it is called the "in lieu" tax. The insurance tax is levied on the premiums written by insurance companies. Therefore, insurance companies pay this tax instead of the income tax paid by banks and corporations.

The California tax-to-personal-income ratio is not markedly different from that in other states, but the contribution from each source may vary significantly. Worth noting are the so-called **sin taxes**: those on tobacco and alcoholic beverages, which many reformers believe are too low. To protect an important state industry, the California tax on wine is probably the lowest in the nation. Although a precise definition of *sin* can never be universally agreed upon, these taxes should be raised if overall revenue shortfalls threaten vital public services.

In times of fiscal retrenchment, one political group may want to reduce services, while another group may want to raise taxes. Both policies will probably be followed simultaneously. Questions about which taxes are raised and by how much depend on state wealth, interest group strength, and the prevailing political philosophy. State wealth can be measured in different ways, and the most common is per capita personal income, on which scale California is ranked ninth. Another measure is fiscal capacity, which includes not only income but also such factors as energy resources and real-estate values. California stands tenth by this standard. But another, more politically relevant ranking is applicable here: tax effort, the ratio of tax collections to tax capacity. California is now twenty-third in tax effort.[6]

THE PROPERTY TAX AND PROPOSITION 13

Long before Proposition 13 burst on the political scene, the property tax was a controversial method of raising revenues for counties, cities, and nonenterprise special districts. The following are typical objections.

1. The property tax does not measure ability to pay. Everyone pays the same rate, regardless of income or wealth. The property tax is hard on retired people living on a fixed income. (However, the state government has moved to relieve this burden: Homeowners 62 and older whose yearly family income is less than $24,000 may postpone paying property taxes until their homes are sold. In the meantime, property taxes are paid by the state government, which recoups its money plus interest when the home is sold. The program also applies to blind and disabled persons, regardless of age.)

2. The property tax taxes income-producing industrial and commercial property at the same rate as residential property. However, California could adopt the split-roll technique, by which income-producing property is taxed at a higher rate than residential property.

3. The property tax taxes **real property**—land and buildings—but not **personal property**. Personal property is either intangible (cash, stocks, bonds, and patents) or tangible (furniture, appliances, cars, clothes, and jewelry). Moreover, some real property is exempted from taxation by the state Constitution. Property owned by nonprofit or charitable organizations (churches, colleges, libraries, museums, hospitals, and retirement homes) is exempt. Land owned by the federal or state governments is not taxed. Whenever any property is exempted, nonexempt property must bear a heavier burden.

4. Assessed valuation varies from area to area. Locations with the lowest assessed valuation may have the highest need for public services.

5. Property taxes, unless paid monthly with the mortgage, are paid twice a year in two lump sums, a highly inconvenient way to pay taxes. (However, when taxes are withheld, as are income taxes, or paid in small amounts, as are sales taxes, people may not realize how much they are being charged. This situation gave rise to the much-quoted statement by former Governor Reagan, "Taxes should hurt.")

The property tax, despite its drawbacks, is not a public menace. Proponents of the tax point out that it is a good revenue producer. Because real property usually

---

6. Advisory Commission on Intergovernmental Relations, *RTS 1991: State Revenue Capacity and Effort* (Washington, D.C., 1993), p. 27.

appreciates in value, the base for the property tax constantly expands. Proponents also point out that real property cannot be hidden from the assessor and that people are used to the property tax, even if they do not like it. Proponents also ask, how might local government otherwise raise money? The income tax is the preserve of the federal and state governments, and the sales tax already falls heavily on the poor.

In June 1978, California voters, furious at rapidly rising property taxes, passed a drastic initiative constitutional amendment known as the Jarvis amendment (Proposition 13). Howard Jarvis and Paul Gann, the sponsors of the amendment, needed approximately half a million valid signatures to put the measure on the ballot—they received 1.2 million signatures. Angry Californians passed the measure by a 65–35 margin, with support high in all areas of the state. Several factors converged to spark this nationally publicized revolt: inflation, rising property assessments, waste in public services, and a huge state revenue surplus. These factors led the state's voters to demand lower taxes and more frugal government.

The provisions of Proposition 13 are as follows:

1. Property taxes shall not exceed 1 percent of the assessed value of the property. This provision reduced property taxes by 57 percent and cut revenues to counties, cities, school districts, and special districts from $12 billion to only $5 billion.

2. The assessed value of all property shall be rolled back to the assessment of March 1, 1975. Assessments may rise from the 1975 figure by 2 percent *per year*. Property is to be reassessed only when sold.

3. Increasing state taxes requires a two-thirds vote, rather than a majority vote, of the state legislature. New state property taxes are forbidden.

4. An increase in local nonproperty taxes requires a two-thirds vote of the qualified local electors. However, local voters may not raise property taxes.

An important and unresolved issue concerning Proposition 13 is the implications of the requirement that property be reassessed to current market value only when sold. If there are two identical houses on the same block, but one is sold and resold many times while the other is never sold, the owners of the two properties will pay widely different amounts of property taxes. In a situation in which a wealthy homeowner stays put and does not sell the property, the principle of horizontal equity is violated (vis-à-vis other wealthy homeowners who sell their homes) and the principle of vertical equity is violated (vis-à-vis less wealthy homeowners who sell their homes). Moreover, some state-aid–to–local-government formulas use assessed valuation as a measure of local wealth. But property turns over four times as frequently in some counties as in others. High-turnover counties therefore show an artificially high assessed valuation, while those with extensive industrial or agricultural holdings that are sold less frequently may appear to be poorer than they actually are.

Many commentators have faulted Proposition 13 (and other tax-cutting measures such as indexing of income taxes and the elimination of the inheritance tax) for reducing government revenues and inducing fiscal stress. The California Taxpayers

This house has not changed ownership since before Proposition 13.
Property taxes are $700.

This house has been resold
three times since Prop. 13.
Property taxes are $1,700.

Same schools; same police and fire protection; same
libraries and parks; same water system
and refuse collection. ...

Association, a probusiness group, has done the most comprehensive study of
state–local tax revenue for both the pre–Proposition 13 and post–Proposition 13
periods. The association found that

> combined state and local spending, as a percent of personal income, has exceeded
> pre–Proposition 13 levels for several years now. In 1977–78, spending was 18.5
> percent of personal income, and in 1991–92 it reached 20.3 percent. In other
> words, state and local government is now a larger share of the state economy than
> at any other time. The long-term effects of Proposition 13 have mostly led to a
> change in the composition of revenues, not an ongoing reduction in revenues or
> spending.[7]

Most of the growth in state–local revenues has been in local fees and revenues.

7. "California Taxing and Spending," *Cal-Tax News* (October 15, 1994): 5.

However, not all analysts would argue that state–local revenues or spending have increased. Tables 10.1 and 10.2 indicate that California is a medium tax-and-expenditure state. One line of reasoning goes as follows: In the years after World War II, California was both a high-tax and high-expenditure state under liberal, progrowth governors such as Earl Warren and Pat Brown. These governors were quite willing to invest taxpayer money on freeway construction, the state water-transfer system, and the public higher-education system. But then Proposition 13 burst on the scene, with reduced taxing and spending emphasized by governors such as Jerry Brown (whose mantra was "small is beautiful") and George Deukmejian (the "Iron Duke with the quickest item veto in the West"). California then became an average tax-and-spend state according to this argument. But more important than characterizing California's public sector is evaluating it. If California is a medium tax-and-spend state, then Californians have been able to keep for themselves more of their personal income. On the other hand, there is arguably insufficient public-sector investment, and the state's neediest citizens have been shortchanged. Moreover, if one is confident in the ability of government to allocate resources efficiently and justly (recall Senator Dianne Feinstein's statement in Chapter 3: "I believe in government"), then state and local government consumption of a larger share of the state economy is a welcome result. On the other hand, taxpayers have less of the money they have earned to spend for purposes of their own choosing.

OTHER SOURCES OF INCOME

California state and local governments receive a substantial amount of federal aid, which is currently more than $22 billion per year. In addition, the state receives royalties from leases for oil and gas production on the state's tidelands, with a great deal of the money going to education. Additional sources of income include personalized license plates, student fees at the University of California and the state universities, charges at state hospitals and state parks, fish and game licenses, and interest earned on state bank accounts.

In 1984 California voters overwhelmingly approved an initiative to establish a state lottery, which has subsequently become the most successful public lottery in the country. Fifty percent of the ticket price must go for prizes, 16 percent for administrative costs, and 34 percent for elementary, secondary, and higher education. Proponents of the lottery point to its strong support among the public and tout it as a painless way to raise money for education. Moreover, participation is voluntary, whereas revenue raised through taxation is coerced. Hence, the lottery is said to yield the most feathers with the least squawk. Opponents of the lottery, on the other hand, cite a long list of particulars. If the lottery has been such a huge success, then this must mean that an even larger number of Californians are losers. Is it proper for government to trick its citizens in this manner? The odds of winning the jackpot in Lotto 6/53 are 23 million to 1. Actually, the odds of winning anything at all are 67 to 1.

These facts are not mentioned to the public in the lottery's glitzy advertising. If the lottery produces compulsive gamblers, then participation is not voluntary for some people. Moreover, pathogenic gamblers will risk financial ruin for what one psychologist calls the "gambler's high" or the "momentary elation experienced while waiting for the roulette ball to settle, the Big Spin Wheel to stop turning, or the silver coating to be scratched off an instant game card."[8] Finally, the Field Poll reports that poorer people or those with less education are the ones most likely to play the lottery most intensively. "Big Spin" finalists appearing on television are often unemployed, on welfare, or in poorly paid jobs. The lottery is not a tax, but it is regressive in effect. In certain respects, the lottery is a "poor person's sales tax." In conclusion, as we noted in the first chapter, the gold-seeking forty-niners, with their get-rich-quick mentality, were the founding fathers of California. The odds are that their legacy is still alive today.

DEBT

Governments, like individuals, sometimes live beyond their means and go into debt. However, state and local debt usually results from the need to finance expensive construction projects. When government borrows money, it issues bonds, which investors purchase. The **bond** indicates how much it is worth, its interest rate, and when the bond is to be redeemed. The two most important bonds are **general obligation bonds** and **revenue bonds.** General obligation bonds are guaranteed, or backed, by the full taxing power and the good credit of the state of California. When Proposition 13 passed, it ended the ability of local governments to issue general obligation bonds. Because the amendment limited the property tax to 1 percent of assessed valuation, local governments did not have the ability to levy unlimited property taxes—that is, they could not make the "full faith and credit" commitment required to back these bonds. Local capital-improvement projects suffered as a result. However, a proposition on the 1986 ballot was passed that authorized local governments to increase property taxes to repay general obligation bonds with a two-thirds vote of the electorate. General obligation bonds are cheaper for local governments because, with their high security, their interest rates are low, and because local governments are not required to maintain the reserve funds necessary for revenue bonds. The latter are issued to finance a revenue-producing project, such as a toll bridge or a college dormitory. The income from the project pays off the bond. Because a revenue bond may be somewhat riskier, its interest rate is higher. All state bond issues require majority approval (local bond issues need two-thirds approval). A bond measure appears on the sample California ballot in Figure 5.1.

State government has increased its amount of bond issues in recent years. This action has two undesirable consequences: Borrowing money leads to large interest payments over the long run; the state government and the state's voters, both of whom

---

8. Ellen Chapman, "A Pandora's Box of Social Change," *California Journal* (June 1986): 293. See also Field Poll, Release no. 1315, December 13, 1985.

must approve bond issues, could be close to an imprudent level of debt. At every statewide election, ballot propositions to float bonds for worthwhile projects are presented to the voters. If these propositions are approved, then the cumulative level of state debt rises. Currently, the state's **debt ratio** is more than 5.3 percent: This is the percentage of general fund revenues that must be used to pay off bond debt. As recently as Fiscal Year 1991, the debt ratio was only 2.5 percent.

SUMMARY

In this final chapter, we have studied state spending and revenue, recent budget crises, tax issues, some principles of taxation, and debt. Proposition 13 of 1978 thrust issues of taxing and spending to the forefront of political discussion. As never before, Californians came to view public money as *their* money, and they wanted to know how it was being spent.

In concluding this chapter, we emphasize that budgeting is political—that is, a budget expresses values and preferences. It is far from simply being an economic or accounting document. A budget is a statement of priorities for both governors and legislators. The programs commanding ideological or interest group support will usually be generously funded.

DISCUSSION QUESTIONS

1. When we classified the state budget according to function, we showed which percentages of the budget are spent on social welfare, education, property-tax relief, business regulation, conservation, and other projects. If you were given complete financial direction over (that is, made "dollar dictator" of) the State of California, on which of these functions would you spend more money? On which would you spend *less* money?

2. Looking at the revenue side of the state ledger, which taxes would you alter? Sales tax? Income tax? Bank and corporation tax? How about the cigarette tax? (Warning: No state can print money, not even those with dollar dictators.)

3. What are some criteria against which different taxes may be judged? In terms of these principles, how would you rate the sales tax and the income tax?

4. State bonds are usually marketed only with large face values. If you had the amount of money necessary, what kind of bond would you buy?

5. Earmarking state revenues for specified purposes is controversial, even if we strongly support the favored state program. What are some of the problems with earmarking?

6. Does California have a structural deficit? If it has one, what if anything can be done about a structural deficit?

GLOSSARY

Absentee voting   If a registered voter determines that it will be inconvenient to go to the polling place on election day, then he or she may request an absentee ballot in advance and vote by mail. (p. 84)

Advanced industrialism   A society and economy that rely on high-technology industry that is itself based on scientific knowledge and research. Because such an economy is knowledge-intensive, a high percentage of the population works in service industries such as education, law, medicine, and communications rather than in manufacturing. (p. 5)

Amendment   An amendment is used to make a change in a law or the state Constitution. (p. 17)

Annex   In annexation, a city attempts to acquire legal jurisdiction over a nearby unincorporated area or over another city. *See also* Unincorporated area. (p. 229)

Appellate court   An appellate court hears appeals from trial courts. In California, the courts of appeal and the California Supreme Court are appellate courts. *See also* Trial court. (p. 194)

Assessment   When real estate is assessed, its value is determined. The property-tax rate will be applied to the value of property later. (p. 226)

At-large elections   In this type of election, the entire city (or county) votes for each member of the city council (or board of supervisors). (p. 76)

Bicameral   A legislature is bicameral when it has two chambers. A unicameral legislature is a one-chamber legislature. (p. 168)

Bond   A borrowing device (IOU) issued by a unit of government to a lender. The unit of government promises to pay the lender the amount borrowed, plus interest, on a specified date. In California, bonds must be approved by the voters. *See also* General obligation bonds; Revenue bonds. (p. 262)

California Progressives   *See* Progressives, California.

Capital   This word has four meanings: (1) It can refer to buildings, to construction projects, or to land on which to construct a building, as in "the budget for capital expenditures." (2) It can refer to the death penalty or crimes punishable by death, as in "capital punishment." (3) It can refer to the city that is the seat of state government, as in "Sacramento is the capital of California." (4) It can refer to the wealth or assets used in business by a person or corporation to produce profits or wealth. If all of this is not confusing enough, there is also a "capitol" (spelled with an "o"). This is the *building* that houses the legislature and the governor. (p. 7)

Charter   The document (similar to a constitution) that provides for the powers of a city or county and also provides for its structure of government. (p. 226)

Civil law   Disputes between private persons or private organizations usually constitute civil law. Examples are breach of contract, dissolution of marriage, defamation of character. *See also* Criminal law. (p. 194)

Clemency powers   The governor's power to grant pardons, commutations, and reprieves. *See also* Commutation; Reprieve. (p. 142)

Commutation   The governor reduces the sentence of a convicted person. (p. 142)

Complaint   When a person is charged with a misdemeanor in municipal court, the prosecutor files a complaint, which is a sworn affidavit of charges. *See also* Defendant; Indictment; Information. (p. 209)

Conference committee   When the Assembly and the Senate pass different versions of the same bill, a conference committee is called to reconcile the differences. (p. 175)

Constituents   The people represented by an elected official. For example, this includes all Californians in the case of the governor, or the residents of a particular state Senate district in the case of a state senator. (p. 108)

Constitutional convention   A group of citizens elected by the voters to make a wholesale alteration of the state Constitution or to write an entirely new document. Their work must be submitted to the voters for approval. *See also* Constitutional revision commission. (p. 44)

Constitutional revision commission   A group of leading citizens and legislators meets to change (revise) substantial amounts of the Constitution. The commission's recommendations must be forwarded to the legislature for approval before being submitted to the voters. *See also* Amendment; Constitutional convention. (p. 47)

Contract cities   Cities may contract with the county for the county to provide services desired by the city. Examples of such services are police protection, helicopter service, street maintenance, and library service. *See also* Lakewood Plan. (p. 239)

Contract lobbyist   A lobbyist who has been hired to represent clients with different economic interests. (p. 102)

Councils of government (COGs)   Regional planning agencies that cities and counties may join in order to deal with area-wide problems, COGs draw up comprehensive area-wide plans and then decide if local governments' applications for federal grants-in-aid conform to the plan. Examples include the Association of Bay Area Governments (ABAG) and the Southern California Association of Governments (SCAG). (p. 245)

Counsel   The legislative counsel is a lawyer employed by the legislature to aid in bill drafting. (p. 122)

Criminal law   Criminal law deals with crimes and determines what punishment (if any) is appropriate. *See also* Civil law. (p. 194)

Cross-filing   A California practice, now prohibited, in which a political candidate ran in the primaries of both the Democratic and Republican parties without revealing his or her real party affiliation. By this means, a candidate could be nominated by both major parties. Cross-filing was later modified and then abolished in the 1950s. (p. 74)

Debt ratio   The percentage of state general fund revenues that must be used to pay off the state's bond debt. (p. 263)

Defendant   The person being sued (in a civil law case) or charged (in a criminal law case). *See also* Civil law; Complaint; Criminal law; Indictment; Information; Plaintiff. (p. 195)

Deinstitutionalization   The policy of moving mentally ill people out of large state mental institutions and into smaller community facilities closer to their homes. (p. 38)

Direct democracy   Initiative, referendum, and recall constitute direct democracy. By means of these three processes, average citizens decide public issues directly rather than through representatives. *See also* Initiative; Recall; Referendum. (p. 116)

Docket   A court's calendar of cases. (p. 208)

Earmarked funds   A significant part of state revenue is earmarked (designated) by law or by the state Constitution to be spent for specified purposes. *See also* Revenue. (p. 252)

Electorate   Can be used to indicate all persons qualified to vote or only those people actually voting in a particular election. (p. 66)

Exactions   Improvements such as streets, sewers, sidewalks, parks, and police and fire stations that cities demand from real-estate developers in exchange for a building permit. (p. 232)

Ex officio   If the law provides that whoever holds office A automatically gets to hold office B, then that person serves in the second office *ex officio*. For example, the lieutenant governor is an ex officio member of the State Lands Commission. (p. 152)

Extradition   When requested to do so by the governor of another state, the governor of California is legally required to extradite (return) a fugitive to the state from which he or she has fled. (p. 143)

Fiscal   The word used as an adjective refers to budgets or to money matters, as in "the governor's chief fiscal advisor" or "the legislature's two fiscal committees." (p. 14)

Flat rate tax   A tax that has the same rate for each taxpayer. (p. 250)

Full faith and credit clause   This provision of the U.S. Constitution requires that civil obligations (e.g., mortgages, leases, contracts, and wills) that are enforceable in a civil proceeding in one state are enforceable in any other state. (p. 48)

General obligation bonds   Bonds guaranteed (backed) by the full taxing power and good credit of the unit of government issuing them. *See also* Bond; Revenue bonds. (p. 262)

Geothermal power Hot steam in the earth is tapped to drive turbines that generate electricity. Used at the Geysers plant in the Napa–Sonoma area. (p. 20)

Gerrymander The state legislature draws the boundary lines for its own districts and for the state's U.S. representatives. When the political party that has a majority in the state legislature draws district lines that will enable the party to win even more seats, a gerrymander occurs. *See also* Redistricting. (p. 76, 182)

Grand jury A grand jury exists in each county. It returns indictments and investigates county government. *See also* Indictment. (p. 209)

Grants-in-aid Through grants-in-aid, the federal government gives money to state and local governments. However, the money always comes with restrictions on how it may be spent. (p. 52)

Gross national product (GNP) The total annual output of goods and services in the economy. (p. 7)

Gubernatorial An adjective derived from the noun *governor.* We can say "the governor's powers" or "gubernatorial powers." (p. 73)

Habeas corpus, writ of An order from a court that requires that a jailed person be brought before a judge so that the judge may determine if the detention is legal. (p. 199)

Ideology A consistent point of view on many topics. Liberalism, conservatism, feminism, and socialism are ideologies. An ideological person is known as an *ideologue.* (p. 184)

Incumbent The person who now holds a particular office. For example, "The incumbent state senator in this district is A. Grizzly Bear." (p. 182)

Indexing When income taxes are indexed, income tax brackets are automatically adjusted for inflation. (p. 256)

Indictment If a grand jury (at the urging of a district attorney) believes that sufficient evidence of a felony exists, then the grand jury will vote an indictment (charges) against an accused person. *See also* Defendant; Information; Grand jury. (p. 209)

Information After a preliminary examination in a municipal court, a district attorney files an information—a sworn affidavit of felony charges—in superior court. This procedure is an alternative to seeking an indictment. *See also* Defendant; Indictment; Complaint. (p. 209)

Information costs These are the costs in time and effort required for a citizen and voter to be informed about political affairs, candidates for office, and so forth. (p. 236)

Initiative A process by which voters can enact laws and amendments to the state constitution and local charters. *See also* Direct democracy. (p. 116)

Item veto The governor may reduce or eliminate (but not raise) any item in an appropriations bill, including the budget. (p. 139)

Judicial review The power of a court to review and to declare unconstitutional (strike down) a law passed by the legislature or an action taken by the executive branch that violates the California Constitution or the U.S. Constitution. (p. 111)

Judiciary The court system. (p. 194)

"Juice" committee A committee of the state legislature that reviews legislation affecting important economic interests such as insurance, horse racing, or alcoholic beverages. Members eagerly seek appointment to these committees (such as the Finance, Insurance, and Commerce Committee or the Governmental Organization Committee) because they want to squeeze money out of these interests. (p. 172)

Lakewood Plan Cities may contract with the county for the county to provide services desired by the city. Lakewood, a city in Los Angeles County, was the first city to contract for services such as police protection, helicopter service, road maintenance, and library service. *See also* Contract cities. (p. 239)

Land subsidence A sinking of the ground, usually caused by excessive pumping of groundwater. (p. 25)

Legislative advocate The formal term used for a lobbyist. *See also* lobbyist. (p. 102)

Lobbyist A person who represents an interest group in Sacramento or in local government. *See also* Legislative advocate. (p. 102)

Local agency formation commission (LAFCO) A unit of county government that approves or disapproves proposals for the formation of new cities or special districts, and proposals for the annexation of territory by cities. (p. 229)

Majority vote When a candidate or ballot issue receives at least half of the votes in an election, a majority vote has been obtained. *See also* Plurality vote. (p. 46)

Mandate, writ of An order from a court that commands a public official to perform one of his or her official duties. (p. 199)

Negative purge The names of nonvoters are removed from the voter-registration rolls by notifying these people by postcard; if the post office returns the cards as undeliverable or if the cards are returned by the person now living at the address, then the voter's name is removed. *See also* Positive purge. (p. 84)

Nonpartisan election An election in which no party labels appear on the ballot. (p. 68)

Office-block ballot An election ballot that groups candidates together under the title of the office sought. This ballot, which is used in California, facilitates ticket splitting. *See also* Party-column ballot; Ticket splitting. (p. 88)

Open-seat race An election in which no incumbent is running for re-election. *See also* Incumbent. (pp. 106, 185)

Ordinance The enactment (law) passed by a local government. (p. 238)

Party-column ballot An election ballot that lists party candidates for various offices in columns. The voter is initially given an opportunity to vote for all of the party's candidates by marking a circle at the head of the column. *See also* Office-block ballot. (p. 88)

Patronage The awarding of a government job to a recipient because that person has worked for or supported a political candidate or political party. (p. 69)

Personal property Property *other than* land and buildings. Examples are cash, stocks, bonds, patents, furniture, appliances, cars, clothes, and jewelry. *See also* Real property. (p. 258)

Petit jury *See* Trial jury.

Plaintiff   The person bringing suit in a civil law case. *See also* Defendant; Civil law. (p. 195)

Plea bargaining   The practice of pleading guilty to a reduced charge or sentence rather than standing trial on a more serious charge. (p. 209)

Plurality   When a candidate in an election gets more votes than anyone else but the candidate does *not* get at least half the votes, then the candidate has received a plurality vote. *See also* Majority vote. (p. 185)

Police power   The power of state governments and local governments to pass laws promoting the health, safety, welfare, and morals of the people (a power much broader than simply providing for law enforcement officers). (p. 221)

Positive purge   The names of nonvoters are removed from the voter registration rolls by notifying them by mail; if they do not respond, their names are removed. No longer used in California. *See also* Negative purge. (p. 84)

Primary election   *Partisan primary:* an election in which each party selects its candidates to run in the general election. *Nonpartisan primary:* an election held for nonpartisan offices such as mayor, city council member, and school board member. If no one receives a majority vote, a runoff must be held later between the two top vote-getters in the nonpartisan primary. No party labels are on the ballot. (p. 65)

Progressive tax   A tax (such as the income tax) that provides that as a person's income increases, the tax rate (expressed as a percentage) also increases. Its opposite is a regressive tax. (p. 250)

Progressives, California   Part of an early-twentieth-century national political movement that sought to control special interests and return government to the people. The California Progressives gave California direct democracy, weak political parties, nonpartisan local elections, and other reforms. *See also* Direct democracy; Nonpartisan election. (p. 67)

Prohibition, writ of   An order from a higher court to a lower court that prohibits the lower court from exercising jurisdiction over a case before it because the proceeding exceeds the lower court's jurisdiction. (p. 199)

Quorum   The minimum number of members of a legislative body that must be present for the legislative body to conduct business officially. (p. 237)

Real property   Real estate is real property, hence land and improvements (buildings) are real property. *See also* Personal property. (p. 258)

Recall   The method by which voters may remove any elected state or local official from office before the end of his or her regular term. *See also* Direct democracy. (p. 116)

Recidivism   Most people convicted of a serious crime have been convicted previously and are likely to be convicted again in the future. (p. 211)

Redistricting   After each U.S. census, all federal, state, and local legislative district lines must be redrawn to provide for equal-population districts. *See also* Gerrymander. (p. 182)

Referendum   A procedure that allows the electorate to vote down or sustain laws passed by the legislature. *See also* Direct democracy. (p. 116)

Regressive tax   A tax (such as the sales tax) that falls most heavily on those least able to pay. Its opposite is a progressive tax. (p. 250)

Reprieve   The governor postpones the carrying out of a convicted person's sentence. (p. 142)

Revenue   Money received by government, usually in the form of taxes. Charges, fees, and intergovernmental aid are also regarded as revenue. *See also* Earmarked funds. (p. 7)

Revenue bonds   Bonds issued to finance a revenue-producing project (e.g., a toll bridge or a college dormitory). The income from the project guarantees the bond. *See also* Bond; General obligation bonds. (p. 262)

Severance tax   A tax on the extraction of a depletable natural resource such as oil, gas, coal, timber, or metals. (p. 255)

Short ballot   A reform suggested by the California Progressives in which a governor, mayor, or county board of supervisors appoints executive officials whose jobs are essentially nondiscretionary. Because these officeholders are appointed, no election is held to choose the officeholder. (p. 76)

Sin tax   Taxes on tobacco, alcoholic beverages, and horse-racing bets. These taxes were originally established not only to discourage the use of these objects but also to raise revenue. They now serve primarily the latter purpose. (p. 257)

Small claims court   A division of the municipal court in which individuals or corporations disputing less than $5,000 represent themselves before a judge. (p. 195)

Special election   An election called to fill a vacancy in public office (resulting from death, resignation, or another cause). Another kind of special election occurs when a school district asks the voters to approve a bond issue or a tax-rate increase. (pp. 32, 88)

Split-roll property-tax rate   Under the split-roll technique, income-producing or business property is taxed at a higher property-tax rate than residential property. (p. 255)

Standing committee   A committee of the state legislature that has a broad jurisdiction. Examples include the finance or natural resources committees. (p. 177)

Ticket splitter   A voter who selects some Democrats, some Republicans, and so forth. Hence, the voter has split the ticket, or ballot. (p. 66)

Trial court   A court in which the trial of a case takes place. Such courts are often called "courts of original jurisdiction" because cases almost always originate there. California's trial courts are the municipal courts and superior courts. *See also* Appellate court. (p. 194)

Trial jury   The purpose of a trial jury is to determine the party at fault (in a civil case) or to determine guilt or innocence (in a criminal case). *See also* Grand jury; Civil law; Criminal law. (p. 208)

Turnout   The percentage of people who vote in a particular election. (p. 86)

Unincorporated area   A part of a county that is not part of a city. (p. 223)

Unitary system of government   When a lower level of government may exercise only those powers granted to it by a higher level of government, the system of government is unitary. This is the legal relationship between California local government and

California state government, but it is *not* the relationship between (any) state government and the national government, which is a federal relationship. (p. 222)

Urgency law   A law to protect immediately the public peace, health, or safety. These laws must pass the state legislature by a two-thirds vote, and they take effect immediately. (p. 119)

User charge   A charge levied on the beneficiaries of a public service that is used to pay for that service. For example, a person visiting a city museum or playing golf on a county golf course might pay a fee to help support that service. (p. 233)

INDEX